You Can Master the Maze of College

Third Edition

John E. Van Brunt
University of Maryland

The McGraw-Hill Companies, Inc.
College Custom Series

New York   St. Louis   San Francisco   Auckland   Bogotá
Caracas   Lisbon   London   Madrid   Mexico   Milan   Montreal
New Delhi   Paris   San Juan   Singapore   Sydney   Tokyo   Toronto

McGraw·Hill

A Division of The McGraw·Hill Companies

You Can Master the Maze of College

McGraw-Hill's **College Custom Series** consists of products that are produced from camera-ready copy. Peer review, class testing, and accuracy are primarily the responsibility of the author(s).

2 3 4 5 6 7 8 9 0 HAM HAM 9 0 9 8

ISBN 0-07-067048-X

Editor: Adam Knepper
Cover Design: Maggie Lytle
Printer/Binder: HAMCO/NETPUB Corporation

YOU CAN MASTER THE MAZE OF COLLEGE
Third Edition

Table of Contents

DEDICATION

This book is dedicated to two people who have been very important to me in that they both stressed the importance of going to college:

To my mother, Hildred R. Van Brunt, who made it clear to me that I was going to college even though neither of us knew what college was. Regretfully, she didn't live long enough to see me get there.

To my uncle, Henry Ward, also deceased, my mother's younger brother, who was the first in my family to go to college. He was a retired teacher from New York City public schools and asked me for years to write a book about how to succeed in college.

ACKNOWLEDGEMENTS

Some people may write books without feedback and support from others. I am not one of them. Several of my friends have been especially helpful to me in getting this book to press. I want to thank each of them for their support. A very sincere thank you to:

Elizabeth F. Jones, my first publisher, and June R. Wyman, friends who read and critiqued this book as it was written.

My former students who have given me feedback on my ideas, which I have used to refine my thoughts and to make them more consistent and practical.

Several colleagues from the College Park campus of the University of Maryland (UMCP) who critiqued sections of this text, including Major Cathy Atwell of the campus Police Department; Mrs. Gaynor Sale, Mrs. Vivian Bland (retired), and Dr. Elizabeth Shearn from the Learning Assistance Service of the Counseling Center; and Mr. Alvin Thompson, Director of the Loss Prevention Division.

Susan E. Bailey, previously at the UMCP Counseling Center's Learning Assistance Service and now Technical Production Editor at the American Psychological Association, for her many suggestions on mechanics, format, style, and content.

x

PREFACE

While writing this book I ran into the problem of which pronoun to use for the third person singular, "he" or "she"? For example, should I say "Your instructor gave you an assignment that he wanted by the end of the week" or "Your instructor gave you an assignment that she wanted by the end of the week"? Other choices included

Your instructor gave an assignment that he/she wanted by the end of the week.

Your instructor gave an assignment that s/he wanted by the end of the week.

Your instructor gave an assignment that they wanted by the end of the week.

After trying "he," "she," "he/she," "s/he," a singular "they" and working to avoid using the third person singular at all, I decided to ignore the semantic problem by alternating male and female pronouns by chapter. One chapter uses "he" pronouns another "she," in random order. Hopefully, I have balanced the two pronouns so that positive and negative situations or examples have been shared equally by both gender pronouns.

The exception to this practice occurs only in an example in which I think keeping the real person in mind is important.

1 THE WORLD'S THE SAME

If you are a traditional-aged college student, you have been in school for the last 12 or 13 years of your life. If you are returning to school, you have at least 12 or 13 years of formal schooling and experience in the "real world." In either case, contrary to popular belief, all of your experiences with life in general--and formal schooling in particular--are applicable in the college setting.

In this book, I will teach you the similarities between your past learning experiences and those you will encounter throughout college and later in life. I will cover educational, academic, or study skills from a very practical approach. The techniques that are presented can be applied in your college classes, in noncredit seminars, at work, in the military, or for that matter, in just about any situation in which you need to learn effectively.

I will show you how to apply these study skills techniques so that you can use them in situations that you face every day. Just learning these skills should not be your objective. Master the techniques to learn more efficiently and effectively.

Be Selfish

Before you attempt to judge whether an idea or technique that I present is useful to you, try it out. See for yourself whether or not you can learn more effectively using the technique than you could without it. Your evaluation of the effectiveness of each idea is crucial. If I suggest an idea or technique--but you don't like the sound of it for whatever reason--you are not likely to use it. If, on the other hand, you can withhold your evaluation until you have given the technique a try, you will probably find out that it really works well.

Look at this book--and education, for that matter-- from a practical side. I already know and use the information that I am presenting to you. If you are reading this text as part of a study skills class, your instructor knows this information too. He has assigned the book to help you learn some techniques to use in studying. Since both of us know this information, you don't have to worry about learning it _for us_. Be concerned about what _you_ get out of the time and effort that you put into reading and studying this text. What is in it for you? What do you want to get out of it? Which skills or information do you need most?

Whenever you read anything, you should have the same questions in mind: What is in the information that I am about to read that is important to me? What do _I_ want to know? What do _I_ need to know? In essence, _what's in it for me_?

Reading, education, and learning are all selfish

endeavors. You read to get something out of the material for yourself. You get an education to help you learn information and skills that will help you get more out of life. You learn to help yourself be able to do or know something that you want or need to know.

In other words, stop thinking or worrying about what others want you to know and learn, and concentrate on learning for yourself. Use the ideas that are presented to help you learn more efficiently, to get more out of reading and listening for you. In essence, I am urging you to be selfish whenever you read--what do you want from your reading and how can you get it?

The World of Work

Throughout this book I will be using examples or applying techniques and ideas to situations both in school and in the work place. I believe that the skills, ideas, and knowledge that you learn in college are directly related to the same skills and knowledge that you will need when you are on a job. That is, the habits, skills, and techniques that you develop in school are the same ones that you will be using when you go to work. The reverse is also true: The habits, skills, and techniques that you use on the job are directly applicable in the college setting.

Let's compare a few specific examples from both work and college and see some of the parallels.

Someone Else Is in Charge

One of the first things that I think of when I compare work on a job and at college is the fact that in both settings someone other than you is in charge. Your boss or your instructor specify what your work assignments will be. He will also indicate when your work should be completed.

Your instructor gives you an assignment, and you don't understand what to do or how to do it. What should you do? If your boss had given you something to do and you weren't sure what you should do, how would you handle that situation? At work you probably would either ask a colleague or your boss for more information. In college the situation is the same--either your classmates or your instructor will help clarify the assignment. All you have to do is talk with one of them before or after class or see your instructor during his office hours.

Evaluation

Your instructor and your boss will both evaluate you and your work. Both have established standards to which they expect you to adhere. Your boss gives out raises for good work whereas your instructor assigns high grades.

At work, if you feel that your evaluation is unfair, you talk with your supervisor. In college, if you feel your evaluation is unfair or if you don't understand what you did wrong, talk with your professor. In each case, the evaluation of your performance will be explained to you.

Work Habits

At work and in school you will be expected to have good work habits. If your boss asks you to complete a report by Friday morning, he expects it to be completed by Friday morning. If your car breaks down or you had a busy week, he still expects the report Friday morning. If too many reports aren't completed on time, you'll be looking for a new job, right?

College instructors also expect your work to be turned in on time. Although your instructor can't fire you, he can lower your grade on the assignment which may cause you to fail the course.

Bosses and professors also expect you to get to meetings and classes on time. I remember one graduate class I took when over half the class came in late for the first class session. The professor was obviously annoyed. He even went so far as to tell us that he expected everyone to be on time. When it happened the second session, he got angry. "Class begins at 3 o'clock," he announced. "At that time I will close the door and no one else will be admitted." A funny thing happened the next class session--everyone showed up at or before 3 o'clock! No one questioned whether the professor would keep his word; they came on time.

Good work habits will be an

asset to you both on campus and in your future employment.

Company Policy

Businesses, organizations, and colleges all have rules and regulations. If, for instance, you want to wear shorts to the office, your boss will probably tell you that it's against company policy. If you want to work a four-day week, you may also find that your company policy specifies that you work a five-day week. Should you want to challenge or change a policy, or perhaps just be exempted from one, there is a procedure for you to follow.

Likewise at college there are procedures and policies to follow. There is also an established protocol for obtaining waivers or exemptions from "normal policy" (see Chapter 11, "Knowing the System," for details).

Your Job

At work you are employed for a specific job. You have duties or tasks that have been assigned to you. If you have all of your work done you are expected to see your supervisor to see if there is anything else for you to do.

In college you also have a job. Your job is to attend your classes, to read your assigned material, and to complete the assignments your instructor has made. If you have completed all of the work that has been assigned, would you ask your instructor for additional work? (Now you know I'm crazy, right? You realize, of course, that you could ask for additional reading material. You know that every college instructor has lots of material that they would like to assign to their students but they know they have to limit the work that they give you. How much would your instructor charge you for extra work? Nothing, right? You could get more education at no additional cost to you, yet you won't ask for more. It seems strange to me that college students have an opportunity to get something for nothing and very few will ever take advantage of that situation.)

Back to the comparison between work and college. If you are at work and your best friend called you to invite you to a matinee that started at 2 o'clock, you would probably tell him you couldn't go because you're at work. If you study in the afternoon, would you also tell your friend that you were working? Would you say "I'm working now. How about a later show"?

Pay

When you are employed your company pays you for your work. College also pays you for working, only the payment isn't made in dollars. Your pay in college is what you learn--the knowledge and skills that you acquire as a result of reading, listening, and studying. At the office it's "If you work, you get paid." In college it's "If you study, you learn!"

The Information Explosion

When I was in grammar school in the 1950s, we were told that the sum total of all of human knowledge would double every 20 years. That is, if you took everything that human beings had learned from the beginning of time, the total knowledge of humankind, what humans had learned for the past tens of thousands of years, would double in 20 years or less. During the 1980s the period it would take to double all of human knowledge was said to be as little as every 10 years! Now, the time it takes for the total of all human learning to double is even less. The world is in an information explosion. New ideas and techniques are being developed in virtually every field that you can think of.

In college classes, students are being asked to know more information than students of 20 or 30 years ago. And even though you are covering more material in your classes, you are learning less of the sum total of all of human knowledge because there is so much more for you to know today.

What does all of this have to do with you? You may think that you have a lot to learn in your classes. Just wait until you are working full time (those of you who are working full time while you go to college already know what I mean). As technology increases, jobs will become more complex. You will need to read and study a lot of different subjects to stay current in the job market.

When I was in high school we were told that we could expect

to hold an average of three different kinds of jobs during our years of employment. I recently read that today's high school students can expect to have as many as 10 different jobs during their working years. Many of the positions that today's students will hold will be eliminated because of technical advances.

Take a look at standard office practices to see a few recent changes in office work. Executives used to dictate letters to personal secretaries. Today they have computer terminals on their desks and they often type much of their own work on their own keyboard. (Typing is now data entry or keyboard entry, a raise in the status of the task.) Many letters and memos that were individually typed and mailed are now sent by electronic mail. Instead of having a file clerk file his memo, today's executive just saves his work to the appropriate computer file.

Receptionists and secretaries used to take phone messages; now it's done by voice mail. Managers who in the past might have had a large clerical support staff now have comparatively few staff backed up by sophisticated automated computer equipment.

With the nature of jobs changing so rapidly and so drastically, students will find it imperative to develop good computer, analytical, and communication skills that can be transferred to a wide variety of employment situations. Increasing the

ability to adapt or transfer skills and knowledge will be as important as the knowledge itself.

My goal in writing this text is to present a variety of techniques that will enhance your ability to learn efficiently. The same skills that you will use for your first-time learning from your textbooks and lectures will also be adaptable to your learning needs when you enter the work force.

You

The focus of this book is on you. You are reading it because you have some interest in learning more effectively than you have in the past. Just simply reading this text will not do you any good unless you are willing to try to implement some of the ideas or techniques. Few of the techniques that are introduced here are hard to understand or implement. However, since many of the ideas will require that you change some of your established learning habits, you will need to make a conscious effort to use them at first. Even after you have tried a technique several times, if you are not thinking about what the best way is for you to learn something, you are likely to slip back into your old habits.

What I am saying is that old habits often die very slowly. The ways that you are comfortable reading and studying have been with you for a long time. Your old habits and skills have gotten you to where you are today. As you read this text and see some techniques that look like they will be effective, you are likely to try them simply because you have taken the time to read and learn them. The problem will come later, when you are not reading this book. Your old habits that have been with you for 10 or more years will almost naturally tend to come back.

To combat the natural tendency to work the way you are used to, I suggest the following:

1. Read only a section or two of this text at any one time. Read, then stop and think about what you have read. How does the information presented compare with the way you usually work? Can you see why the technique that you read about should work for you? If not, reread the section to get a better understanding so that you can really use the technique in your own learning.

2. Finishing a chapter is not as important as understanding the ideas that are presented in each section. Read to learn, not simply to finish the chapter or a class assignment.

3. Each time you go to class or read anything, stop and think about what you expect to learn from it. Are there any new learning skills that you want to apply in the class or in the reading assignment?

4. Try to use some of your new techniques as you read and study this book. What better place to practice new learning skills than in the book that is supposed to give you more effective study skills?

5. If you have trouble using any of the procedures that are suggested, don't get frustrated. Talk to your instructor about the problem you are having, or talk with one of the learning specialists that are on your campus.

6. Do not try to use all of the techniques that are suggested in a chapter at the same time! Changing habits is hard. Going overboard in your attempt to improve by changing everything is not an effective way to make permanent modifications in your behavior. Try one technique and get comfortable with it before you try another. Slow, steady changes made one at a time will help you change the most in the long run.

When I say that you are the focus of the book I mean just that. My aim in writing this book is to help you learn to learn more effectively and to try to put some enjoyment back into your learning. What you think and feel about learning is extremely important. If you can enjoy your learning, if you are in control of your own learning, you are likely to want to learn even more.

As you look back at what you have read in this chapter, what difference does any of the information that you have read make in your thoughts about learning more effectively? Has anything that you have read suggested any ways for you to learn better? Seriously, stop for a minute and reflect on what you have read in this introductory chapter. What have you learned from reading it?

If you did not stop to think about the questions that I just asked, why are you bothering to continue reading? This book will not do you any good if you are only going to sit and read. The questions that are asked are there to help you get involved with your own learning. It is the involvement in reading, the involvement in your own learning, and the thinking about what you have read that will help you learn better.

Academic Dishonesty

Before I wrap up this chapter, let me remind you about one area of unpleasantness that everyone in higher education would rather avoid--academic cheating or academic dishonesty.

A large percentage of students who have gone to college indicate that they have cheated at least once while they were in college. Each year thousands of college students end up in serious academic trouble because they have been caught in some form of academic dishonesty. If a student is caught for cheating or some other form of academic dishonesty, the negative consequences can be failure in the specific course in which the dishonesty occurred--often with a notation like "XF," which denotes failure due to academic dishonesty and/or dismissal from the college or university. There also may be

a notation on the transcript that the dismissal is because of academic dishonesty.

The three most common forms of academic dishonesty are plagiarism, cheating, and falsifying information. Each can lead to an "XF" in a course as well as dismissal from the school.

Plagiarism

If you knowingly use someone else's words for your own and do not reference the source you are guilty of plagiarism. Even if you have changed some of the words that you use in your own written form of the material you may be guilty of plagiarism.

Direct Quotes

If you use information from another source exactly as it appears in the original copy, you must quote the source of that information. You can use either quotation marks or indentations to show that the material is being quoted from someone else. The material that is quoted could be a paragraph, a sentence, or even a phrase. As long as the original idea or material was written by someone else, be sure that you reference the source.

Paraphrasing

Even if you make changes in material that you gathered from another source, you may still be guilty of plagiarism. When the content or the ideas that are expressed in your writing are essentially the words of someone else, you also must give the original author credit for his work. The information does not have to be marked with quotation marks or set off by indentations, but the author still must be cited.

Specific Details

If you are using specific information that you have gathered from your research such as the number of gallons of oil that were imported to the United States during 1990, you must cite the source of your information. Only when the details that you present are considered "common knowledge," such as saying that the divorce rate in the United Stated is about 50%, can you avoid making a citation.

Citations

A citation is information that an author presents to show where he obtained the material that he is presenting. Usually that means that the author of the original work, the title of the book or article, the publisher, and the pages used are listed. Style manuals will tell you the specific information that you must provide and the specific form of the citation. Although there are a number of different style manuals that you can use for your papers, the Publication Manual of the American Psychological Association presents a simple form that I highly recommend.

Cheating

Cheating refers to using some kind of unauthorized assistance on an assignment or examination. Using "cheat sheets" or "crib notes" on an exam would be one example of cheating. A second example would be looking at someone else's test paper or signaling information to another student during an examination. Taking a break during an examination to go to the restroom to look up information either from your text or notes is also cheating. So is using someone's paper or assignment to create your own paper.

Many years ago a graduate assistant of mine caught two students cheating on an out-of-class assignment. There were almost 500 students in the class that semester. Each had a three- to five-page assignment using the SQ3R study method. When the papers were graded, my graduate assistant thought that he had seen material in one paper before. He went through the 500 papers and found the second matching paper. Most paragraphs in the two papers matched perfectly, although they were arranged in different orders.

Think about that example for a minute. Almost 500 papers were being graded and the grader remembered seeing the first paper when he read the second one. Sound amazing? Not really. The graduate assistant was an ex-English teacher in training for a college level teaching position. College instructors have excellent memories for written material. They can often find exact references years after they have read a particular article even though they have not used that material since. No, they do not have photographic memories, they just tend to enjoy reading and value what they have read. They remember a lot of information that they don't have to know. That habit of remembering material that has been read before carries over to times that the instructor is correcting student papers.

Having someone take an examination or class for you is the last form of cheating that I want to mention. A few years ago, after a class examination, students were asked to show picture ID cards after they left the examination. When the smoke cleared, six students were present who were not enrolled in the class. There were also six examination papers from students who were not physically there. All twelve students ended up in academic trouble.

Students have also had someone take an entire course for them so that the instructor would see the same face in class and during the examinations. Some students have had someone else take examinations for them, such as the SATs. When caught, all are guilty of cheating and could be prosecuted.

Do your own work and get the grades that you have earned honestly. The penalty for cheating is not worth the benefits you may get.

Falsifying Information

If you provide false information on official college documents or in class papers or reports, you are guilty of academic dishonesty. Probably the most common form is students creating or copying someone else's data for lab reports. Although this offense may not seem particularly bad or dangerous, keep in mind that it can lead to the "XF" grade or to academic dismissal.

Suppose you are dismissed from College A. Later you decide to apply for admission to College B. On the application to College B there is likely to be a question like "Have you attended or been dismissed from any other college?" Since colleges do not share their academic records with each other, you may be tempted to say "No" to the question. If you say you haven't been dismissed and later someone finds that you were dismissed from another school, you will be academically dismissed from College B. You will be dismissed even if you have taken classes and earned A's and B's in all of them!

Report Academic Dishonesty

Reducing the incidence of academic dishonesty is the job of everyone who is involved in higher education--faculty, staff, and students. If an instructor can show that you knew about cheating, such as when you allow another student to use your paper, you too can be charged with academic dishonesty. Even if a student who used your paper says that you weren't aware that the guilty student copied from your paper, you still may have to suffer the consequences of getting a lower grade, doing another assignment, or receiving an F in the course. If you allow someone else to use one of your assignments as a model for their own, try to arrange to see his final copy so you can protect yourself. This does not mean that you cannot work with other students, only that you keep yourself out of academic difficulty by not unknowingly being guilty of collaboration in some form of academic dishonesty.

Who do you call if you are going to report academic dishonesty? Call the specific instructor, the department head or the dean of the college in which the incident occurred. If you cannot easily find that information, talk to someone in your campus Judicial Office. Do remember to specify that your name is to be kept confidential.

Rights and Responsibilities

When you attend college, both you and your college have almost entered into a contractual agreement that has implied rights and responsibilities for both you and your college. Usually your rights and your college's responsibilities are mirror images of each other. Similarly, your college's rights are probably the opposite of your responsibilities. For example, you have a right to know your college's degree requirements before you sign your admissions application. That means that your college has the responsibility of publishing its degree requirements so that you will know exactly what courses you will have to take and pass in order to graduate.

Your campus will probably have a formal statement of your rights and responsibilities printed in your college catalog. Those rights and responsibilities are much more than just words that are written in your college catalog; they are the guidelines that will be present on campus to help you earn your college degree.

Student Rights

In general, your rights as a student include, but are not limited to

1.   the right to freedom of expression without bias or prejudice;

2.   the right to know your college's degree requirements, policies, rules and regulations, course requirements, and how you will be evaluated and graded in each course;

3.   the right to be graded fairly and equitably without bias or prejudice because of your gender, race, age, personal or political beliefs, religion, or marital status;

4.   the right to appeal any grade, policy, or regulation that you believe unfairly puts you at a disadvantage compared with other students;

5.   a right to have your instructors be prepared to teach their courses in a fashion that is consistent with

the course description in your current college catalog;

6. a right to expect that both your person and your property will be reasonably protected from harm while you are on campus.

Student Responsibilities

Just as students have rights on campus, they have responsibilities that go with those rights. As a student, your obligations include, but are not limited to

1. the responsibility to complete all required course assignments and to turn them in by the time specified by your instructors;

2. the responsibility to attend your classes and examinations on time and, for discussion-style classes, to be prepared for each class session;

3. the responsibility to personally complete all assignments without using resources that have not been approved by your instructors;

4. responsibility for both your self and your actions while you are on campus or when you are representing your campus;

5. the responsibility to know and follow the campus rules and regulations.

(Adapted from UMCP Codes of Conduct)

Summary

In this book, I have presented information and techniques to help you learn practical skills that you will be able to use both in college and in your future work. The skills that lead to success in both fields are incredibly similar. Since the way that you have learned to learn has become more or less a habit to you, changing what you do when you read and study will take a little systematic effort. The basic idea is to get you to focus your attention on what you want to learn and to have you develop a strategy or strategies that will ensure that you learn what you want to learn.

I mentioned a brief warning about academic dishonesty to remind you of the seriousness of the issue and hopefully to prevent you from being tempted to cheat in any of your college courses.

Lastly, I presented a summary of students' rights and responsibilities in college. The purpose of this text is to help you make use of your rights and to fulfill your responsibilities--to learn all that you can as you work your way through the maze of college.

2 SETTING GOALS

Going through life without goals is a little like the game pinning the tail on the donkey. You are going to pin the tail on something; the question you have when you play the game is "What? What will I pin the tail to?" During your life you will do things such as have a job, go places, live somewhere, know people, buy things, have a family, etc. My concern here is about where you are going. You are spending your time, energy, emotions, and money doing something for some reason. To what purpose?

Have you ever talked with people who are 60, 70, or 80 years old? When you ask them questions about their lives, what kinds of things do you hear? Isn't one of the items often "I wish I had...."? "I wish I had taken more time to be with my kids," "I wish I had saved more," or "I wonder what would have happened if...." Yes, there are also many things that the person is happy about, but there often are a number of things that come under the "I wish I had..." category.

There is a high probability that you will live to be 60 or 70 years old or older--people are living longer and longer. When you reach that age and look back on your life, how many "I wish I had's" do you want to have?

If you are a college student, you successfully completed high school. Think back on that experience. Did you get all you could from your three or four years in high school? Educationally, did you learn all that you could have learned? Personally, did you grow and mature as a person as much as you possibly could? For most of us the answer is no. We could have done more in high school but we didn't. Despite the fact you didn't accomplish all that you might have in high school, you made it to college.

Put the idea of goal setting and your years in high school together and think about them. When you entered high school, did you have clear goals about what you wanted from those three or four years? Did you know where you were going and how high school would help you get there? Without specific goals it is difficult to get the most we can from a given situation. You have seen that in the past; now, what about the future?

Without knowing what you want from your college experience it will be difficult for you to maximize what you get from college. You will be investing at least four years of your life in your college education. You also will be spending a great deal of money for that education. What do you want for all that time, effort, and money?

Long- and Short-Range Plans

Most businesses have long-term plans that govern how they allocate their financial resources to make the most profit possible over an extended period of time. Governments try to make long-term plans so that schools and other services will be available as the population in their geographic area expands. Sports teams try to ensure long-term winning by developing plans to improve their players and records. In the "Arts," orchestras, museums, and theaters have long-range plans on how they will improve.

Virtually every organization has plans on how to improve, with a great many having both long- and short-term goals for guiding that improvement. At the same time, most of the people who work in these organizations have not attempted to plan their personal lives out ahead of time. When asked about planning specific goals for their own lives, very few people will be able to show you a written set of goals. Why not?

Planning assumes that you have the ability to make decisions about how you will use your time, energy, abilities, and financial resources to reach the goals that you specify. It also means that you believe that you have some control over your life and that the control you exercise will make a difference in what happens.

Not all people believe that they can control or make any difference in their future. For example, my father believed in predestination, that everything in life had been determined ahead of time and that there was nothing that he or anyone could do about it.

Things would happen because they were meant to happen that way. When something happened that was either good or bad, it didn't matter that much because that was what was meant to be. Today there are still a lot of people who share my father's views. "Why try, why plan, it won't make any difference." Hopefully, I can show you that you can make a difference in what will happen to you in the future---that by setting goals and working toward them, you can increase the odds of getting more of what you want from your life.

Of course, just because you set goals for yourself does not mean that you will reach them. Your goals along with a lot of effort can make a difference. Your goals set your direction. After that, work is needed to reach those goals. Let's look at three examples from the sports world to see what I mean.

In the 1968 Summer Olympics that were held in Mexico City, a young swimmer named Mark Spitz was to lead the American swim team to victory by earning four or five individual gold medals. Unfortunately, he earned only two gold medals, both as a member of the men's freestyle relay team. When you read the news articles about that olympics, you get the feeling that Mark Spitz was a colossal failure. He let America down.

For the next four years Mark Spitz worked to redeem himself. He trained everyday, averaging over six hours a day in a pool. Sometimes he swam as many as 14 hours in a single day. When you take a world-class athlete and train him as intensely as Mark Spitz trained for those four years, is it so surprising that he would go on to earn seven gold medals in the 1972 Munich Olympic Games?

Mark Spitz was in the news again during 1991. He decided that he wanted to compete again in the 1992 Olympic Games in Barcelona, Spain. He was 40 years old! In competitive swimming, 40 isn't just old, it is old, old--ancient. Twice during 1991 he competed against world-class swimmers and lost. Did Spitz make it to the 1992 American Olympic team? No, Mark did not make the team. However, as far as he was concerned, he had a dream and he tried. If he hadn't made the attempt, he would have been disappointed in himself.

The next example is a boxer named Cassius Clay. Cassius Clay won the 1960 Olympic light heavyweight boxing gold medal. He went on to professional boxing and alienated a lot of sports writers and sports fans with his boastful statement "I'm the greatest." In 1964, Clay won the professional boxing heavyweight championship of the world from Sonny Liston. Shortly afterward he converted to The Nation of Islam (the "Black Muslims") and changed his name to Muhammad Ali.

In 1967, Muhammad Ali's title was revoked when he refused to be inducted into the armed services. In 1974, Muhammad Ali regained the heavyweight title, which he held until he lost it in a title bout during February of 1978. Seven months later he regained the title in a rematch. He retired from boxing the next year. A year later Ali came out of retirement in an attempt to win the heavyweight title a fourth time! Although he didn't win that title bout, he made millions in his attempt. He did try.

The third example is Wilma Rudolph. When Wilma was four years old, she developed double pneumonia and scarlet fever. She completely lost the use of her left leg. Doctors said that she might never walk again. For the next four years she went through physical therapy that included daily leg massages from her mother. At eight she was walking with the aid of a leg brace. By high school she had become an all-state champion in basketball--she was all-state four years in a row. She made the 1956 Olympic team and was on the women's bronze medal 400-meter relay team. In the 1960 Olympics in Rome, Wilma Rudolph became the first woman athlete to win three gold medals, winning the women's 100-meter and the 200-meter races and anchoring the winning women's 400-meter relay team.

Not everyone is going to be a world champion. Do remember, however, world champions are made, not born! A great deal of time, energy, and effort goes into the making of any world champion. You don't have to aspire to be a world champion. The point is, if you don't aspire to something, how are you going to control where you are going and how you will get there? Many of your dreams can come true. More of those dreams will come true for you if you help them along.

Take a few minutes to fill out the Life Goals Work Sheet. Write a list of the things that you want to accomplish during the rest of your life. If you think that some of your ideas are silly or crazy or impossible, remember, if you can think of them, some day someone will do them. That someone could be you. So write your list (you don't have to show it to anyone, it's just for you). Do remember to think about goals in your personal life, goals for your career, as well as goals that relate to your formal and informal education.

When you have completed what I call your "life list," your long- term goals, look the list over and think about how your college years can help you accomplish some of those goals. Use your life list to create a list of goals that you want to complete while you are in college. These are your short-term goals. On the short term College Goals Work Sheet, specify educational goals, career goals, values you want to maintain, and personal goals that you want to complete or at least work on while you are earning your college degree.

Use your short-term, or college goals, to help you select your college major, your minor, and your elective classes; the kinds of activities and organizations that you participate in while you are in school; and the kinds of jobs you take to help finance your education.

Suppose that one of your long-term goals is to have a middle management position in a major business or corporation. Although you eventually want to go to work in the business world, you really love American history. You decide to major in history, but at the same time you create a minor that consists of the core required business courses. To create the business credentials that you want you could join several student organizations and work on their finance committees, later becoming the treasurer. For work, you could get a position as a teller in a local bank. During your four years at the bank you could be promoted to head teller and become partially responsible for hiring and training new employees. You would gain experience working with both money and people. By the time you graduate from college you would have the kind of credentials that show your ability to successfully plan and implement a short-range multifaceted project--you.

Once you have established your college goals, move on to your semester goals. Use the Semester Goals Work Sheet to target your goals for this semester.

Implementation

Once you have identified your goals---your goals in life, college, or in reading this text---it is up to you to implement a strategy that will help you reach those goals.

Life Goals Work Sheet

Priority   Task

_____   _____

_____   _____

_____   _____

_____   _____

_____   _____

_____   _____

_____   _____

_____   _____

_____   _____

_____   _____

_____   _____

_____   _____

_____   _____

_____   _____

_____   _____

_____   _____

_____   _____

_____   _____

_____   _____

_____   _____

_____   _____

College Goals Work Sheet

Priority   **Task**

_____   _____

_____   _____

_____   _____

_____   _____

_____   _____

_____   _____

_____   _____

_____   _____

_____   _____

_____   _____

_____   _____

_____   _____

_____   _____

_____   _____

_____   _____

_____   _____

_____   _____

_____   _____

_____   _____

Semester Goals Work Sheet

Priority   Task

_____   _____

_____   _____

_____   _____

_____   _____

_____   _____

_____   _____

_____   _____

_____   _____

_____   _____

_____   _____

_____   _____

_____   _____

_____   _____

_____   _____

_____   _____

_____   _____

_____   _____

_____   _____

_____   _____

_____   _____

Use the techniques that are presented in this text, especially those that relate to managing your time, to see what impact they will have on your reaching your goals. If you like the result that you get from using a technique, you will probably use it again.

Remember, goals are neither right nor wrong. They are simply your goals; they are guides. If you can specify a goal, great. It will give you some direction in which to channel your efforts.

Now, are you willing to do all the work that is necessary to reach that goal? What are your plans, what is your strategy for reaching each goal? Even if you don't achieve your goal, can you enjoy the quest, the attempt, the challenge? Many times when people reach their goals they say that reaching the goal wasn't half as important to them as making the attempt. Enjoy the process of working toward your goal as well as the results that you achieve. So, what are your goals and how do you plan to achieve them?

Using This Book

You are reading this book for some reason. Why? What do you want to get from it? If you are taking a study skills course and your instructor has assigned it to you, you will probably learn how to be a better student even if you don't really care about what you read. If, however, you stop and think about how a book on study skills can help you get more out of college, and to get more out of life than you could without it, you will get a great deal more from the time that you spend reading and studying the suggestions that are here.

The ideas that are present are not all "theoretical." Most of the techniques or procedures are very practical and will work for you both in college and out in the world of work that you are planning to enter. Before you spend a lot of time reading this book, take a few minutes to think about what you want from it for the time, energy, and money that you have and will invest in reading and studying the material that is here. What skills do you want to improve? Why? Are you really willing to try out some new or different ways of learning?

Summary

Goals can help you channel your time and energy to get more of what you want from your life experiences. Set life goals to establish the direction you want to go, the skills you want to learn or the things you want to accomplish during your life. Set college goals to guide you through the selection of your major, college courses, and extracurricular activities.

3 MANAGING YOUR TIME

The biggest academic skill problem college students expect to have and report having had in college is managing their time. The problem comes up in many ways: not having enough time to do the things you want; not getting the grades you want on tests, papers, or projects; not turning in assignments on time; not getting enough sleep; not being prepared for your classes; not...; not...; not!

Time is a resource that you can use a lot of different ways. When you know what you want from your time and your life, it can be an easy matter to control your time to get what you want. The first step has to be knowing what you want. If you have not read the chapter on goal setting (Chapter 2) and completed the goal-setting exercises, you can still continue with this chapter, though it would be best to have established your goals first.

To Do Lists

One of the problems that people have in controlling their time is that there is often just too much to do. Many of us have been taught to believe that the harder we work, the better we will be perceived by both ourselves and by others. When we have a lot to do, we bury ourselves in our work or in working hard on as much as we can. When the pressure is on we work harder and harder, but we never seem to get caught up. The problem is that we will probably never have enough time to do everything that we want or need to get done!

If you don't have enough time to get everything done that you want to, or if you find that you seem to be working all the time and important things aren't getting done, try creating a "to do" list.

Make a list of all the things that you need, want, or should do for the day. Be sure to include everything that you want to get done for school, for work, for church, for or with your friends and family, and for yourself. Don't worry about the list getting to be too long, getting things done comes later. First you need to know all the things that you want to do.

When you have completed your list look over the things you have on it, and decide how important each item is. Use "A" to indicate those items you think are most important, "B" for the things that are important, and "C" for the remainder, the items you feel are least important. Note, "important" is part of each ranking--most important, important, and least important. Because you want to do something it is important to you. However, everything is not equally important to you, some things are just more important.

Once you have written your list, go over it and mark your priority ranking in front of each item. Try to limit your top priority A ranking to only two or three items, those that you really need or want to get done. If you marked everything on your list A, most important, you haven't helped yourself. If everything is most important, then mark them "A-1," "A-2," "A-3," etc. One way or another you have to decide what your priorities are. Which of your tasks do you want to target for special attention? If you target only a few items for completion, you have a good chance of completing them. Those become your A's. Once you have selected your A's, go back and mark the rest of the items on your list either B or C.

How do you select your priorities? Sometimes that isn't easy. First you start with your life and semester goals. If you have decided that music is a significant part of your life and that you want to commit time each day to playing the piano, then finding time to practice on the piano becomes a daily priority. If completing your college degree with a B average is a priority in your life, then study time becomes a top priority. If taking a trip to Europe this summer is one of your year's priorities, then going to work and saving for the trip may be a daily priority.

It all comes down to what you want! In deciding what you want, you may need to take other people or agencies into consideration. If you are on a scholarship that requires that you maintain a 3.5 grade point average, getting C's in your courses will cause you to lose your scholarship. Study time becomes really important. If you are an officer in a student organization, time to do work for that club will need to be a priority for you. If your parents or family are helping you with your college expenses, their expectations will probably figure into your priorities. Remember, however, these are your priorities. Others may figure in to or may need to be considered when you decide on your priorities, but the rankings you use are your priorities!

Once you have decided on your priorities, you need a game plan for getting the A's completed. Finishing everything on your "to do" list is not important. Completing the A's is your target. When you have available time, time that is not committed to class or work, try to get the things that you marked A done. When using to do lists, it is better to complete part of an A than it is to complete three C's or even three B's! "Wait a minute," you say, "getting three tasks finished is great!" Remember, you looked over the tasks on your list and you decided on the priorities. You are the one who said the A tasks were more important than the B or C tasks. Completing B's and C's before the A's means that you are not working on the tasks that you yourself said were most important. If you want time to work for you, help it by completing your A's first.

Prime Time

The idea behind prime time is that each of us is different. We behave differently. We have different biological clocks within us. However, we all have times of the day when we are at our best, when we can tackle anything successfully. Likewise, we have times when we have little energy. Prime time is your best time. On any given day, when are you at your physical and mental best? That is your prime time. Can you accomplish your most important tasks during your prime time?

If you are a morning person, can you take your most difficult classes early in the day? Can you get your heaviest studying done in the morning? If you are a morning person, you most likely run out of gas at night. Why would you try to study at night when you don't have the energy to study effectively?

Similarly, if you are tired shortly after you each lunch, don't take chemistry at 1 o'clock in the afternoon. Find some things of lesser importance to do then.

Most people tend to have their greatest amount of energy in the morning after they have had a good night's sleep. If that is true for you, why not take advantage of your morning hours for your difficult work and use your evening hours for rest and relaxation?

If your best time is at night, getting up late, taking afternoon classes, and studying at night makes sense. On the other hand, taking a class at eight in the morning would not make sense for a night person. The important point to remember is that you need to know

yourself well, to know how to use your day most effectively.

Swiss Cheese

Large tasks such as a term paper are difficult for people to complete. The size of the task itself isn't the problem. It is the way we go about completing the task.

Take the term paper, for instance. When you decide to work on the paper, you think about all the work that has to be done, getting to the library to find your references, reading the material, getting all the writing done. The term paper looks or feels huge. If you sit down to work on it, you'll be there for hours, or days, or maybe even months. Since you are not crazy, why even start? As the paper gets put off longer and longer, it becomes more of a monster. As it becomes more of a monster, you tend to put it off even longer.

When you have a large task that needs to be done, break it into small pieces or sections that are more manageable. With a term paper, for instance, break it down into component parts, the first of which is probably choosing the subject.

Choose the subject as soon after the assignment is given to you as possible. Think about having just been told by one of your instructors that you have a 40-page term paper that must be turned in at the last class period. The longer you wait to get started the

To Do List

Priority   Task

_____   _____

_____   _____

_____   _____

_____   _____

_____   _____

_____   _____

_____   _____

_____   _____

_____   _____

_____   _____

_____   _____

_____   _____

_____   _____

_____   _____

_____   _____

_____   _____

_____   _____

_____   _____

_____   _____

You may want to photocopy this form to make daily work sheets greater the pressure you feel, in part, because the end of the semester is getting closer. When the assignment is made, find some time, _make some time_, to select your topic. You can do that anywhere: while you are in the shower or soaking in the tub, while lying on the grass on the mall, while canoeing or hiking, anywhere! Once you have chosen your topic, stop! You have completed one part of your assignment. When you are ready to work on it again, your task will be to decide what it is that you want to do with the topic.

If you need information, you will probably need to get to a library. What library? When that is known, stop. Again, you have completed part of the term paper; you now have a topic, know that you need to do some research, and know where you will do it.

An alternate way of helping or forcing yourself to select your topic early is by making an appointment with your instructor to discuss the topic and your thoughts concerning the assignment. If you have an appointment for, say, Monday morning at 9 a.m., you have to have something ready to discuss.

Once you have your topic and have thought about what you want to do with it, the next step is probably to go to the library to do some research. If you have never been to that particular library, just getting there and learning how to do research there will be a task in itself. How do you use a library efficiently? Yes, the computerized card catalog can be used, but there may be an even faster way of getting what you need. Reference librarians have been trained to locate information efficiently. They know reference books and abstracts that most of us would never be aware of. Use the librarians knowledge to help you gather information. (Take notes on what you are told for later use.) Now stop. You've gotten some work accomplished, you now know where to find the information that you need.

When you make time for more term-paper work, you will be gathering information. Locate the information you need, scan it to be sure that each item is appropriate, and then photocopy everything you need. Then, of course, you stop. Work has been accomplished. Next, collate the photocopies and stop. When you read your copies, mark them with underlines and/or notes that will help you when you are getting ready to put the paper together.

Using the swiss cheese approach identifies small tasks that you can finish in a reasonable amount of time. You can complete a small task and feel good about your accomplishment. When you feel good about your work, you tend to put it off less and maybe even look forward to doing more of it in the future.

At some point in your work, you may have a large block of time available for the main assignment. When you do, you will already have accomplished

Scheduling Work Sheet

	Monday	Tuesday	Wednesday	Thursday	Friday	Saturday	Sunday
5							
6							
7							
8							
9							
10							
11							
12							
1							
2							
3							
4							
5							
6							
7							
8							
9							
10							
11							
12							
1							
2							
3							
4							

many smaller tasks. In essence, you will have punched a lot of holes in the main assignment that will make the job more manageable. When you sit down to work, a lot of the initial planning and work will already be completed.

The larger the task you need to complete, the more important it is for you to divide the task into small, manageable segments that you can tackle easily.

Schedules

Schedules help us to use specific blocks of time effectively. Most professional people, managers, and executives use some kind of schedule to remind them of the things that they want or should be doing. Pocket sized weekly and daily schedules such as "A Week at a Glance" can be excellent tools to help you make the best use of your time.

Accountability and Schedules

Take a scheduling work sheet and try to account for the last seven days of your life. In one-hour blocks, write down on the work sheet how you used your time for the past week. Don't worry about little things, like the time it takes you to brush your teeth, just account for activities that took up half an hour or more.

When you have completed the schedule, summarize the time that you spent on each of the different activities that you engaged in on a separate piece of paper. For the sample schedule on the next page, the summary would look like this:

Activity	Time
Class	18 hours
Misc./unplanned	11
Church	1
Reading	4
Commuting	10
Sleep	55
Friends/social	15
Study	17
Laundry/housework	2
TV time	10
Lunch/dinner	13
Work	12

The sample summary has accounted for all but 11 hours of time. Don't be surprised if you find out that you have more hours that you simply cannot account for. Use the information that you have and see what that tells you.

Suppose you created this sample schedule in hopes of answering the following questions: Can I work more hours--I really could use the extra money (four more hours should do the trick)? My grades aren't what I'd like them to be--where can I find another six to eight hours for studying? I want to join the campus chorus--can I afford the five hours of practice time?

In essence, you want to put an extra 15 to 17 hours of activities into your week. Two of those activities have set

Sample Time Schedule

	Monday	Tuesday	Wednesday	Thursday	Friday	Saturday	Sunday
5	Sleep	Sleep	Sleep	Sleep	Sleep	Sleep	Sleep
6	Sleep	Sleep	Sleep	Sleep	Sleep	Sleep	Sleep
7	Sleep	Sleep	Sleep	Sleep	Sleep	Sleep	Sleep
8	Commute		Commute		Commute	Sleep	Sleep
9	Hist	Commute	Hist	Commute	Hist	Work	Reading
10	Friends	Math	Friends	Math	Friends	Work	Reading
11	Math	Lunch	Math	Lunch	Math	Work	Church
12	Lunch	Study	Lunch	Study	Lunch	Work	Lunch
1	Engl	Study	Engl	Study	Engl	Lunch / Work	
2	Psyc	Astr	Psyc	Astr	Psyc	Work	
3	Study		Study		Study		
4	Study	Study	Study	Study	Commute		
5	Study	Study	Study	Commute	Study		
6	Commute	Study	Commute	Dinner	Dinner	Dinner	Dinner
7	Dinner	Commute	Dinner	TV	Friends	Friends	Laundry
8	Work	Dinner	Work	TV	Friends	Friends	Laundry
9	Work	Study	Work	TV	Friends	Friends	TV
10	Work	Study	Work	TV	Friends	Friends	TV
11	TV	TV	TV	Reading	Friends	Friends	TV
12	Sleep	Sleep	Sleep	Sleep	Friends	Friends	Sleep
1	Sleep	Sleep	Sleep	Sleep	Reading	Sleep	Sleep
2	Sleep	Sleep	Sleep	Sleep	Sleep	Sleep	Sleep
3	Sleep	Sleep	Sleep	Sleep	Sleep	Sleep	Sleep
4	Sleep	Sleep	Sleep	Sleep	Sleep	Sleep	Sleep

hours: work, Saturday afternoon; and chorus, Tuesday and Thursday evenings. Study time can go anywhere. If you add the items that you want to your schedule, you will have less flexible time for unplanned activities. Is that okay? Tuesday and Thursday evenings are available for chorus if you reschedule some of your study time. Extra work on Saturday is possible because that time isn't committed now. Where will the new and rescheduled study time fit in, Sunday afternoon and evening?

There is enough time to add all the things you want to add. You simply won't have a lot of free time in your schedule. If that is acceptable, then you can add the work hours and the campus chorus and still provide time for extra studying.

Many people find that by simply filling in a schedule they learn a lot about themselves and where their time "disappears." The basic schedule is simply a work sheet that shows the 168 hours that we have available to us each week. The work sheet becomes a tool to use to account for where your past time has gone and how you plan to use your time in the future. It is not necessary nor is it desirable to change your entire schedule to make this analysis helpful to you. Just seeing where your time goes can help you understand a lot. Once you know where your time is going, try to make small changes that will get you more of the activities that you want. Remember, it is your time. What do you want from it?

8- to 5-Schedule

Your use of time in college can seem very different from other periods in your life. In reality, time usage in college is not much different than it is or has been in the rest of your life. In high school, you probably went to school at or before 8:00 and got out about 3:00. When you stop and think about it, the hours for high school, junior high, and elementary school were all about the same, 8 or 8:30 to 3 or 3:30. When you enter the work force you will probably need to be at work at or before 8:30 a.m., and you won't leave to go home till about 5:30. The work week comes out to be about 40 hours on the job (8 to 5, 8:30 to 5:30, or 9 to 6 all come out the same way--40 hours).

Your work hours will only be a little more than the total hours you have been putting into school work. When you total your number of school hours, the time you spend in school and the time that you spend on homework, the total number of hours in classes and homework and your future work hours are very similar.

In elementary school, in junior high school, in high school and at work most of us had schedules that resembled a 40-hour work week. In college, schedules seem to be different. We can set our class schedule to have "8 o'clocks" or to avoid "8 o'clocks." We study just about any time of the day or night that we want. For most of us, before and after college we have a pretty definite schedule. In college, however, we do what we want, whenever we want.

Why not use the schedule that the rest of the world uses while you are in college? Create a standard work week with college being your job. You go to class and study between 8 and 5 or 9 and 6, Monday through Friday. You have 40 hours to commit to your classes and your study. With that work schedule you get every evening and weekend off! You have no studying to do at night or on the weekend! Isn't that the way your life is going to be after you graduate--no work at night or on the weekend? Why not try that schedule now?

Using the class-related activities in the sample schedule you find 18 hours of class time and 17 hours of study. If you add in the additional study time that you need you will find that a 9-to-6 schedule will give you enough hours for all of your college work. Changes will, however, be needed to fit all the work into the 9-to-6 schedule, but it could be done. The benefit to the 9-to-6 schedule, of course, is that you will not have to bring work home, and you get your evening and weekends off! Try it. It works!

Time Off First!

If you have ever worked full time or if you have watched your parents and their use of time, you probably know about getting time off or vacations from work. When you work full time, what is work like the week before a vacation? Yes, it is hectic. There is a rush to get all the work done before you leave (in many cases your vacation is contingent on getting your work completed before you go on vacation). The week before a vacation often requires extra work hours to get all of your work completed to get your time off. There is a great deal of pressure and stress from all of the additional work.

How do you get through that week? By thinking about the vacation, naturally. Right? By knowing that the vacation is coming you can get lots of extra work done almost effortlessly, because you know that you will have the next week off. Almost any task becomes easy, or at least easier, because you know the vacation is coming.

Why not begin your college schedule by protecting time for fun, for "time off"? Protecting time off means that regardless of how busy you get, you know that you have time scheduled <u>for the good things</u> in your life. When exam time comes, you still have time scheduled for the things you like. Protected time is <u>never</u> to be given up! You can reduce work time or sleep, anything except protected time.

If you get to believe that you will always have your protected time, you can have an extremely busy schedule and stay mentally and physically healthy because you still have time for yourself. Need to study 40 or 50 hours for finals? No problem, you still have your protected time to relax! Protected time becomes a given in your life.

Note, by using the concept of protected time, all you have done is reverse the usual work-first-then-play with a modified regardless-of-how-much-I-work-I-still-get-to-play rule. The major change is a change in the way you look at everything. Hard work becomes less of a problem, in part, because it is balanced with play. You motivate yourself by knowing that you have earned the time off. You know there is enough time for your work and for personal time.

Using Scheduling

Schedules are not magical. They are tools that you can use to control your time. Try planning a week's schedule and then compare your planned schedule with what actually happened that week. Did you spend most of your time as you had planned? If not, what happened that caused you to change your plans? If you did not follow your schedule, were you pleased with how you actually spent your time? If not, why not try harder to keep your next week's schedule.

On the next four pages, there a two sets of schedules, each with a work sheet that you use for planning your week and one for recording how you actually used your time. Compare your schedule plan with how you actually used your time. If you followed your proposed schedule, pat yourself on the back and try to do it again.

If you didn't follow your schedule, what did you learn from your analysis about yourself, why didn't you use time as you had planned? Adjust your schedule for next week and try again.

Repeat the planned schedule with the evaluation and study of how you actually used your time until you learn how to help yourself to control time as a resource to get done those things that you really value.

Behavior Modification

Psychologists call the motivational technique of using rewards and punishments behavior modification. The actual idea of using rewards or punishments as an incentive for work obviously goes back to long before the field of psychology ever existed. Psychologists just labeled the various aspects of the technique and showed us how to use behavior modification more efficiently.

I use behavior modification as a technique of "last resort" in managing time. When all the other time management techniques won't work for you, or rather, when you can't or won't let the other techniques work for you, use behavior modification. It is all but guaranteed to work for you! It works for you because you change the consequences or outcomes that follow completing or not completing the desired task.

Let's try an example to get a feel for how and why behavior modification works. You enroll

Planned Schedule Work Sheet

	Monday	Tuesday	Wednesday	Thursday	Friday	Saturday	Sunday
5							
6							
7							
8							
9							
10							
11							
12							
1							
2							
3							
4							
5							
6							
7							
8							
9							
10							
11							
12							
1							
2							
3							
4							

Actual Schedule Work Sheet

	Monday	Tuesday	Wednesday	Thursday	Friday	Saturday	Sunday
5							
6							
7							
8							
9							
10							
11							
12							
1							
2							
3							
4							
5							
6							
7							
8							
9							
10							
11							
12							
1							
2							
3							
4							

Time Analysis Work Sheet

As you review your planned
schedule, summarize how you
planned to use your time.

What did you like about your
planned schedule?

    Activity   Hours

_____

_____

_____

_____

_____

_____

_____

_____

_____

What didn't you like about
your planned time schedule?

_____

_____

_____

_____

_____

_____

_____

What needs to be changed to make your planned schedule more to your
liking?

_____   _____

_____   _____

_____   _____

_____   _____

Time Use Work Sheet

As you review how you actually
used your time, how did you
spend your time?

What did you like about the
way you used your time?

    Activity   Hours

_____

_____

_____

_____

_____

_____

_____

_____

_____

_____

_____

_____

_____

_____

What didn't you like about the
way you used your time?

_____

_____

_____

_____

_____

_____

What needs to be changed to make your schedule more to your liking?

_____   _____

_____   _____

_____   _____

_____   _____

_____   _____

Planned Schedule Work Sheet

	Monday	Tuesday	Wednesday	Thursday	Friday	Saturday	Sunday
5							
6							
7							
8							
9							
10							
11							
12							
1							
2							
3							
4							
5							
6							
7							
8							
9							
10							
11							
12							
1							
2							
3							
4							

Actual Schedule Work Sheet

	Monday	Tuesday	Wednesday	Thursday	Friday	Saturday	Sunday
5							
6							
7							
8							
9							
10							
11							
12							
1							
2							
3							
4							
5							
6							
7							
8							
9							
10							
11							
12							
1							
2							
3							
4							

Time Analysis Work Sheet

As you review your planned
schedule, summarize how you
planned to use your time.

What did you like about your
planned schedule?

Activity   Hours

_____   _____

_____   _____

_____   _____

_____   _____

_____   _____

_____   _____

What didn't you like about
your planned time schedule?

_____   _____

_____   _____

_____   _____

_____   _____

_____   _____

_____   _____

What needs to be changed to make your planned schedule more to your
liking?

_____   _____

_____   _____

_____   _____

_____   _____

Time Use Work Sheet

As you review how you actually
used your time, how did you
spend your time?

What did you like about the
way you used your time?

Activity   Hours

_____

_____ _____

_____ _____   _____

_____ _____   _____

_____ _____   _____

_____ _____   _____

_____ _____   _____

_____ _____   _____

_____ _____
                                        What didn't you like about the
_____ _____   way you used your time?

_____ _____   _____

_____ _____   _____

_____ _____   _____

_____ _____   _____

                                        _____

What needs to be changed to make your schedule more to your liking?

_____   _____

_____   _____

_____   _____

_____   _____

in a beginning level chemistry class. What happens if you don't study chemistry the first day of classes? The answer is nothing happens, your life goes on as usual. What happens if you don't study the next day? Nothing happens that is different or unusual. What happens if you don't study chemistry for the entire first week of the semester? Again, nothing happens just because you did not study. What happens if you do not study the entire first month of the semester? Maybe you fail a quiz or a test. What actually happens to you?

Nothing, no calls go to your home, no letters get sent to you from the Dean's Office, life goes on. (Some schools will send out deficiency notices if you are failing at midterm time, but few, if any, call you in to find out why you are not doing well in chemistry.) What happens if you don't study for the entire semester? You probably will fail the course. But what actually happens to you because you did not study chemistry? The answer continues to be nothing; nothing occurs just because you didn't study. You probably are still eligible to enroll the next semester. You, and possibly others, are probably disappointed in your chemistry grade, but nothing specific occurs because you did not study chemistry.

Using behavior modification, something undesirable will happen as a direct consequence of not studying. If you do study, something positive will happen. For example, you could have your roommate hold 20 dollars with the understanding that she will get to keep the 20 dollars if you do not study chemistry for one hour each day. If you do study, you can watch TV for an hour. Studying chemistry controls what will happen. If you do not study, your roommate now has the 20 dollars. (Note, the money was in your roommate's possession to hold so that you would not change your mind and not pay off.) If you do study, you get to watch TV.

In the first example, without any direct consequences to your behavior, or lack thereof, you might have avoided studying chemistry. In the second example, would you have risked losing 20 dollars just because you did not study? (If need be, increase the amount of money you have your roommate hold until studying chemistry becomes less painful or more pleasant than whatever the consequence you set.)

Most of our behavior has been shaped by the use of rewards and punishments. When people drive their cars most drivers go above the speed limit. People easily go 5 to 10 miles an hour over the posted speed limit. Why? Most of the time you will not get a ticket for going just a little over the speed limit. Go 20 mph over the speed limit and sooner or later you will get a ticket.

You dress the way you do, in part, because of the positive (and sometimes because of the negative) comments you get. Why do you smile at people? Because, most of the time, they smile back at you. In behavior modification language, they positively reinforce you for smiling at them!

Behavior modification, then, is the use of rewards and punishments to control behavior. The rewards and punishments can either be external or internal: external-- Mom said be nice to your younger sister or else; internal--you were nice to your sister because it felt good to you.

Behavior modification usually has at least two parts that are connected together; one is a consequence of the other. More specifically, a reward and/or a punishment is made contingent on whether or not a target behavior occurs. If..., then....

Target Behavior

The first step in using behavior modification is to specify the behavior or task, the target behavior, that you are interested in controlling. Some of those behaviors might be studying, reading, working on a term paper, cleaning your room or apartment, etc. When you use behavior modification, however, you must be very specific about what you mean by your terms.

A target behavior should be specific, measurable, and observable. That is, define the target behavior or task such that another person could look at you and determine whether or not you are actually doing the task. Take studying for instance. The specific target behavior you have in mind might be to read and study Chapter 3 of your chemistry text. If you are working on a math problem for your calculus class, you are not working on the target behavior--studying Chapter 3 of the chemistry text.

Measurable means that the behavior or task can be quantified. If your target behavior was to improve the quality of your studying, how would you determine if you were accomplishing your objective? You can't observe the quality of your study, nor can you measure it. If, however, you said you wanted to study Chapter 3 of the chemistry text, you could determine that there are 35 pages in the chapter and that you had completed 18 of those pages. Although the measurement aspect of behavior modification may not seem to be important now, it will become important later.

Going back to the four sample tasks mentioned earlier, we can convert each to a specific behavioral definition:

Studying	Study 35 pages of chemistry
Reading	Read two chapters of Hamlet
Work on a term paper	Locate and photocopy four articles for the term paper
Clean room or apartment	Vacuum the bedroom, put clothes away

The more specific you can be about your target behavior the

easier it will be for you to determine whether or not you are actually doing the task that you say you want to be doing. Remember, the aim of your use of behavior modification is to get you to do more of the things that you say you want to be doing.

Rewards and Punishments

Once you have determined your target behavior, decide what the reward will be for completing the behavior. For a small task, you earn a small reward. For a large task, select a large reward. For example, if you read 10 pages of your psychology text, you earn half an hour of television time. If you complete one math problem, you can make one phone call to a friend. If you complete your chemistry lab report, you get to go to the ball game. If you get to your 8:00 class on time, you can have pizza for lunch. If you earn a 3.0 for the fall semester, you get to visit your friend in Florida during the semester break.

The important aspect of the reward is that it be something that you want to earn. Your reward does not have to be expensive or something that everyone else wants as a reward. It is your reward, you have to value it, to want it. You can work to earn time listening to your stereo, or going to the movies, or playing tennis, or for a piece of candy, or time with your friends, etc. If you do not earn the reward, however, you don't get it! No fair saying that you get a donut for completing a math problem and then eating the donut even though you did not do the math work.

Punishments are used the same way that rewards are only in reverse. If you do not complete the target behavior, then you have earned the punishment. If you do not study chemistry for an hour, you do not get to watch television that evening. If you do not complete three math problems, then you do not get to go out that night, or you do not get to have your best friend over, or you cannot have dessert at dinner, or you cannot listen to your stereo that day, etc. Again, use a small punishment for a small target behavior and a large punishment for a large target behavior.

The rewards and punishments you select must be important to you. You have to be willing to make them contingent upon completing or not completing your target behavior. If you really enjoy going to the movies, you might have an excellent reward. However, are you willing to give up going to the movies if you do not complete something like study?

Rewards and punishments can be the reverse of each other. If your reward is watching TV, then if you do not earn the reward, your punishment is not watching TV. If your punishment is not going to a movie, your reward is earning the right to go to the movie. The idea is to come up with a motivational system that will work for you, that will get you to do the things you say you want to do but, at present, are not doing.

Wait a minute! All this is a silly game. I do not have to do any of this. Yes, in a way behavior modification is a game. You are setting the rules of the game, setting the rules such that you will win your game. If you are failing chemistry, you and I both know that you could be passing, even doing well, if you studied more. In this case you are playing a game and you are losing! You could stay in and study, you could leave your friends and study, you could go to the library instead of watching TV, you could get a tutor to help you, you could see your teaching assistant for help, you could..., but you do not do any of these things. As long as you are playing games with yourself, why not play the game and win?

Behavior modification is almost guaranteed to work for you. It will work for you <u>if</u> you really want the reward, or if you want to avoid the punishment. Your definition of your reward is therefore extremely important. A reward is a reward if it changes your behavior. If you have watching TV as your reward for doing math homework and you do not complete the homework, the reward is not strong enough (or the punishment of not watching TV is not strong enough). If you establish a reward and it does not work to motivate you, increase either the reward or the punishment until you are motivated.

Perhaps some examples of rewards and punishments in action will help you to use this technique better. Most of the students that I have worked with have had little difficulty coming up with punishments for not doing their target behavior. Rewards, for most, were harder to come up with.

I had a commuting student (let's call him Tim) who was sleeping through his 10 a.m. class. Tim wasn't sleeping in class, he was at home sleeping in his bed. Tim's mother woke him up at 7:15 and then left for work. Tim simply went back to sleep. In essence, Tim was saying that it was his mother's fault that he was sleeping through his class. Tim had a younger brother Paul who agreed to wake Tim up in the morning. He was to knock on Tim's door three different times, the last time being 7:15 just before he left for school. Tim was to be up and dressed by the third call. If Tim was not up, Paul had permission to pour a bucket of cold water on Tim! Note, Tim would be up either way-- either he would be up before the third call or he would get up soaking wet. (Could you really stay in a wet bed?) Of course, Mom said that Tim would have to clean up the mess, air the mattress, etc. if he ever got the punishment.

Tim got up and dressed before the third call the first day of the program. He wasn't up by the third call the second day and got soaked. The program now changed to two calls instead of three. Tim was up the next two days, but on the third day he got soaked again. Again the program changed. Now it was one call! He had to be up and dressed by the first call! (Can't you see your brother or sister calling "time to get up" and tossing the bucket of water at almost the same time? How do you avoid getting wet? By being up and dressed of course.) Tim taught himself to be up and dressed by 7:15 to avoid getting wet.

Can't get up in the morning? I bet there are lots of people who would be willing to toss water on you if you didn't get up!

Here are some other, shorter programs that I have seen:

•Study one hour for half an hour of TV time.

•Pay a roommate if you do not get up on time.

•Study calculus for one hour before going to school for a piece of pizza at lunch.

•Study two hours before going to a party Saturday night.

•Study three hours during the day in order to go out with your fiance that evening.

•Study three hours each day to earn the use of your car over the weekend.

•Study 15 hours a week in order to go home for the weekend.

Sometimes you may need to bring other people into your plan. Ideally you design and implement the plan yourself. If you still cannot get your target behavior completed, perhaps you are cheating by taking the reward (or avoiding the punishment) even though you have not earned it. Try having someone else handle the reward. For example, put 10 dollars in an envelope and give it to your best friend to hold for you. Tell her the conditions of your contract and that if you do not fulfill the contract, the contents of the envelope are hers to keep. Here are some other examples of behavior modification programs that I have helped create:

•Two roommates were to be given $5 each if the student was not up by 7 a.m. or if she went back to bed before noon (all three were up every weekday at 7, the student never had to pay off).

•A student who wanted to lose weight arranged to give her father $1 for each piece of candy she ate at home (Dad collected $12 the first day). After that she did lose weight because she stopped eating candy.

•A student arranged to have a 10 dollar check mailed to the General Motors Corporation if she did not have a paper completed by 9 a.m. Monday morning. The check did get mailed.

•A graduate student eliminated grammatical errors from her thesis by agreeing to pay a nickel for each error a friend found in her work (she paid $.25 on the first page, $.20 on the second page, $.05 on the third, page and never had any other mechanical errors on the rest of the thesis).

Start Small

Behavior modification works best as a teaching aid if you start with small tasks and build yourself up to larger projects. In psychology they call the idea <u>successive approximation</u>. Start with a small change and earn the reward. Then gradually increase the target behavior to earn the same reward. If you are concerned about your study time, try studying for 10 or 15 minutes to earn a reward. Once you consistently get the reward slowly increase the amount of study time to 20 minutes, then 30, 40, 50, etc.

Accomplishing small tasks and then gradually being asked to do more and more is the way most of us were taught to work. When you were a child, say two or three years old, if your parents were out raking leaves in the fall, you might have helped out by picking up a leaf and taking it to one of your parents. They smiled, took the leaf, praised you, and asked you to get another one, then another one. Later you brought them two leaves, then a hand full, then an arm full. As you grew older you were asked to do more until you had responsibility for raking the whole yard. Sound familiar? Your tasks were probably different, but the process was the same.

If you are having difficulty controlling or managing your time, try starting with just writing a daily "to do" list. Just write down the things that you need, want or should do. If you make the list, you get your reward. When you have written a list each day for say a week, increase the task to writing the list and prioritizing the items on the list. The third week make your goal to write the list, to prioritize it, and to work on one of the A's. The fourth week try to complete one of the A's. Finally, try to complete all of the A priorities on your list.

Let's review behavior modification First establish your target behavior. Next, make a reward and/or a punishment contingent on whether you complete the behavior or not. If the program doesn't work at first, adjust the reward and punishment to make it work.

Causes of Time Problems

People are often the cause of their own problems. Difficulties in managing time can often be traced to other kinds of problems that, in turn, cause us to have problems with our time.

<u>No</u>

Saying "no", or rather not being able to say no can be a problem that creates difficulties with our time. If you can't say no at times, you can lose control of your time. People can ask for more and more of your time until there is little or no time left for you. If your friends ask you out often, or your boss needs some extra work hours, or your parents want you to come home for the weekend, or your instructor wants to move up your final exam, or your chorus director wants some additional rehearsal time, etc., your priorities can easily get lost. Sometimes we have to say no to people we really care about if we are going to accomplish the tasks that we have set aside for ourselves.

A single "yes" doesn't mean that your time schedule or plans are doomed. Several yes's are the problem. Being able to stick up for yourself is called being assertive. Many times we have to assert ourselves to keep from being caught up in activities that will destroy our plans.

Saying no can be difficult. It isn't necessary to say no every time someone asks you for things that will take up your time. Sometimes you can delay whatever the request is and everyone gets what they want. For instance, when your parents ask you to come home for the weekend, you might say "This weekend I'm pretty tied up, how about next weekend?" If your boss needs extra time, can you give her time on a day that you can afford it? When your friends want you to go to a party with them, how about meeting them at the party after you get your studying finished?

If you have a lot of trouble being assertive on your own behalf you might want to read the section about assertiveness in this text or join an assertiveness training group to learn skills that really are necessary in life. Your campus Counseling Center probably offers programs in assertiveness. If you need

this skill, why not take advantage of their service? Remember, being assertive does not mean that you can't help or be with others, it just means that you need to consider your own needs and stick to them when they are infringed upon by others.

Murphy

Remember Murphy's Law? Murphy's Law states that if anything can possibly go wrong, it will, when it is least convenient. Using Murphy's Law you can predict the future! When do you suppose your typewriter or word processor will break down? Yes, the day before your term paper is due. When will you have a major fight with your boyfriend or girlfriend? The answer is just before finals. When will your car break down? When you really need it, of course!

When things go wrong I blame it all on Murphy. (It's much easier than taking the blame myself. Besides, I can have fun with Murphy. I can try to beat Murphy.) If you leave your term paper to the last minute, Murphy will definitely get you. However, if you target getting the paper completed a week ahead of the due date, Murphy never shows up! If you are ahead on your studies when finals arrive, your boss doesn't want any extra hours and you won't get into a fight with your boyfriend. When you plan for things to go wrong, they rarely do. However, when you're running late or can't afford to have things go wrong, they do.

In the business world they call this contingency planning. When you have work that has to be completed by a given date, build in time for things to go wrong. It's not negative thinking, it's being practical and remembering that regardless of how well we plan, we can't think of or control everything. If you plan ahead and build in contingency time, you can control Murphy.

The Pleasure Principle

Sigmund Freud is credited with formulating the pleasure principle. Basically it says that given the choice between two or more activities, you will do the one that is most pleasurable for you. Because you are a student, when you are given a choice between studying chemistry and being with your friends, you will, of course, study chemistry! Sure you will! If you are given a choice of sleeping late and studying, you sleep late. If the choice is between watching your favorite television program and reviewing for an exam, ...

When your choice is between two things that you don't like, you will choose the one you dislike least! If your choice is between studying chemistry and studying calculus, you will choose the one that is less painful or less "bad."

The problem with the pleasure principle is that immediate pleasure doesn't take long-term pleasure into account. Young couples who want to own a home have difficulty coming up with the down payment, in part, because they want to do other things, such as have dinner out, that consume money that they need to save for the down payment on their house. Studying tonight deprives you of time with your friends today but will get you a higher grade on your exam and help you graduate in a few years. Can you balance your short-term, intermediate and long-term goals? Can you get some of the "good things in life" now, tomorrow, and in the future? Can you schedule in both work time and time to enjoy yourself now?

To do lists can often be helpful in helping you prioritize all the things that you want to do. Once you have that list you can try to balance work and play so that you get both short- and long-term pleasure.

Tolerance Limits

The idea behind tolerance limits comes from engineering and manufacturing. If you are manufacturing nuts and bolts, the nut must fit the bolt. The nut must be loose enough to go onto the bolt, but, at the same time, it must be tight enough to stay on after it is tightened.

When you are working on an assignment, when is it good enough to turn in; what are your instructor's minimal expectations? You have been in school for years. You should have a pretty good idea of what your instructor expects of you. If you don't, why not ask her? Ask her if you could see a sample of an acceptable paper!

When you take a job, don't you want to know what the boss expects of you? In school it is the same; you need to know your instructor's expectations.

The other side of tolerance limits is perfectionism. When have you exceeded expectations but you can't stop because your work isn't good enough? When are you needlessly reworking something that is already really good? You need to have realistic expectations for yourself. Papers can always be improved. Authors I know have often said that their material could have been better, but it was good enough. Their work was published, but they know that it could have been better. Don't throw your standards away, just balance them with the expectations of those whom you are working for.

Tolerance limits are the boundaries of acceptability of your boss, your instructor, and of your own expectations.

Planning Is the Answer

If you are having difficulty making time work for you, you really need to sit down and think about your part in the dilemma. What do you want? If you haven't taken the time to create a list of long-term and short-term goals, take the time to plan ahead, to know where you are going. Planning controls the strategies that you use to make time work for you instead of against you. Once you have your plans made, all you have to do is to implement them. If you have difficulty with the implementation of your plan, if the time management techniques that have been discussed do not work for you, it may be time for you to talk with someone, such as a counselor, at your campus learning center to find out why you are having so much trouble controlling your time.

Procrastination

Procrastination is working on anything but the task that you want or should be doing, regardless of how desirable or socially acceptable your current task is. If you are supposed to be working on your term paper and you are cleaning your room, you are procrastinating. If you are supposed to be cleaning your room and you are working on your paper, you are procrastinating. Helping a friend with her homework may sound good, but it is procrastinating if you are supposed to be doing your own homework.

We have many different reasons for putting things off. Some of those reasons include fear of failure, fear of success, lack of goals, lack of motivation, wanting to be somewhere else, wanting to be doing something other than the current task, and problems with just getting started. The first, fear of failure, blocks us from trying because we may find out that we really are not good enough or capable enough to do the task in question. The fear of success can mean that others will raise their expectations about us or that we will have to set even higher goals in the future. Lack of goals and motivation suggests that completing the task has little or no meaning to us. If we are doing something that we do not really want to be doing, it can be difficult to get started.

When you find that you are procrastinating, stop and think about what is causing your procrastination. Consider the cost, to you, of not doing whatever it is that you "should" be doing. What benefit are you getting from procrastinating? Yes, if you are not doing a task that you want or should be doing, there is some benefit that you are deriving from "not doing." If you are not studying, people feel badly about all the hard work you have to do or how difficult the work you have to do is, etc. By not studying you get attention. If you often procrastinate about the same task, try making a list of the costs of not completing the work and the benefits that you are getting from your procrastination.

Try creating specific goals that you want to accomplish. Connect the small goals together into a larger package that has more meaning to you. For instance, you keep putting off working on a term paper because you know it will take a lot of work, energy, and time. Try connecting the term paper to the reports that you will have to write after you graduate and go to work in the business world. (The business world runs on proposals and reports. Those who write well get ahead!) Your assigned term paper is no worse than reports that you will be writing in the future. The paper has been

assigned to help you improve your thinking and writing skills so that your business reports will be easier to write.

You might try being selfish. Ask yourself What's in it for me? What will I learn from writing this paper? Whatever you are putting off, what will you learn or earn from completing it? Try thinking about your pride of workmanship or pride of authorship. (A number of years ago there was a lot of criticism about the quality of American manufactured automobiles. Workers, it was said, had little pride in their work on the assembly line because they did not really feel they were of significance, their little part in the manufacturing process was invisible. Ford Motor Company attempted to counter this belief in the manufacture of their Taurus model. General Motors created Saturn. In each case, groups of workers assembled each car. Workers took pride in their work. The quality of the work was excellent!)

An unusual technique for stopping procrastination is conscious procrastination. Just sit and do nothing! Try it. Just sit, and force yourself to do absolutely nothing. No thinking about fun things, no day dreaming, no planning about what you are going to do. Just sit and do nothing. (It is very hard to do nothing. Actually it is impossible to do nothing. You will think about something.) Hopefully, it will not take you long to want to do something, anything, even study chemistry! Remember chemistry? That's what you were procrastinating about.

Time Visual Displays

Working on big projects can be frustrating, in part, because it is difficult to see progress being made. When confronted with large tasks, some people like to create visual aids such as charts and graphs to help them see that their work is moving ahead. Community fund drives often use a large thermometer to show the public how much money has been ^contributed to date. Computer specialists sometimes use flowcharts to plot their course of action. Project managers often use Pert/CPM or Gantt charts to keep track of complicated programs. You can adapt these charts to help you visualize your progress and maintain control over the project or task.

Visuals are a way of creating a road map or the path you plan to take to complete your project. They can be as useful as a road map is when you take a long trip by car.

Before beginning a long automobile trip most travelers trace out their planned route on a map. Auto clubs like AAA will supply premarked maps to their members. Travelers use the marked route to find their way to their destination.

Why not create a road map for yourself, to help you get through your work? Creating the map or plan may not be as easy as you might think. You will have to know the steps to complete, the options that will be available at different points, time lines, etc. Creating your map will be something like creating an outline for a paper. It will take time and a lot of thought. Once completed, however, your work will become easier because you will know where you are going and you can easily plot your progress through to completion.

Flowcharts

A flowchart is a graphic image of the path you plan to follow while completing a project. It shows the task from beginning to end in a simple diagram. Each step that needs to be implemented too complete the project is should on the chart.

Review the sample flowchart and the "conventions" to use when you create a flowchart.

Gantt, Pert, and CPM Charts

In the government and in business large projects such as government and military contracts or large building developments are often observed, followed, or controlled through the use of visual displays known as Gantt, Pert, or CPM charts. The Gantt, or bar, chart was first used by Henry Gantt in the early 1900s. Activities and events are listed on the vertical axis of the chart, whereas starting and ending times are plotted on the horizontal axis. That is, each horizontal bar in the chart represents a different kind of activity and shows when and how

A flow chart for a required departmental seminar paper might look something like this:

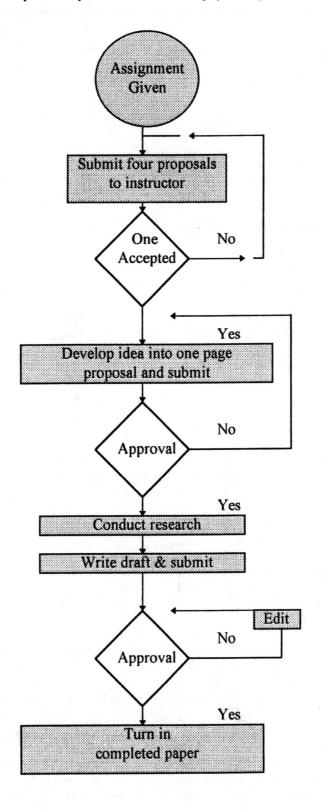

Circle	Label (Assignment Given)
Rectangle	Process or execution (what is to be done)
Diamond	Decision point with options (where to go with either a yes or a no)
Line	Path to be taken (where to go next)
Arrow	The direction of the flow

Conventions to Use When Creating a Flow Chart

long that activity should take. You can then compare your planned progress with your actual work to control getting your final product completed on time.

Pert (Program Evaluation and Review Technique) charts were developed by the Navy during the late 1950s. At about the same time, DuPont created a similar technique that is called the Critical Path Method (CPM). Often the two techniques are combined into a single Pert/CPM chart. Events and activities are identified and plotted sequentially.

Completion time for each activity is estimated and plotted using three different estimates: most likely completion time, an optimistic completion time, and a pessimistic completion time. The chart shows the interdependency of all the specified activities as well as the critical path--the sequence

of necessary activities that will take the greatest time to complete.

In each of the visual display charts, you can plot your actual work progress against your planned timetable. If you see that you are behind schedule, you can begin thinking of ways of making more time available for your paper to get back on your planned timetable.

The visual display becomes a tool to use to see your work progress. As work is completed you actually get to see progress on your time chart.

Friends & Coworkers as Models

Some of your friends may be using other techniques to help them complete things that they value. People have a lot of different techniques for getting work done. Most people also enjoy being asked for advice. When you see someone

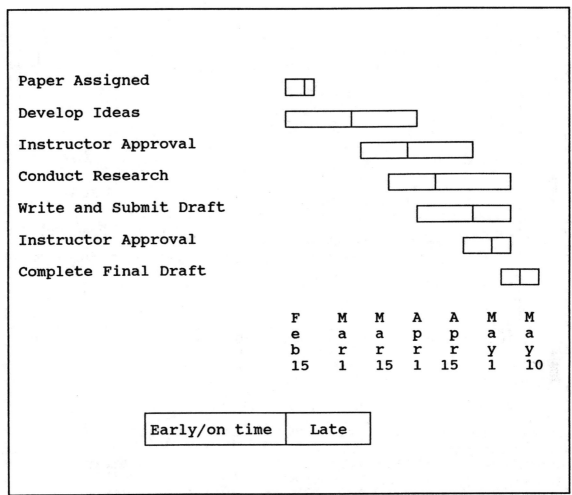

Figure 1 Gantt Chart for Seminar Paper

you know who seems to be getting a lot done, why not ask them how they do their work so efficiently? Teachers, counselors, coworkers, bosses, and even strangers will often offer advice if they are asked for it. All it takes is caring enough about learning how to get more out of your time and a little bit of assertiveness to ask for advice.

54

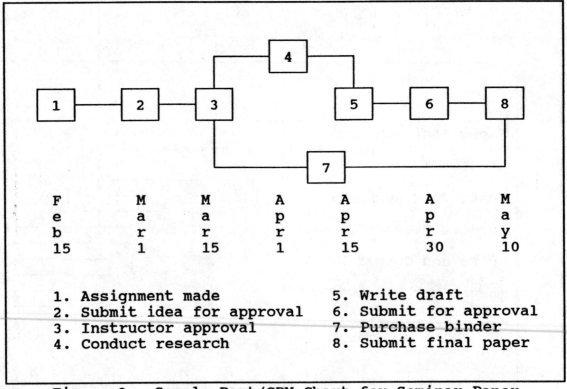

Figure 3.   Sample Pert/CPM Chart for Seminar Paper

In your major field there may be time-saving techniques, procedures or skills that you are supposed to know. In many of the sciences you are expected to know how to use certain computers, computer programs, and support services. Your instructors, advisor, and students ahead of you in your program could be sources of additional information about managing time-saving techniques.

A Pert/CPM chart for the required departmental seminar paper could look something like the diagram above.

Summary

Time is a resource that you can use to get the things that you want out of life. To get the most that you can out of the time that you have available, you need to know what it is that you want--you need goals. Once you have identified your goals you can use to do lists and schedules to help you decide how you can best use your time to reach your goals.

The key to efficient use of

time isn't working harder, it is working smarter, working on the most important things first. If you use To Do Lists, identifying your priorities will help you to focus your attention on your most important tasks. Schedules will help you see where your time is going. Visual displays can show you whether or not you are staying on schedule.

The key to effective time management, however, is planning--planning what it is that you want to accomplish. Time management then becomes creating and implementing a strategy that will get you to your goal.

4 THE STUDY ENVIRONMENT

You have been a student for at least 13 years. During that time you have heard a lot of different things about the room or place that you study in. Almost all of us have heard that our study room has to be quiet. We are supposed to sit on a straight-back metal or wooden chair. The light that we use for reading should be positioned so that it does not shine in our eyes. The temperature of the room should be between 68 and 72 degrees and there should be good ventilation. There is a list of supplies that we should have available to us when we study that includes a dictionary, a desk encyclopedia, a world atlas, pencils, pens, a calculator, lined and graph paper, etc. The desk at which we study should be free of all distractions--no mirrors, no pictures. The desk should not be next to a window, and no bed should be in sight. Lately, I guess the list includes a word processor or a personal computer.

I've just described your study room right? Sure I have. If I am honest with you, I have to say that I have seen very few student rooms that are like the one that I just described. And yet, study skills books tell you that is the way the room should be.

Have you ever been in a busy office? What is it like there when they have a deadline to meet? Is everything neatly organized? Is it quiet? Is anyone concerned about the amount of light or the heat?

Are people running to look words up in the dictionary or trying to locate places in the atlas? Is everyone sitting up straight, working at a desk that has no distractions on it?

No, busy offices aren't like that at all. Often there is a lot of confusion especially when there are deadlines to be met. Life can be very stressful and hectic, and yet work seems to get done.

If that is true, then why do students have to study in a sterile environment, at a desk that has been cleaned so that nothing remains except the things that are absolutely needed to get studying done?

The truth is that most of the things that I mentioned above are not essential to successful study at all. Although there is a little bit of educational research to support some of these traditional beliefs, there is no strong evidence to support any of them. Let's look at each area of concern and see what is best for you.

Quiet

Usually the first thing that we are told about our study room is that it must be quiet. In the office people can work with music and noise, but students are supposed to work in quiet. Strange, isn't it?

It is true that some people like to work in quiet. It is equally true that others like to work with noise or music around them. Quiet is supposed to be helpful because there aren't any sounds to distract you. Without distractions, you are supposed to be able to concentrate better.

Have you ever been awake in bed at 3 o'clock in the morning? It's quiet then. Is it really totally quiet? No, there are sounds such as the furnace starting and stopping in the winter or the air conditioner or a fan running in the summer. You can hear cars on the street, water dripping from the bathroom faucet, the house creaking as it settles or the refrigerator starting or stopping. You can even hear a train that may be a mile or more away. The trouble with quiet is anything that is "nonquiet" is distracting.

Systematic noise, on the other hand, can mask sounds that you might be interested in. A running fan or air conditioner produces a boring hum that hides other sounds such as people talking that could take you away from your work. Music can be helpful in hiding other sounds as long as the music itself isn't a distraction. Instrumental music that you don't really like or hate will block out distracting sounds. Vocal music or talk radio stations tend to be distracting because you will tend to listen to the voices.

You have been to stores where they have soft music playing. Why do they play music? To cover up the sounds of business, to create a pleasant, nondistracting atmosphere for you to spend your money in. After you have been in the store for a little while, do you hear the music? No, it blends in and almost isn't there.

The same thing happens at work. The sounds of work---the telephones, the computers and printers, people talking---all blend together into background noise. If we want to listen to any one of them, we can. We can also work with them and be productive. So too with study. You can study with music and noise.

I had one student who recorded a classical music tape with the same piece on both sides of her cassette. Another used popular music--she took an instrumental piece and recorded it over and over on both sides of her cassette. The music became work or study music. When each student played her tape, it reminded her that it was time to be working. The music became background noise that was both comfortable to be with and a masking noise that blocked out sounds that would have been distracting.

How much sound is good for you? If you use music for a background to your studying, how loud should you have it so that it facilitates your work but does not distract you? It is up to you; you have to decide what amount of sound will facilitate your work and what amount will be distracting.

The Straight Backed Chair

"Sit up straight when you read!" That's what your teachers and parents told you.

Sitting up straight was supposed to help your posture and, at the same time, help you concentrate better.

When you look at research on reading, however, there are no studies that show that sitting on a straight-backed wooden or metal chair helps you read better. You can read sitting on a straight-backed chair, in a lounge chair, standing up or lying down. You can even read standing on your head! (It is a bit difficult to hold the book, of course, but you can still read!) You and I both know that the position that you get your body in really doesn't matter. You also know that the more horizontal you get, the greater the probability that you will go to sleep. If you want to go to sleep, go to sleep. If you want to study lying down, study lying down.

What you sit or lie on and the position that you are in when you study doesn't count. You can read and study in any position that you can get your body into.

Light

Study skills books often tell you that your light source should be of a certain wattage and location. When I was in school I remember being told that my reading light should come over my less dominant shoulder (Because I am right handed that means that my reading light should come over my left shoulder). This recommendation was made to avoid glare from the light while reading and to prevent shadows from covering the text.

Let's look at the problem of light a different way. Have you ever been to the beach? Have you ever read a book or a magazine while sunning yourself at the beach? What was the light like there? Millions of candlepower were coming from the sun, reflecting off the water, the sand, even your skin. Could you read? Yes, you could. With all the glare? Yes, you could read even though the light source wasn't what it was supposed to be.

What is the smallest amount of light that you can read with? 100 watts? 60 watts? 40 watts? Have you ever tried to read by candle light? One candle power is about the smallest readily available source of light I can think of. Yes, if you want to, you can read by candle light. The actual amount of light you need really depends on what you want or like.

In the office, light can be anywhere from bright fluorescent overhead lighting to poor desk lights. People read computer screens in dark rooms and in brightly lit rooms. Whatever light a person wants, gets, or is comfortable with is what she works with. What does all of this mean in terms of light to study with? You do need light to see the print on the page. Use whatever amount and placement of light that you are comfortable with.

Temperature

I have been told that the temperature in the place that you study should be between 68 and 72 degrees. The reasoning is that if it is too cold you'll be concentrating on being cold and not on studying. When it is too warm, everyone knows you'll get sleepy and fall asleep.

Remember reading at the beach? What was the temperature at the beach that day? Could you read?

If you live in the north, have you ever needed public transportation in the middle of the winter? When the temperature was, say, 20 degrees, did you have any trouble reading the sign on the bus that told you that it wasn't the one that you wanted?

The building that I work in was built in the late 1920s. In the winter, rooms can be either hot or cold. When the air conditioning is on during the summer, it can be either hot or cold, too. Unless the building gets to be over 85 or 90 degrees in the summer, I am expected to work. If it gets into the low 60s during the winter, I am also expected to work. The same is true of most other offices that I know of. That is, regardless of the temperature, you are expected to get your work done.

When you read and study, don't worry about the temperature. Try to get a temperature that is comfortable for you if you can. You can read and learn at any reasonable temperature.

Equipment and Supplies

Items that you are supposed to have at your desk include things like a dictionary; a desk encyclopedia; an atlas; various kinds of paper, pencils, and pens; erasers; a calculator; etc. The truth is, you don't really need any of these items to study effectively.

Two examples should help to clarify the point; (a) the dictionary and (b) the atlas. When you read and come across a word that you do not know, do you stop and look the word up in your dictionary? Wasn't that what you were taught to do in school? Of course, when most people run across a word that they do not know while they are reading they simply skip the word and keep on reading. Students, however, are supposed to look up the word in the dictionary.

Think about it for a minute. You have a vocabulary of 5,000 or 6,000 words or more. How many of those words have you ever looked up in the dictionary? Not many, right? Take a look at one word that you use regularly,"the." What does "the" mean? The <u>Oxford English Dictionary</u>, a two volume dictionary that has print so small that it comes with a magnifying glass to read with, has three columns of definitions of the word "the." There are about one hundred definitions for the word "the." How long would it take you to go through those definitions to find the one that the author meant in the passage that you were reading?

Most of the time when you are reading and you find a word that you do not know, you simply guess what it might mean. When you have seen the word used several times you begin to "know" what it means. If you really must know what a new term means when you are reading a textbook, the author will probably tell you what it means within the actual text. If the new word is part of the subject matter, it will probably be defined in the glossary, if there is one.

When you are reading a book and the author mentions a place that you haven't heard of before, do you stop and look it up in your atlas? Probably not. When you read a history textbook do you know where all the places are that the author discusses? Do you look them up in the atlas? I can make a case for looking these places up so that you will know where they are and perhaps get a better appreciation of the world. Still, most people do not stop reading to locate new places.

None of the other supplies are needed when you study either. You do not need anything but your textbooks.

No Distractions

The desk at which you study should be free from distractions such as pictures and mirrors. It should be located so that you cannot see either a bed, a picture or out a window. The idea is to avoid distractions such as pictures of people that you care about.

Can you really find a place to study that has no distractions? Suppose you bought a new desk

that had no imperfections. Wouldn't you be bothered by having everything perfect?

I remember reading about astronauts who were being trained to experience weightlessness by floating in large tanks of water. Apparently they would spend hours wearing their space suits floating around in tanks of water to get the feel of what prolonged weightlessness would be like. It was a boring experience with nothing to do. There were no sounds, there were no distractions. What happened? After a while the astronauts reported hearing things that weren't there, songs that they enjoyed, etc. Because there weren't external distractions to occupy their thoughts, their bodies created internal activities to keep their minds occupied.

When you don't have external distractions to take you away from your study, you too will create internal distractions that you can use to keep yourself from studying. There are always things in our lives for us to worry or think about. It is almost impossible to be someplace and not have potential external or internal distractors around you.

Even the library has its distractors that you can use to avoid study. When I first got to graduate school in 1965 I often went to the graduate library to study. The building had marble floors. What kind of shoes did women wear in the mid 1960s? High-heeled shoes with spiked heels. The heels had metal ends or taps on them.

(In the library it seemed that they had pneumatic hammers on them--tap, tap, tap.) How could someone walk across a marble floor in high heels and not be distracting?

Distractions will be with you until the time they put you in your coffin so learn to work with them. Your office won't be quiet and your boss won't want to hear about why you were distracted. If your work doesn't get done, you'll be looking for another job. You can be in the ideal study environment or the perfect work place and still not get any work accomplished. Create an acceptable work place or study environment for you, one that you can work in. The rules for that environment are minimal: light, enough for you to read comfortably; something for you to sit on; and your work.

The One Critical Ingredient

I have tried to eliminate all of the myths about what you should have, where you should be, and what your study area ought to be like. There just isn't sufficient evidence that shows that most of the traditional necessities for study really help. There is, however, one important or critical consideration, aspect, part, or feature of the study environment. What do you suppose it is?

The critical ingredient in the study environment is you, all aspects of you. It includes your attitude, your goals and objectives, your abilities, your interests, your thoughts and feelings, your personality-

-all of you. In the perfect study environment you could get nothing accomplished if you didn't want to. On the other hand, you could study in a busy shopping mall, waiting for a bus on a busy street, in a recreation room with people playing games, in the living room while your family or friends watch TV, at the office during your coffee break, etc.

When you find that you are not studying, stop and think about why you aren't getting the work done that you want to. Is it really too noisy? Is it really too warm? If you need to change something, change it and get to work. If you aren't going to work, to study, stop playing at it and go and do something else. Why spend an hour or two or three getting nothing accomplished except getting frustrated? If you want to or need to work and are having difficulty getting started because of "distractions" or not being in the "right" place, try using some of the techniques that are presented in the chapter on textbook reading. The environment probably isn't the problem, you are.

Summary

When it comes to the place that you study, the location can be anywhere you want it to be. The things that you may have heard about the study environment such as needing quiet or lack of distractions, study in the same place or some specific temperature setting will make little difference as long as you want to study. You will need light to see, of

course, that's about all. You
can read and study sitting
down, lying down, or standing
up. Where you study doesn't
count. That you do settle down
to study and that you work
effectively does. Use any
study area that makes you feel
comfortable, that helps you to
get your work done. The place
isn't important; you and your
thoughts are.

64

5 TEXTBOOK READING TECHNIQUES

In this chapter, I will review a number of different techniques for learning material from textbooks and other written sources. Because anyone reading this book can obviously read, why include a chapter on textbook reading techniques?

As we have learned to read and study in school, most of us have learned some "bad" habits, the worst of which is that whenever we are given a reading assignment, the most important thing to do is to finish reading the material. If our assignment is something like "Read Chapter 4 of your history book" or "Read section three of Chapter 7," the tendency is to concentrate your efforts on getting all the pages of the assigned material read.

So far, everything sounds good. What's the problem? The concern I have is, have you learned the material you were assigned? The answer I often receive when I ask this question is "I read the assignment." Then I explain that I understand that you said you read the material. The question I am asking is not "Have you read the material?" but "Have you learned the material that you read?" The response to the question is often a look of bewilderment, of disbelief that I have asked such a stupid question.

Try looking at my question this way. Does read equal learn? Pictorially the statement would look like this: READ = LEARN?

Most students have learned that just because you have read something does not mean that you have learned it. We can read material, have understood the words that we read, but not have learned the content of material we just completed.

The real statement or answer to the question "Does read equal learn?" is "No, just because you have read something does not mean that you have learned it." In other words, READ $\neq$ LEARN.

So what? After you have read the text material you will go back and learn it, right? You may have underlined the text or used a magic marker to mark all the important material. That means that you have seen the material once and that important things are marked to simplify learning later. When test time arrives, you will go back and learn the material that has been marked.

Again, this sounds good. You go through the assigned text material, mark what you think is important, and then, at a later date, go back to learn. The trouble with the system is that now you have to go over material that you do not know to learn it for "the test." You are going to actually learn that material for the first time. First time learning takes a lot of time. Students often find that there is too much to be covered just before the test and end up not knowing as much as they need to for the exam.

Learning for yourself is not the same thing as studying for the exam. When you learn for yourself you are learning to know more, to have better skills that you want to be able to use or know in the future. When you study for the exam you learn what you think your instructor wants you to know. You learn for someone else and probably do not care if you are able to maintain that learning for any extended length of time.

That is what school is all about, right? Learn the material that your instructors want you to know so that you can score high on the class examinations. If you get high grades on the exams, you will get a high grade for the course. The high grades for your classes translate into a high grade point average, which in turn means a good job with a good salary.

Sounds great! The problem, however, is that the world of work is beginning to learn that a college degree does not mean that the person has college level skills! The field of education is a good example. In the past, teachers at most levels of public education had a good command of the English language. When they wrote notes to parents, the note was clear and free of grammatical errors. Today, many parents and school systems are extremely concerned about the academic skills of their children's teachers. Because of the concern for teachers' skills, many school systems have instituted English and mathematics competency tests that prospective teachers must be able to pass before they can be hired. Even though the teacher applicant has a college degree, he is still required to demonstrate his ability in basic skills!

Businesses are also questioning the skill level of college graduates, in part, because new graduates sometimes cannot perform as expected. Good grades are respected, but the applicants' skill level will not be assumed from their college grades. Increasingly, applicants are being tested or otherwise asked to demonstrate their knowledge and skill level.

What's the Point?

The point is that most of us do not learn from simply reading. We need to do something with the material that we read to really learn it, to make the information our own! When we read we need to incorporate the incoming information with our past learnings. We need to integrate the new with the old.

When we read we need to provide thinking time for learning. We take some information in and then work it over in our head to make it become part of us. Look at the way you talk about information that you read but didn't learn. You say "It didn't sink in." "It" will rarely just sink in. You have to work at making "it" get into your head, to become part of your personal collection of knowledge and skills. You have to internalize your learning.

Reading Once Is Not Enough

Many students seem to feel that there is something wrong with their reading or learning skills if they cannot comprehend material that they have read only once. Most of us have heard about photographic memories that enable some people to be able to read or mentally photograph written material so that all of the information can be recalled weeks, months, or even years later. Regretfully, that kind of learning is not possible for most of us. There will be times, of course, that you can read some material only once and find that you can understand almost all of the ideas or concepts that have been presented. This can happen if you are familiar with the ideas that are covered, if the information is easy for you to understand, or if you are really interested in knowing the information that you are reading.

Sometimes, of course, we can read something once and remember it forever. For instance, when I was a teenager, I remember reading in the Ripley's Believe It or Not section of the newspaper about Captain Cook and his voyage around the world. Captain Cook was an Englishman who was hired to sail around the world and bring back to England a record of what he had discovered. One of the places that Captain Cook visited was Australia. I don't know exactly where he went, but I do know that while he was there he saw some kangaroos. Keep in mind that Captain Cook had never seen a kangaroo before. He saw this weird animal hopping about. It didn't look like any animal he had ever seen before. He asked one of the local people what it was and was told "kangaroo." Now, if Captain Cook were a good explorer, he probably asked someone else what that animal was and again was told "kangaroo." He wrote down in his journal that he had seen a kangaroo and described the animal in detail.

Stop and think for a minute. What language did Captain Cook speak?

English, right? After all, he was an Englishman. When he talked to the people he met in Australia, what language did they speak? Good question, right? I never have known what language it was. What I do know is that the natives he spoke with did not understand English. "But they told him the animal he had seen was a kangaroo didn't they?" No, they didn't. When Cook asked what the animal was, they said "kangaroo," or "I don't understand." That's right, in the natives' language, "kangaroo," or something that Captain Cook wrote down as kangaroo, means "I don't understand."

So what? The point of the story is that I read this piece of information sometime in the 1950s and have remembered it. Kangaroo has never been the correct answer to any question that I have ever been asked in class--not in elementary school, or high school, not in college, and not in graduate school. And yet I remembered it. We all can remember some of the information that we have read one time. Unfortunately, only a very small portion of what we read, probably much less than one percent of our total reading, will be remembered for long periods of time without our ever having to work at retaining or remembering the information.

For most students, simply reading is not enough to ensure learning. Research on reading suggests that there are at least two factors in mastering and retaining material: (1) The reader must see or hear most of the information that he wants to learn, and (2) the reader must do something with the information after he has read it in order to maintain the learning over time.

Study skill methods have been devised to help ensure that learning, not just reading, has taken place. The methods themselves do not guarantee learning, they just provide a structure that can be used to help us master material if we want to. The structure, in turn, can be used as a tool or an aid to help us learn more effectively.

SQ3R

SQ3R is a study technique that was developed by Frank Robinson. The letters stand for Survey, Question, Read, Recite, and Review--SQ3R. The technique will take a little time to learn and even longer to be comfortable with. However, the procedures of the method do seem to work for those who use them. Learning

SQ3R should pay off for you by helping you to master material that you want to keep for an extended period of time.

The SQ3R method and each of its parts will be explained in detail so that you can understand and see the logic behind each step. Get a good feel for the method, in general, and then back up and master each step. Once you understand the method and how and why it helps in the learning process, you can use it on your own textbooks.

SQ3R starts you off with an overview of the material that you want or need to learn. After the overview comes mastering small sections of the information. Finally, you are asked to bring all the little pieces together again to produce "the whole picture" or a summary of the information that you have read. That's all there is to it--overview, learn each section, and then pull all of the sections together in a review.

Survey

Before you begin to read an assignment, look over the material to get a general idea of what it is all about. More specifically, read the chapter heading to get a condensed summary of the main idea of the chapter. (Telling you to read the chapter title may sound simple minded, and it may be. However, a very large number of students never seem to read the chapter title and use that information to help them learn better. The chapter title tells you the main idea that will be covered in the chapter. Read the title to begin focusing your attention on the concepts that the author is about to present.) After you read the chapter title, read the introduction, if there is one. Next read all of the subheadings; look at words that are in italics or boldfaced print; and glance at charts, graphs, and pictures. Finally, read the summary of the chapter.

You should be able to survey most textbook chapters in less than 15 minutes. This time investment is something like the warm-up exercises that you do before starting athletic competition. You warm up physically and mentally in sports so that your body and mind are ready for the competition ahead of you.

Did you ever play tennis, basketball, or ping-pong (table tennis for the purists), or any other two-person contest? Do you remember learning to play the game by competing with people who were better than you were? Suppose there was someone you regularly competed against, let's call him Carl. If Carl was significantly better than you were, you probably lost to him all, or almost all the time. The next time you played against Carl, didn't you try to think about the things that you could do that would help you to win? Didn't you think about what not to do? Didn't you mentally review games that you had played with him in the past? In essence, you mentally and physically prepared to win, perhaps even thinking about or

visualizing the victory. If you kept playing, you eventually got better and, hopefully, beat Carl.

The Survey step is part of your mental preparation to learn the text material before you. You learn the essence or main idea of the chapter before you go back to learn the details.

Have you ever worked on a picture puzzle? You have a puzzle that has 500 pieces. What is the first step in putting all the pieces together? Answers to that question include things like dump the pieces out of the box, find the corner pieces, find the edge pieces, and get the border completed.

If you stop and think about it, don't you look at the picture on the cover of the box before you get started on the actual puzzle? Sometimes you look at the picture and say that the puzzle is too easy or too hard for you. When you have decided to work on a specific puzzle, you use the picture to tell you where different colors or objects go. (Real picture puzzle fanatics get puzzles that do not have pictures on the boxes. They even get puzzles that don't have straight edge pieces to guide them in completing the picture.) The point here is that even when doing recreational activities like picture puzzles, we use the "big picture," the central thought, to help us do better.

When working on a picture puzzle you rely on the picture on the box to help you put all the pieces together. Likewise, in surveying you are creating a mental picture of the essence of the chapter so that you will know how all the pieces of the chapter fit together.

In reading research on human learning, researchers talk about advance organizers, things that people can do before they read that will help them learn material better. Surveying, getting the main idea of the chapter, before you read is one of the techniques that has been shown to aid us in learning. When you survey and learn the main idea of the chapter you create a structure or foundation on which you will assemble the rest of the information that you want or need from the chapter. Now, instead of receiving isolated bits of information from the reading material, you have bits and pieces that fit into the general structure that you have created during the survey.

The survey then is a technique to use to get you started in learning the information that you are about to read. Your survey should give you a general idea of what the author is going to say so that you can (1) remember what you already know about the subject and use that starting point to learn the rest of the material and (2) understand how each section of the material fits together and know where the author is going.

Question

After you have completed your survey of the chapter, go back to the beginning of the chapter

to begin systematic learning of the material. Read the first heading or subhead and turn that heading into a question.

Suppose you are reading an American History text and have been assigned the chapter on the Civil War. It is possible that the first heading in the chapter could be Harper's Ferry. The Question step of SQ3R has you change this heading into a question. The question you ask might be "Who is Harper Ferry?" This really isn't a good question to ask but it meets the requirement of creating a question. When you read the text you find out that Harper's Ferry isn't a "who," it is a "what," a place. You made a mistake with your question, why? Why did you think it was a person? Were you really paying attention when you surveyed? Are you studying or are you playing at studying?

Have you ever made a mistake before? Did you learn from your mistake? I hope so. I hope you learned at least what not to do so that you won't make the same mistake again. It is the same with the Question step of SQ3R. If you ask a bad question you find out it was a poor question when you read. Hopefully, you find out why your expectations were wrong and get yourself back on the author's track, to the author's thought process, to the author's ideas.

Back to the example. A better question to have asked would have been "What happened at Harper's Ferry?" If you stop and think about it, an even better question would have been "How was Harper's Ferry related to the Civil War?" Or, since this is the beginning of the chapter, "What happened at Harper's Ferry that caused or led up to the Civil War?" As you read you will be looking for the answer to the question that you asked. You will become involved in your reading because you want to get something from it.

Please keep in mind that reading is a personal or a very selfish activity. You read for yourself. You read for information that you want to know or to entertain yourself. You read not for your teachers, not for your parents, not for your boss or friends, you read to get something out of the material for yourself. Your instructors assign materials to be read to give you information and skills that you can use for the rest of your life. Later in life, after school, your boss will give you information to read to help you become a more productive worker or team member. When you join the work force, you will seek out material to read that will help you get promoted to a better, higher paying job or into another field that interests you.

The Question step in SQ3R is there to help you focus your attention on the most important aspect of the reading material, the main idea. The heading is a condensed summary of the main idea that the author will present. By reading the heading, by thinking about it, by creating questions, you will be zeroing in on the essence of

what the author is trying to get across to you.

Think about your textbooks for a minute. Why were they written? To help you learn the subject matter, right? Wrong! They were written to make money! They make money for the author, the publisher, the bookstore, the paper companies, etc. If they were written to help you learn, wouldn't "they" have done things to help you learn more effectively? For instance, have you ever bought a new textbook that was professionally underlined? A chemist writes a chemistry text and then a different chemist comes along and underlines and marks the most important information to help you focus your attention on the material that is really important. Wouldn't professional underlining help you focus your attention on the really important material?

One of the few things that most textbooks have in them to help you learn is headings. Headings are used to break up the book and chapters into smaller and smaller chunks. Each heading tells you the focus point of the next piece of information. So read the heading, and give it the attention that it deserves. It is giving you a condensed summary of the main idea that the author will present next.

Textbooks contain a tremendous amount of information. Most people cannot or will not learn all of the information that is presented. If you are not going to or if you do not need to learn everything, why not concentrate on the most important material that is presented, the <u>main idea</u>. The question you ask should point out the most important idea or concept that the author will be trying to get across to you. By reading the heading you will be starting to organize your thoughts about the information that you know will be coming. Even before you read, you will have begun getting your thoughts focused on what the author is about to say.

Take a look at sports again. Before you play a game like tennis, what do you do? Warm up. What does warm up mean? Warming up means getting your muscles ready to perform or work effectively when you are ready to compete. You warm up physically and mentally. You "psych" yourself up to play the best that you can.

Remember reading the children's book about the little engine? The little engine had a long line of freight cars to pull up the mountain. It was hard work, but he got the job done by saying, "I think I can, I think I can." In sports we use positive thoughts to help us play better. We try to "psych" ourselves into playing better than we have before.

A different example. Did you study a foreign language in high school? Did you learn it? Many, if not most, of the students I talk to about how they studied their foreign language say they did not learn the language because they had no real use for it. They told themselves, "I can't learn this. I have no use for it."

Students can spend hours and hours proving that they can't learn a language that they could easily learn if they wanted to.

What happens when you play a game saying "I can't win, I can't win"? You lose, right? If you say, "I think I can, I think I can," does it mean that you will win? No, just thinking that you will win is no guarantee that you will win, but it helps!

Research on reading shows that one important aspect to learning is our intention to learn. If we intend to learn, we may. But if we don't intend to learn, we rarely do. The Question step of SQ3R helps you concentrate on what is in the reading assignment <u>for you</u>. It helps you to create an intention to learn. It tells you what you want to know when you complete the reading.

<u>Read</u>

Once you have your question in mind it is time to read the section of material under the heading. Your reading ought to be different than your reading was before you learned SQ3R. You should be an active, aggressive reader who is looking for something. You will be reading to get the main idea of what the author is saying. You will be reading to get the answer to the question that you asked.

When many people read they sit back and wait for the author to tell them something. Sure enough, the author spews out a great deal of material. There are names, dates, formulas, facts, concepts, etc., etc., etc. It is very easy to get overpowered by all of the information that is presented. What is important? How much of the information do you have to know?

The question that is created using SQ3R helps you separate the information you read into different "levels," main ideas, supports, and details. The heading of the section told you what the main concept of the section was. You read to understand that idea and the supporting information that goes with it. The details of the section are not important. The main idea is! Once you understand the main concept that the author has presented, you can decide how much additional information you need to support or "round out" your understanding.

Reading is an active, thinking process. You need to concentrate your energies to get from your text what you want or need. Focus on what you want from the text, what is important to you, what you can use from the information that is in front of you.

You may find that there will be times that you need to go back over material because although you got the main idea, you know that you need to get more supporting material to go with it. If you need to read a section a second time to get more information, read it a second time. Remember, most people cannot get all the ideas that they need from their text in a single reading of the

material. If you need more information, read the text again.

Recite

After you have read the heading or subheading and changed it into a question, you read the material to get the main idea of that particular section. In the Recite step of SQ3R you summarize the essence of the material you read to see if you really understood and learned the information in that section. Reciting means that you summarize, <u>in your own words</u>, what you have just read and, hopefully, learned.

Have you ever read something, perhaps underlining or using a magic marker while you were reading, only to discover that when you finished you didn't learn the information that you just read? When you looked at the pages you had supposedly read, they were underlined, you know that it was you who did the underlining, but you do not remember ever reading the material.

When people read, some of the time they are not attending to the material that they are reading. Their eyes move across the page, they seem to be reading, but nothing is actually happening. They look like they are reading but, in fact, their minds are elsewhere, and they are not attending to the text that was in front of them. The idea behind the Recite part of SQ3R is to prove to yourself that you know and understand the information that you have read. Reciting gives you feedback as to whether or not you have learned the material the way you want to know it.

You may be thinking that it is not how well you want to know the material that is important. What is important is knowing the information as well as your instructor wants you to know it. It is the instructor who will be asking the questions and giving the grades, right? Wrong. Your instructor already knows the information. You are taking the class to learn something, to develop skills and knowledge to help you later in life. What is really important is you knowing the information as well as you want to know it! You set the standards! You say how well you want or need to know the material.

Yes, your instructor will assign a grade to you on the basis of how well you know the material that he has assigned to you. You should have some idea about how well he wants you to know things. After all, you have been through more than 12 years of schooling. You have had instructors before and have some idea about what "A" quality work is, what "C" work is, and what is not acceptable. If you are unsure of what this particular instructor's expectations are, try reviewing one of his old exams from previous classes (many campuses have a central file of old exams that are legally and ethically available to you for review, some departments have exam files, and some instructors readily make their old exams available to current students). Use the old exam to

give you an idea about what your instructor wants you to know from the course materials.

Now, how well do you want to know the course content? Think about the instructor and his expectations, think about how the course contents relate to your life, think about the expectations that others have for you, and decide the level that you want!

Let's move from reading and classroom expectations to sports. Hopefully, you have played basketball, softball, or football. Perhaps you have bowled on a team, run track, or participated in some other team sport. How do you feel if you have personally had your best day ever but the team lost? Yes, you feel good that you had a good game but, often, you are really disappointed that the team lost. In team sports we have our own expectations and the expectations for the team.

In sports you use feedback to indicate how well you are doing. If you are shooting foul shots in basketball, you watch where the ball goes and either try to duplicate what you just did or make some kind of change to make the next shot. If you missed the foul shot because the ball fell short, you compensate by using more force on the next shot. If you are playing tennis and you have hit several balls that go beyond the end line, you try to take something "off" the next shot. When you make a strike in bowling, you try to remember everything that you did when you rolled the strike and then, hopefully, duplicate it a second time for a second strike.

In most sports we are usually watching something, often a ball. When the ball does what we want it to, we try to duplicate what happened. When the ball doesn't go where we want it to, we use our visual feedback to make corrections and try again.

Feedback is an important part of all sports. We use the feedback we get to improve our game. When the feedback says we have done the best we have ever been able to achieve, we still try to do even better.

Think about "world class" athletes. An athlete sets a world record. What does he say? Yes, he says he is happy, he thanks his coaches, etc. He also says "I can do better!" A world record means that no human being in all of recorded history has ever equaled the performance of the record setter. And yet, most record setters turn around and try to better their own world record. The feedback they have received says that they are the best ever, and they still want to do better.

Is this the way you tackle your textbook reading? Are you trying to learn more and better than ever before? Does the feedback you get when you read say that you have accomplished what you wanted to, that you have learned what you wanted to learn?

"What feedback? I don't get any feedback on how well I know the information until I have an exam!" That's the point! The way that most of us read does not provide any feedback as to whether we have learned the material we just supposedly processed. We wait for our instructor to tell us if we know the information well enough. The feedback we get in the classroom is often weeks behind our supposed learning. Yet in sports we want the feedback that tells us how well we are doing as soon as possible.

Let's take a look at a new version of bowling that I have developed and hope to market. The two popular forms of bowling are duck pins and ten pins. In duck pins you get three balls to roll each frame, and each ball is a little larger than a softball. In ten pins you get to roll only two balls each frame, and the ball is about eight or ten inches in diameter. In my version of the game you get to roll only one ball each frame and that ball is the same size as the ten-pin ball.

My game is very similar to the other two. When you arrive at the bowling alley you exchange your shoes for bowling shoes just as usual. I will assign you to a lane, again, as usual. You select a ball from the rack and bowl as you would when you bowl ten pins. Remember, however, in this game you only get to roll one ball each frame. When you release the ball and it hits the alley, or the gutter, a curtain will drop down blocking your view of the pin action. You will hear the noise of the ball striking the pins, the pins will be reset, and the ball will be returned through the ball return. As the ball returns, the curtain will raise up, and you will be ready for the next frame.

Each frame will be similar. When you release the ball the curtain will come down, pins will hopefully fall, the pins will be reset, the ball will be returned, and the curtain will go up for the next frame. Each of the ten frames will be the same. Because you usually bowl three games when you go to the bowling alley, you bowl your usual three games and leave. You return the bowling shoes, pay your bill, address an envelope to yourself, and leave.

I think this is a great game. As the owner, I will see customers finish their games much faster. More people will bowl on each alley meaning that I will make lots of money!

"Wait a minute," you say, "I don't like the game. I won't know how well I have done! How could I ever improve my game?" That's what the envelope is for, to give you detailed information about your game. In about four weeks, my computerized reporting system will send you a detailed report on your bowling. The report will include each ball's velocity; the force with which it struck the pins; the angle of impact; the direction, velocity, force, and spin of each pin; and, of course, your scores for each frame and each game. You will receive more detailed information on your bowling than you have ever had before.

"That's crazy. I won't know how well I did until weeks after the game." True. It will be just like the way you tackle your school work. You will not receive any feedback about your reading until weeks after your studying has been completed! You study tonight for a test that you will take in a week or two. You will receive feedback perhaps a week later that tells you how well you learned the material you study tonight. My bowling game is stupid, right? Your way of studying without feedback is....

Our lives are, in part, based on or controlled by the feedback we receive. We smile at people because when we smile others smile back at us. When we drive we watch the speedometer. When we exceed the speed limit we know that there is a good possibility that we will get a speeding ticket so we slow down to just a little above the limit and watch for police cars and radar traps. We dress up for job interviews or first dates because we know that first impressions are important. In our romantic relationships we give and receive signals that tell, or rather are supposed to say, what kind of behavior is or is not acceptable. We dress the way we do, in part, because of the feedback we have received. (Parents often do not understand that both positive and negative comments will affect what their children will wear. Ever say something like "I did it just to get a reaction from my parents"?) On the job we try to get positive responses such as pay raises from our boss while we try to avoid negatives such as being fired.

In most of life we expect and often desire and request feedback-- except in school. We don't want to find out that we supposedly read a piece of material and don't understand or remember what it was about. Somehow we feel bad, stupid, or even worse when we get feedback in school that says we need to work harder, to know more, etc. But on the ball field we don't feel the same way. When we make a mistake playing ball, we work harder to improve our skills so that we won't make the same mistake again.

Reciting when you read tells you whether or not you have gotten what you wanted from your reading. If you learned what you wanted to know, do you stop and "feel good" about your accomplishment? My experience with students says that most students don't. They don't get feedback; and, if they do, few seem to take time to pat themselves on the back and say something like "well done," "good work," or "boy, I learned a lot." In sports, of course, when we have done something special, we get excited, we scream and shout, we tell our friends, etc. Learn something in school, however, and nothing happens!

Join the rest of the world and value and use feedback to learn more of what you want to know. School, or learning, is there to help you achieve what you want or need to, to be successful in life. As you read, get feedback that tells

you whether or not <u>you have learned what you wanted to learn</u>. When your feedback says you successfully learned, stop and think about how well you have done. When you haven't learned what you wanted, stop and think about what you can or should do to master the material the way you want to know it.

Reciting can be done out loud, silently to yourself, to another person, or in writing. I would highly recommend any of the first three and reserve writing a recite for material that is particularly difficult for you. Writing is very slow and cumbersome. It will take a lot of time to write out good recites. "Brain speed" and speed of speech are much faster and can give you rapid feedback as to how well you have learned your material.

The essence of the Recite step is to read, to think about what you have read, and to evaluate whether or not you have learned at a level that is satisfactory to you. It is active, efficient learning. It is feedback that you can use to evaluate how well you know the information that you have just completed.

Review

Using SQ3R you survey the chapter, then go back and create a question from the first heading. You read to answer the question and then try to recite a satisfactory answer to your question. When you know the material at the level that you want to know it, decide whether you want to tackle another section. If so, go on to the next section. Create a question from the next heading, read the section, and recite what you learned. Continue to question, read, and recite until you have completed the chapter or are ready to stop reading. At this point stop and review the material that you learned in each of the recites. Pull together the information that you have learned and fit it into the total of all the information you already know.

In the recite step you mastered small pieces of material. In the Review step, you first go over each of the sections that you mastered earlier. Even though you mastered the material in each recite before you went on to the next section, you will have forgotten some of the information that you need. You can go back and reread part of the text that you need to, to refresh your memory. You can also put all the pieces you learned together in a summary of the main ideas of the chapter or the main idea of the sections you read. In essence, the review is used to pull all of the information that was covered in the study session together to understand how all of the parts go together.

Here is another question for you. When you study, what is the best part of studying? For many or most of us, we would say "getting finished." Getting finished is the best part of the study session. How often do you get finished with your studies? I'm never finished. There are always more assignments to do!

If there is always more for you to do, studying becomes or appears to be a never ending task. One of the reasons for putting off studying is the feeling that once you start you will never be able to finish. If you break your studying material into parts and aim to complete pieces, studying becomes much easier. When you read, read and master one section. Recite to show that you have learned what you wanted from your text. When your recite demonstrates that you have learned what you wanted to know, decide whether you want to master the next section. If you go on, read and master the next section. When you have "had enough," stop and review. Review all the material that you covered in that study session. What did you learn and how does it fit into what you already know?

Chunk Learning

Using SQ3R starts you learning information in logical chunks rather than having you try to concentrate on everything that you read. Probably the worst habit you learned in school is to read your texts one chapter at a time. In most textbooks the amount of information that you would be expected to learn from your book would greatly exceed your mental capacity. That is, you would be trying to take in more material than you could possibly absorb in a short period of time.

Leave textbooks for a minute and think of what you know about electric circuits. If you took all of the electrical appliances in your home and plugged them into the same circuit and turned all of the appliances on, what would happen? Yes, the fuse or circuit breaker would blow. The situation is almost the same when you are reading a textbook. You can take in too much information and almost blow your mental circuits. What happens with reading is that when you take in too much information, much of the information that you are trying to learn gets mixed up. Yes, you learn some things correctly, but at the same time you only partially learn a lot of the material that you need to master.

Haven't you ever read a textbook, perhaps using a yellow marker to highlight important sections, only to find that when you completed the reading you didn't know the material? You have highlighted important material but you can't remember reading it. If your task was to read over the text and highlight information to study later, you may have accomplished your task. However, if you thought that you were learning the information that you were "reading," you failed to reach your goal.

When you read, you can only take in a limited amount of new information and assimilate it. The assimilation aspect of reading is extremely important in college-level learning. Your instructors will want you to know the basic facts as well as what they mean, why they are important, how they fit into the bigger picture, etc. College-level learning is not just rote memory of information such as names and dates. College-level learning means that you are able to synthesize new information with the old, that you are able to analyze and integrate ideas, concepts and theories, etc. College-level learning means that you are supposed to think about the information that you are learning. When have you stopped to think about the material that you have read?

Chunk learning means that you take in a logical chunk of information and then think about it, that you try to make the new material fit into the sum total of all that you already know. The reading process then becomes read and think, read and think, read and think. The reading brings in new thoughts, ideas, and information; the thinking gives you time to process the new material and make it your own.

Using SQ3R allows you to use the structure from your textbook to create logical chunks of information for you to read, learn, and integrate into your personal knowledge base. Each heading and sub-heading will contain only a few main points with a limited number of supporting ideas that logically go together. Use that structure to help you learn and assimilate all that you can.

Underlining and Notetaking

Most students that I have known either underline or highlight as they read. Their rationale is that they are marking important information so that they can review it later. Very few students learn material better just because they underline or highlight. Underlining itself does not significantly increase learning. Underlining or highlighting can help learning if the material is marked after the student has learned the information. That is, first learn the information and then mark it for easy access later. Read the material, recite it, and then mark it.

In most cases taking notes from your textbook will not be as productive as you might think. Two points to consider: (1) Writing good notes takes a great deal of time. If you were to read one page and reduce that page to 50 or 100 words, it would take you between 5 and 10 minutes to make your notes. How many times could you have talked through a summary of the material in the same 5 to 10 minutes that it would take you to write it? Would you know the information better if you had written it once or if you had recited it four or five times? (2) How much did you pay for your textbook? Thirty, 40, or 50 dollars? If you paid that much for the book, why would you want to rewrite it? The information that you want to learn is already down on paper! You can refer to it any time that you want to.

If you want to mark your text, fine. Just don't confuse marking the text with learning the information. Remember, most people who underline do not know the information that they are underlining. They are simply marking material to come back to later. If you mark, mark (underline or highlight) after you have mastered the material that you want to know. You might even try to indicate information that you expect to find on your next exam. After the exam you can see how well you predicted what your instructor would ask. Your textbook marking system would both help your learning and guide your test preparation.

Speed Reading

Speed reading involves a variety of techniques that can enable you to go through many pages of written material in a very short period of time. Speed reading, however, does not permit most people to read a 50 page chapter of chemistry in one hour at the level of learning that most chemistry professors will accept. On the other hand, speed reading can help you to save a lot of time and effort if it is used appropriately.

Speed reading might more appropriately be called selective reading because not every word of the material is read. Usually a speed reading program will teach you to "read in phrases" or to read "groups of words" and to zig-zag down a page, taking in clusters of information. In essence, speed reading programs teach you to read selectively.

If you want to read selectively, you can already, if you think about it. Try reading a chapter of a nonfiction book by (1) reading the introductory paragraphs, (2) read every heading and subheading, (3) read the first sentence of every paragraph until, (4) you reach the summary; there you slow down and read everything that the author has written. You have rapidly processed the chapter and should know most of the main ideas that have been presented. You have carefully chosen selective portions of the chapter to read. In a way, you have been speed reading.

In English we usually write the main idea of a paragraph in the first sentence of the paragraph, the topic sentence. We then fill in the paragraph with additional information to support the point we made in the first sentence. If you simply read the first sentence of each paragraph, you are usually getting the main idea of each paragraph without all the details that the author is using to prove his point. You are reading selectively to get the main ideas; you are speed reading.

Years ago my mentor and I were teaching a group of adults a variety of reading techniques including how to speed read. Each week students had to read a textbook on the history of labor in this country as part of the total training program that they were participating in. My mentor wrote multiple-choice comprehension questions to check how well the students were retaining the material that was assigned. The average comprehension score on each test was about 70%. Then we asked the students to read one

chapter by reading only the introductory paragraph, the first sentence of every other paragraph and the summary, after which they took the comprehension test for that chapter. Their scores were equivalent to the scores they had obtained when they had read every word of a chapter. This makes sense when you remember that in our exercise, they had read the topic sentence of each paragraph and had therefore covered all of the main ideas that had been presented.

Effective Reading

By the time that you reach college you should have three or four different reading rates. However, you probably are not very aware that you have different reading rates, so you cannot use these different rates to help you become an efficient reader. I categorize your reading rates as follows:

•Critical reading rate--slow, thorough reading that you might do when you are reading a lease, a legal contract, or very difficult text material such as statistics.

•Textbook reading rate--for many people this is their typical reading rate for most material, slow but.... Comprehension of most of the text material is very important.

•Light reading rate--the kind of reading you do when you read a novel or the newspaper; every word isn't important.

•Speed or rapid reading rate--

getting through the written material rapidly to get the gist of it, to get the main ideas that the author is presenting without getting bogged down in the details.

If you want to be an effective reader, stop and think why you are reading before you begin. What do you want from the material that you are about to read? Then, select the rate that is most appropriate for your purpose.

Suppose you own a car with a manual transmission, a five-speed transmission. Would you drive from New York City to Los Angeles in first gear only? Would you drive from New York to Los Angeles in fifth gear only? I hope your answers were no to both questions. Each gear has a different purpose. You shift gears as road conditions change. Similarly in reading, you should shift gears as your needs change. Read slowly and thoroughly when you need to see all the details; read rapidly when all you want is the essence of what the author is saying.

Concentration

When you are studying you need to be able to focus your attention on learning the information that is in front of you. You need to be able to concentrate on learning the ideas and concepts in the textbook. Unfortunately, there are times that we just can't seem to get ourselves together and settle down to read and learn. During those times we say things like "I couldn't concentrate," "the material was boring," "I was distracted by personal problems," and "other things were more important than studying."

In most cases, when you sit down to study and can't concentrate, you or something about you is at the heart of the problem. Lack of concentration is caused by your attending to things other than your textbooks. A few of the areas that may be the cause of your inability to concentrate are lack of motivation or interest in the subject matter, personal and physical problems, and the favorite, distractions. Let's take a look at some of the things that we do to avoid concentrating.

Lack of Motivation or Interest

I was surprised when I heard my first student tell me the reason that he wasn't motivated to study. He came to college to major in engineering. He had had excellent grades in high school but was failing most of his courses in college. His classes were too big and weren't interesting. Although the student wanted to be an engineer he wasn't willing to do the necessary work to pass his classes to earn the degree that would lead to his goal.

Motivation is the spark that gets you going. When you lack the spark it can be very difficult to work effectively. If the lack of drive is causing you problems, how about creating some motivation by thinking ahead to your goals and about how your academic work will pay off in the long run?

Let's take the case of the engineering student again and update it to the 1990s. What will be the starting salary of a top engineering student in 1995 or 1996? It is likely to be around $35,000 per year. Would a potential salary like that get you motivated? Why not calculate your probable starting salary and then write it on a card that you tape to the bathroom mirror or on your alarm clock to remind you of one of the reasons that you are going to college? An alternative to posting your starting salary would be to describe what your life would be like if you stopped going to college now and got a full-time job versus finishing college before you started work. Would there be a difference in the kind of job that you might get? Would there be any difference in salary? Hopefully there would be a big difference in both the job and the salary. By seeing that difference you could create a spark to get your school work done.

Lack of motivation itself is rarely the problem that causes loss of concentration. Usually there are a variety of factors, such as not being sure of what you want to do, is the effort going to be worth it, etc., that cause you to start thinking about things other than the text that you should be studying. It is the thinking about your alternatives that causes you to lose your concentration.

Personal Problems

Personal problems can range from a lack of motivation, to arguments we have had with our parents or friends, to being lonely or depressed, to difficulties with roommates, etc. Personal concerns get our attention and are difficult to put aside just to get some studying completed. The difficulty is that although the personal concerns are important to us, many of them have been with us for a while and will continue to be with us in the future. Meanwhile, the semester you are in continues to roll by.

Suppose you are in a long-term on-again--off-again relationship. When the relationship is going well, it is easy to study effectively. However, when a break-up occurs it feels as though your world is coming apart---studying becomes impossible. When you sit down to study, your relationship problems are in your thoughts constantly. You try to read, but the words just don't make any sense. As days and weeks go by the pressure to study increases and your mental gymnastics intensify. You get stressed. Studying disappears entirely.

Logic-Tight Compartments

When personal concerns are getting the best of you, try creating some logic-tight compartments. Logic-tight compartments? You have heard of water-tight compartments in submarines and on ships, haven't you? Logic-tight compartments work the same way except that thoughts are isolated instead of water.

I believe in the Fifth

84

Commandment---Thou Shalt Not Kill. I also believe in the death penalty in certain circumstances such as when a person is guilty of multiple killings. Logically, it is impossible to fit these two beliefs together. I don't have any problem holding these two incompatible beliefs because I keep them in two separate logic-tight compartments and rarely take them both out at the same time except for this example. As long as I keep the ideas separate, I don't have to come up with any explanation to myself or to anyone else to resolve the incompatibility of the two concepts.

Now suppose it is time for you to study. That long-term relationship you had that recently ended comes back into your mind and "prevents" you from studying. Could you put the relationship in a logic-tight compartment for a couple of hours and get some studying done? That is, can you put your concerns about your relationship on hold for two hours, study, and then come back to your problem? The problem won't solve itself while you study and you won't forget it, will you?

Another way to look at it is to say, there is a time and a place for everything. Now is the time to study; later I'll get back to my problem. First you focus your attention on some studying, then you focus on the problem. Each gets your full attention in sequence, not together.

Lists

Another alternative to controlling personal problems while getting your studying done is to create a list of the things that are bothering you. By writing things down you are acknowledging to yourself that an issue is important and that you do not want to forget it. Once you have the list of problems, you know that you won't forget them because you have written them down. You can talk yourself into studying knowing full well that you will get back to your problems later.

Counseling

If, after trying to control your thoughts by separating personal concerns from your academic work, you find that you still cannot concentrate on studying, try talking with a counselor on campus to see if they have other suggestions about dealing with your concerns.

Physical Problems

Physical concerns such as being tired all the time, not being able to sleep, having problems with drugs or alcohol, having colds, being depressed, having headaches, etc. can also be the cause of concentration problems. The best way to handle these concerns is to go to the campus Health Center to see a doctor. I suggest the Health Center because the staff there has experience in dealing with the complex combination of health and academic concerns, especially the impact of stress on your ability to concentrate.

Distractions

"I couldn't concentrate because of all the distractions." What kinds of distractions? They could be anything that you want them to be---noise, movement, heat, cold, thoughts about your friends, wishing you were watching TV, being hungry and lots more. Distractions when you are studying are often things that you use to prevent yourself from studying. What this means is that when you have decided that you don't want to study, you <u>will</u> find some excuse to use to keep you from studying.

Lists

Of course, there are times that when you are trying to study, something occurs to distract you. Once the distraction is over, can you refocus on your work and begin to study again? If you find that you are often distracted, you might try creating a list of the things that tend to distract you. When you begin to see a pattern of things that distract you, you can try to develop a strategy to avoid or overcome the distraction. For example, if you find it hard to begin studying, start by reading a small portion of your favorite subject and then switch subjects. If you get restless after studying for a while, try breaking your studying into small chunks and recite while you walk around or stand up. If sounds are distracting you, can you find an alternate study area in the library or in another area of the library? If you get distracted by remembering all the things that you should or could be doing, write a list so that you won't forget them and return to work; if you get tired whenever you begin to study, try a little exercise before you study.

Be Your Own Best Friend

Another way of looking at problems with distractions is to imagine it is your best friend who is having the problem that you have. What would you suggest to him if he were distracted by the same problem? Funny how often we can tell our best friend how to solve his problems, but we can't seem to solve our own. Talk to yourself; talk through your problem as you would if you were conversing with your best friend.

Make Yourself Concentrate

A different way to overcome distractions is to teach yourself how to get back to work after your concentration has been broken. You begin by studying as usual. When you get distracted, you must read either one paragraph or one page and then you must stop! Let's use a one-paragraph requirement and see what happens. You begin to study and get only half a page finished before you get distracted. Now you must read one more paragraph and then you must stop studying. Mark where you stop, underline if that is what you normally do, but after reading that single paragraph you must stop.

"One paragraph? I'll never get any work done," you say? If you have a problem with being distracted, look at what you would have done. After you were distracted, you started to work again! True, you only got a little bit of studying completed, but you did get some work accomplished without a great deal of pain.

The next time you study do the same thing---read until you get distracted, and then force yourself to read one more paragraph and stop. After you have done this five times, increase the required reading to two paragraphs. After five more study sessions, increase the required reading to three paragraphs and then to four and so on. You will teach yourself that the distractions are not the main concern. You will always get distracted from your work. Successful people have learned how to get back to productive work quickly and efficiently after they have been interrupted.

Retention

When we learn in college, we have two different steps to be concerned with: (1) learning the assigned information and (2) retaining the material that we have learned. If you are concerned about long-term retention of information, try breaking the learning process into the two component parts.

First You Learn

In school, most students are concerned about how well they are doing academically. When they study, they are often studying "for the exam." Many of these students focus their attention on questions like "will it be on the exam?" or on the grades they will get on their examinations, rather than on trying to learn the course information that they will need both for their exams and their general education.

Once you have learned the material that you have been reading you can begin to be concerned with retaining that information for the future. As easy as that statement may sound, most students seem to get the order reversed---first they are concerned about retaining information for their examinations and then they wonder if they know it. If you keep the order correct, the learning process is much easier.

Let's try an example. Have you ever been to a party with a lot of people that you did not know? Hopefully the host introduced you around to everyone. When you met someone later, did you remember their name? Probably not. A second question for you: did you ever really know their name? When you were introduced, did you listen to your host when he introduced you and hear who you were introduced to? If not, if you never heard the person's name, how could you possibly know it later on? Get the name first and repeat it to see if you really have it right. If you do, you stand a chance of knowing it later when you meet the person again.

With your textbooks, first learn a small section of the assigned material. Once you have learned it you can begin to be concerned about hanging on to the information for an extended period of time.

Think back to course examinations that you have taken. When you have not gotten the correct answer to a question, did you really ever know it or had you just "seen" the material before? If you have usually had objective or multiple-choice examinations in school, you have probably gotten used to the idea of being able to recognize the correct answer on a test. When you study, you study to "sorta know what looks right." In college, your instructors will be requiring you to be able to do more than just recognize information. They will want you to know the information and to be able to use that information in a variety of ways.

Forgetting

In college, you will be expected to remember and use a great deal of information. If you are a full-time student, you may be carrying five different classes in which you are assigned readings that could easily total over 2,000 pages (history and literature majors can easily have 4,000 to 6,000 pages of required reading in a single semester). When your exams arrive, your instructors can easily appear to be demanding that you remember every single bit of information that has been mentioned either in class or in your textbooks. When a course is especially demanding, you may get the impression that you seem to forget everything that you have learned.

Perhaps an example will help me make the point. You enroll in a basic accounting class. You go to class regularly and read the assigned material. You even get your homework turned in on time. Five or six weeks into the semester, your accounting instructor is rattling on and says, "Remember when we talked about debits?" You sit there and look at him not comprehending anything; you remember hearing the word before but you have forgotten what it means or why it is important. Panic!

Unfortunately for students, forgetting is a perfectly natural process. When we say we have forgotten something we usually mean that some information that we had previously known is no longer remembered. As students, however, we often misuse the word forget.

To forget means that at one time you actually knew the information. Many times when I hear students talk about forgetting, it is apparent that they never really knew the material well in the first place. Take the accounting example above. Just because you read the assigned material on debits does not mean that you know it. Even if you complete your accounting homework correctly, that does not mean that you really understand what a debit is. So when the instructor mentioned debits in the fifth week of class, you could have had several different kinds of forgetting:

1. You never saw the information before.

2. You remember reading or hearing the information but you never really learned it.

3. You read the information and "sorta" learned it or at least thought that you had learned it.

4. You really learned the information but have not used it in two or three weeks---you forgot what you had learned.

Note that in the first three cases of forgetting you never did master the information, so how could you forget it? Only in the fourth alternative did you actually forget. In other words, much of the time when we say that we have forgotten something, we never really knew it in the first place. When you seem to forget a lot, are you forgetting or is it that you never really learned?

The Law of Exercise

One of the few "laws of human learning" that I have seen is called the Law of Exercise--- the more you use information, the longer you will be able to retain it. An alternate version of the same idea is "use it or lose it." That means that if you want to retain information you have to review it fairly regularly or else it will disappear from your memory.

Our conscious minds seem to have a limited storage capacity. We store information there that we need for whatever reason. If material is stored and we don't use it, somehow it gets deleted from our current memory files. The memory space gets used for storing something else.

Try picturing your mind as though it were a computer hard disc with a manager who is to keep everything in the best condition possible. Material can be stored as long as it is considered useful. What does useful mean? Unfortunately, I don't know. It has something to do with how well the information was known in the first place. It has something to do with how often you use the information. It may also have something to do with how important the information is and whether you intend to store it or not.

The manager of your mental disc cleans house regularly, throwing out material that no longer seems "useful" so that the space can be used for potentially more important information. There's that word "useful" again. "But he tossed out formulas that I needed for my final exam," you say. "They would have been more than just useful, they were really important." "Sorry about that" says the manager, "how was I to know they were important? You never used them."

While our brains do not work exactly as this discussion indicates, there is more truth in the example than fiction. Whether we like it or not, we will forget names, dates, formulas, ideas, events and whatever else there is if we do not use or review them. For a student this means that it is essential for you to provide yourself with time to review material that you want to keep in conscious memory. Instructors schedule their exams throughout the semester in an attempt to make you review course material every four or five weeks so that you won't forget it. Even after you complete your college education the problem with forgetting will continue to plague you. If you don't use information or a skill, it will disappear.

During a semester, one way to slow the forgetting process is to spread your study time out. Instead of studying accounting twice a week in three-hour chunks, study four or five times each week for an hour or two. By spreading out your study you learn, begin to forget, relearn, begin to forget, relearn, begin to forget, etc., etc., etc. Your memory manager doesn't throw the information out as fast because it is getting regular usage.

Memory Aids

While people generally learn and remember the same way, there are lots of individual differences that you can use to help you retain information that you want to keep. Some techniques that you may want to consider include group study, writing, favoring your learning style, and mnemonics.

<u>Group study</u>. Most adults earn their living working with other people. Students, on the other hand, are usually encouraged to study by themselves. Why not read and study first by yourself and then get together with some other students to talk about the information that you all read? You can ask each other questions and help one another learn difficult material. Learning does not have to be an isolated occurrence that can only happen in the privacy of your room.

<u>Writing</u>. Generally speaking, writing down information that you want to learn can take a great deal of time as I have mentioned several times in this text. However, some people feel that when they write something down it becomes more a part of them. They had to concentrate while writing the information down and they had to spell all the words that they used.

Flash cards can be an easy way to have a little bit of writing pay off. On a 3 x 5 index card write a main idea, concept, or formula that you need to know. On the reverse side, write a brief summary of the important information that you want to retain about the subject. Reading the key word or the main idea then becomes a test question--Harper's Ferry becomes, "Tell me all I am supposed to know about what happened at Harper's Ferry."

I know a number of people who swear by notes as the only way to really learn effectively. They use their notes to organize information logically. In the chapter on "Listening" there are several different forms of notetaking described that you may find to be helpful.

<u>Mnemonics</u>. Occasionally it will be beneficial for you to trigger words or sentences to help you remember isolated facts. I guess the classic mnemonic is remembering the names of the lines and spaces in the treble clef in music: "every good boy does fine" for the lines E, G, B, D, F; and, face (F, A, C, E) for the spaces. In many academic subjects there are a few mnemonics around to help you retain a few selected bits of information. Usually the time and effort that it will take you to create a mnemonic that you won't forget could be better spent learning the actual information.

Learning Style

Learning style refers to the way that you prefer to learn. Your learning style may be visual, auditory, experiential, or some combination of the three. If you favor a <u>visual</u> learning style, highlighting with color markers, graphic or pyramid notes (see examples in the chapter on "Listening"), the use of charts, drawings, and flash cards may be helpful additions to your study skill techniques. If you prefer <u>listening</u> as your primary channel for learning, recording some of your lectures, using audio-recorded textbooks, reading your notes out loud, and studying with a friend using a question and answer format could all be helpful. Those who prefer to roll their sleeves up and "get into it," to <u>learn by doing</u>, need to involve themselves by being as active in their learning as possible, perhaps walking around while studying or using flash cards.

A different kind of learning style relates to how you prefer to organize and use your time.

<u>Slow and steady</u> pacers will tend to study fairly evenly all semester with only a slight increase in study time during examinations.

<u>Fast starters</u> can begin studying before the semester actually begins but slow down to hold on at the end of the semester.

<u>Strong finishers</u> may do little studying for the first half or two thirds of the semester but buckle down to get the work finished at the end of the semester.

Use what you know about yourself, about the way that you prefer to learn, about the way you like to get things accomplished, to help you adapt the basic strategy of learning or mastering information in logical chunks. How can you make that technique work best for you?

Summary

The basic idea of this chapter is to get you to focus your attention on learning logical sections or chunks of information and on creating a feedback system in which you demonstrate mastery of the material that you read. The SQ3R method of studying was recommended because it is simple to learn and can easily be adapted to a variety of learning situations. In the SQ3R study method you first survey a chapter and then you go back to master the individual parts of the chapter. To read a subsection, first change the subhead into a question, then read to answer the question, to get the main idea. When a section has been completed, recite the information that you have learned and evaluate how well you have learned that information. If you are satisfied with your learning, read the next segment the same way. When you finish your reading, review all of the information that you have learned from each of the sections.

Problems with concentration focused on what role you have in creating the distractions that interrupt your ability to concentrate. Last, retention was presented as an issue to be concerned with only after basic learning has occurred--first you learn, then you use or review the information that has been learned in order to retain it over time.

6 LISTENING AND NOTETAKING

Students in a classroom situation often confuse listening and notetaking. Students put a tremendous amount of effort into taking detailed notes of what they think the instructor has said. The measure of their success in class appears to be the quantity of notes they have at the end of each class session. The more notes they have, the better off they think they are.

The problem with this approach is that the emphasis is on notes and notetaking instead of on learning. The rationale for this strategy is that the notes can be studied later to get ready for a course exam. Research on notetaking confirms the fact that notes are indeed an excellent external storage place for information. However, if you ask a student who uses this approach "What did the instructor say today?" you rarely get a good summary of the points that the instructor made. Notes store the information but have little to do with what the student has learned.

A number of years ago, I taught a study skills class that required enrollment in an American History course, The History of the American Revolution. The aim of the study skills class was to apply the skills discussed in this book to the history class.

The history class met for three hours before the first study skills class. As part of the agreement with the history professor, I attended all of the history class sessions. The professor was an excellent lecturer. He lectured without notes and presented ideas that pulled together the material he presented with the information we were supposed to learn from the reading list. He challenged students to understand what life was like for the various people who lived during the Revolutionary War. He tried to get students to understand not only what happened but why it happened as it did. A great deal of detailed information was presented during each class session. As you might expect, during the lectures all of the students in the class took notes. Virtually all of the time, all of the students were writing notes about what the instructor was saying.

At the first class session of the study skills course I asked the students what the instructor had said for the three hours that he had lectured. There was no response. A few students tried to find their notes from the history lectures. Later we discovered that the students had a total of over ten pages of notes from the three hours of lecture but no one could summarize what the instructor had said.

What do you think the professor said during the first three hours of the class? Remember, the title of the course was The History of the American Revolution.

No, the instructor didn't

mention the Boston Tea Party, taxation without representation, the Stamp Act, or Lexington and Concord. He didn't mention the ride of Paul Revere. In fact, he didn't even mention the American colonies or the New World! He talked about English nobility in the year 1200! For the first four or five lectures we heard about the English concept of the "divine right of kings" (the power of the King of England emanated from God). The King ruled through his nobility, each rank of which was described in detail. Later, the professor talked about the Magna Carta, how in 1215 the nobles of England took the power to raise and collect taxes and the power to go to war from the King. In England, this system remained for centuries. However, in the colonies, landowners questioned the right of English nobility to govern the thirteen colonies. They demanded a say in their government. The desire for dissemination or filtering of power down to landowners, the instructor said, led to the Revolutionary War.

Why didn't the students know that the instructor talked about material that seemed so far off target? When they reviewed their notes, they had the information written down. Since the information had been received, why wasn't any of it available for class discussion?

The obvious answer is that the students hadn't learned the material that had been presented to them. They were "recording machines," writing down as much of the course material as they could but learning very little.

After college you will enter the work force. In staff meetings, proposal sessions, sales conferences, etc., you will be expected to listen and know what is being said. Will you really have time to write everything down and consult those notes every time someone asks you a question? When your boss wants a summary of a meeting she wasn't able to attend, will you have to run to your office to get your notes? Since you will be expected to listen and learn in the work force, why not use that same expectation while you are in the classroom now?

The students in the history class were told to listen and learn, to reduce their notetaking to a minimum. They were told to listen to the ideas behind what the instructor was saying, to understand the concepts he was trying to get across. The details of his presentation weren't the essence of what he wanted the students to know. Details were fillers to round out or fill in the information that would be needed to understand the main idea of what was said. "Listen to the Professor," I said, "and understand the ideas, concepts, issues, etc., that he is trying to get across to you. Don't worry about the details, they aren't important."

A week later, the history instructor called me and asked "What did you tell them? I can tell every student who is taking the study skills class! They never take their eyes off me. What did you say?" (Picture the classroom from the instructor's view. Forty students writing furiously while a dozen watched his every move. If you were the lecturer, who would you like to talk to, the tops of forty heads or the eyes of the dozen "attending students"?)

After any history lecture, I could ask one of my students to summarize the history lecture and I would receive a detailed summary of the material that had been covered. The students had listened and learned! That is the purpose for going to class, to listen and learn. After you have learned, then be concerned about retaining what you have learned. First, however, you need to learn.

The first part of this chapter will focus on how to listen effectively. Later, after you have gotten comfortable with listening and learning, go on to the section on retention to learn more effective ways of retaining what you have learned from listening.

Listening

In any discussion of effective listening, you need to understand the meaning of the words hearing, listening, and auding. Hearing refers to your ability to know that a sound has been made. Sound waves reach your ear and are transformed into nerve impulses that are sent to your brain. If you clap your hands, the sound waves from the clapping will reach your ears, and your brain will register the fact that you heard the sound.

Listening refers to your ability to understand the sound that you heard. When you heard the sound of your hands clapping, you knew that the sound you heard was your hands clapping.

Auding, to most of us, is what we mean when we talk about good, or effective, listening. Auding means that you are able to understand the meaning behind the sound that you identified. When you clapped your hands, you understood that you were hearing the sound of your own hands clapping as an example of understanding the difference between hearing and listening.

In this text, when I talk about listening, I really mean good listening, or auding. Listening means that you understand the meaning behind the words that are being used. You listen to understand the ideas and concepts that are being conveyed to you. You, the listener, take the responsibility to get the information that is being presented. Listening is an active, interactive skill not a passive, lay-back-do-nothing activity.

When I was an undergraduate student, I was allowed to take a graduate statistics course instead of a required calculus class. The statistics class met once a week for three hours. The instructor lectured to us while he wrote on the blackboard. He talked rapidly. He printed material on the board in beautiful block letters in lines that were perfectly straight. After a few minutes, it became apparent to me that he was talking about one concept while he was copying text from 3 x 5 cards that was significantly different from his lecture material. I really didn't understand some of what he was saying and I couldn't listen to him and copy what he was writing at the same time. I started copying from the board. I noted that everyone else was copying too. Our problem was that the instructor was printing faster than we could write! At one point he went back to erase a board and students hollered "Wait, we're not finished yet." The professor waited impatiently for the students to get caught up. Then he quickly erased the board and started printing again.

After an hour and a half the instructor gave us a break. He left the classroom, and we stayed to finish our copying. As we completed the notes, students left the room and gathered by the soda machine. No one seemed to understand any of the material, not the lecture and not the text on the blackboard. We grumbled as students will and went back to class.

When the break was over, the boards were erased and the whole process started again. The instructor lectured and printed, and we wrote as fast as we could.

After class, many of us met again by the soda machine,

lamenting our choice of classes, our ignorance, the instructor, the situation, and just about everything else. We concluded that the problem we had was our lack of the required textbook for the class. The material had to be there.

We bought the required text, read the assigned material, and returned to class not understanding much of anything. The instructor started up again printing on the board while he lectured to us. One of the older students raised his hand with a question but the instructor couldn't see it because his back was to us. The student waved his hand. Nothing happened. Finally, the student called out "Mr. _____ (I forget his name), I have a question."

The instructor stopped writing and turned around. "Yes?" The student said "I don't understand anything that you have said. I have copied the material you wrote on the board and I don't understand any of that either!" The instructor just looked at the student a minute and said, "You must have understood some of it." "No I didn't understand anything. I've never seen any of it before."

World War III had just begun! With each response, the student and the instructor raised their voice just a little. Before long they were shouting at each other. After five minutes of shouting, the student turned to the rest of us and said "Come on, you agree with me. Tell him!" Just about everyone in the class shrank down in their seat an inch or two; no one said anything. The verbal battle started up again. The student tried to let the instructor know that no one had understood anything he had said.

The instructor pressed for specific examples and for clarification, after all, this was a graduate class, someone had to understand something. By this time the instructor was sweating and he had turned red. The student was shouting, trying to make the professor understand. Several requests for class support ended with one very mild "I didn't understand much" from one other student.

The controversy ended when the student gathered his books and left the classroom. His parting comment was "You all deserve what you get!" He walked out the door and slammed it shut.

The instructor was obviously flustered. He shuffled the 3 x 5 cards he had in his hand. He loosened his tie and unbuttoned the top button of his shirt. After several minutes he said "Does anyone agree with him?" Nothing happened, no one said anything.

The professor realized that something was wrong, but he did not know what it was. He asked for someone to summarize what he had covered in the previous class session. No one responded. He asked specifically what he had said about one specific statistical concept. No one responded. He

resorted to calling on a student. The student flipped through his notes and found the material that had been requested. He read the information back. (Have you ever heard someone read something that they couldn't understand? The reading was awkward, halting, and difficult to understand.) We followed the reading in our "notes"; we didn't understand either.

The professor stopped the student and said, "In your own words, what does it mean?" The student finally said, "I don't know."

The instructor asked all of us "Can anyone explain the idea in your own words?" No one responded.

Can you imagine the professor's frustration? He thought he was teaching 30 graduate students, and no one seemed to understand what he thought was a basic concept. He paced back and forth, obviously upset. Finally he walked over to his jacket and pulled out a piece of paper. He held it up to us saying "This is my appointment letter. This is Psychology 667 isn't it?" We all nodded our heads. "This is the fourth graduate statistics course for statistics majors." "No!" came our reply. "This is the introductory course for nonmajors!"

The course that the professor had been hired to teach had not had sufficient enrollment to be offered. Our class had been overenrolled. The department had simply divided students in our class in two and created a second section. Unfortunately, the letter that was sent to the instructor still contained the old class number!

During the first class session, the instructor had reviewed material that should have been covered in <u>three graduate statistics classes</u>. He had tried to prepare us for the new material he would present in his class. No one had understood the information he presented and no one tried to stop him until the fourth hour of lecture! We all had our excuses. We had all lost a great deal of time and suffered a lot of frustration because we had not been effective listeners. We had not let the speaker know that the message that he was sending wasn't getting across to us.

(Once the confusion was over, the professor explained that he would have to make up for the time that had been lost and that he would make sure that we received all the information that we were responsible for regardless of the administrative error. When the class ended, I realized that the instructor was one of the best I had had as an undergraduate student. Too bad we started with such a frustrating beginning.)

Hopefully, this chapter will help you to become a better listener than I was in the above example. My focus in this chapter will be on **listening and learning**. I will review some of the problems people have in listening effectively, present techniques for improving your listening

skills, and lastly, look into the issue of notetaking.

Problems in Listening

The problems that we have in listening can be categorized or concentrated into three different areas: problems that are caused or have their beginnings with the speaker; problems in transmission and reception; and, problems that are centered on you, the listener. Learning to correct, remove, avoid, and/or adjust to these problems is the sign of a good listener.

Speaker Problems

Some of the problems that we have in listening may have their origin with the speaker. Speaker problems are divided into two groups, those that are characteristics or qualities of the speaker and those that are related to the speaker's delivery:

Speaker Characteristics

age
interest in the subject
appearance
mannerisms
beliefs
mood
dress
national origin
gender
political orientation
health
religion
interest in the audience
race
socioeconomic class

Delivery Problems

accent

organization
delivery style
speed of speech
enunciation
tangents
examples used
tone
eye contact
vocabulary used
intent to communicate
volume

Other factors such as the time of day, the weather, and the temperature in the room can all have an effect on the speaker's ability to get the message across. How? Many of those factors act as screens coloring or biasing the speaker's point of view. Others, such as the lack of eye contact or perceived lack of interest in the audience, tell the listener that the speaker really doesn't care whether the message is understood or not.

Good listeners know that there is nothing they can do to change most of the items listed above, that is, you are not going to change your instructor's age, health, accent, organization, etc. You can demand that the speaker's volume be increased or perhaps slow down a rapid speaker, but you can control or change little else.

Your lack of influence on the speaker could cause you to become frustrated when you are trying to listen and learn from a bad speaker. The task of a good listener is to work your way through the problems that are presented by the speaker in order to get the message or information that is there. Yes, it is hard to listen to a speaker who is not organized. Yes, it is difficult to listen to someone who is saying things that you do not believe in or agree with. However, good learners are concerned with learning from the speaker first and evaluating what was learned later. They learn to identify speaker biases and characteristics that cause them difficulty in listening. They learn to listen through these biases. They learn to screen out the speaker variables, to listen "in spite of" the speaker. Good listeners first hear what the speaker is really saying, then evaluate what was said.

When you are having an argument with someone, it is very difficult for most people to hear what the other person is really saying. We tend to get so caught up in presenting our own side of the issue that we cannot hear the other person. The next time you are in an argument with someone, before you present your side, try to summarize what the other person said. It is amazing how often we have missed the point.

A good listener gets past the idiosyncracies of the speaker and hears the message that the speaker is trying to get across. Once the message has been received, the listener is free to do with it what she wants. In class, you are responsible for listening and learning what the instructor has said regardless of the things that she may say or do while she is lecturing.

I remember taking a history class from a woman professor

who had a "pageboy" hair cut (short hair with "bangs" that came down and across her forehead). As the professor lectured, her bangs would slip down her forehead and begin to obstruct her eyesight. While she spoke, she would toss her head back, flipping the offending hair out of the way. The hair would stay in place for a few minutes and then begin to slide down her forehead only to be flipped back with another toss of the head. On more than one occasion, the professor tossed her head twice in a row when the hair wouldn't stay up. We compared notes at the end of class to see how many times she had tossed the hair back (counting started when the professor began to lecture).

On an average day the instructor tossed her head between 65 and 70 times during an hour-and-fifteen-minute lecture. Our counting was so accurate that we rarely had different numbers at the end of a lecture.

In short, we had a great time watching and counting the number of times the instructor tossed her head during lectures. It was great fun, until the midterm exam! Our test scores weren't all that good. (The professor never asked us how many times she tossed her head during an average lecture!) During the second half of the course the instructor never tossed her head again! Well, to tell the truth, I really don't know whether she tossed her head again or not. Counting her head tosses hadn't given me a

good grade on the exam. We all stopped counting and focused our attention on what the professor was saying. Needless to say, our grades on the final examination went up significantly.

When you finish school and go to work, you will have meetings, seminars, sales interviews, etc., in which the speaker will do things or say things that could mask the message you will be responsible for receiving. Promotions, salary increases, and even your job will depend on your ability to stay clear of the speaker distractions and biases to hear the information that you need to know. While you are in college, develop or improve the way you attend to the message that the speaker is attempting to get across. Learn to focus on what is being said and not on the speaker or the things that she does that interfere with your understanding.

Problems in Transmission

Problems in transmission relate to difficulties in getting the message from the speaker to the listener. In a telephone conversation, the transmission problems could have something to do with the speaker in the sending phone, interference or lack of transmission in the telephone wire, problems with your telephone, or general noise around you. During lecture, the biggest transmission problems are the distractions that can occur in the classroom. Students may be talking or wrestling with their books, there may be a faulty microphone or audio system, etc. In some cases, the instructor may be aware of the distractor and do something to correct the problem. If not, can you do something about it?

My favorite distraction story is about Romeo and Juliet, two students who were taking my study skills class. They were very much in love. They sat in the center of the second row and never took their eyes off each other. They talked to each other during the entire lecture! That is, they both talked softly to each other while I lectured. At the next class session, the other students moved their chairs to the side of the couple or pulled chairs in front of them. Some of the students sat to my left or right; a few even sat behind me next to the blackboard. No one sat behind Romeo and Juliet.

The second class was similar to the previous one; I lectured while Romeo and Juliet talked with each other. Toward the end of the class period, I ended the day's lecture early. I then proceeded to chew out the class, everyone, that is, except Romeo and Juliet. Virtually every student in the class had been inconvenienced or worse by the talking, and not a single student had done anything to stop the distraction. Even when students moved their chairs to avoid some of the annoyance, most were still having difficulty seeing the board and keeping in visual contact with me. I asked why no one had asked the two students to stop talking or why someone hadn't thought to ask me to do

something. I apologized for allowing the talking to continue but noted that we had been talking about active learning and that they certainly hadn't been active on their own behalf. Similar situations would occur in other classes or later in life when contracts and jobs would be at stake, and, as good listeners, they would have to do something in the situation that would allow them to hear what the speaker was saying.

When you are having trouble hearing the speaker because of distractions such as other people talking, stop and think about what you can do that will enable you to hear better. You might have to get up and change your seat. You might need to talk to the instructor after class or during her office hours and ask if something can be done to make the room quieter. You are in the class to learn as much as you can. Take responsibility for getting the most you can out of the situation.

Problems With You, The Listener

The third problem area in listening has to do with the listener, with you. Characteristics or aspects of the listener that could cause difficulty in listening might include the listener's

    age interest
    beliefs
    mood
    education level
    national origin
    gender
    political affiliation
    health

race
hearing
religion
"listening"
vocabulary
socioeconomic class

Other factors that might influence your ability to listen include the time of day or night, the temperature, the weather, how tired you are, how comfortable you are in your seat, etc. These factors have an effect on how well you can listen. Although you have some control over some of the factors that are listed, others are beyond your control. What you can control, however, is your ability to listen regardless of your age, education level, etc. You can learn to identify your own biases so that you can listen through or in spite of your biases. Once you have accurately received the information that is being sent, you are free to do anything that you want to with it.

Remember, the important part of listening in college is to develop or hone your listening skills so that when you join the work force you will be able to be successful in your field. When your boss talks to you, you will need to be able to hear the message that is being sent regardless of the way it is sent, the distractions that may be present, or what you think about it. First the message must be received accurately, then you need to decide what to do next. Use your college classes to improve your ability to hear what the speaker is actually saying.

Effective Listening

Listening is a very active skill. When students talk about listening in class, they often say things like "I sat and listened" or "I just sat there and took it all in." They have difficulty in being specific about what they mean. To me, being an effective listener means that you are doing at least four different things at about the same time.

Listener 1: Listen!

First, an effective listener is taking in the information that the speaker is sending. We have already seen many of the difficulties that may be involved in that simple statement. Even when you have tried to be a good listener, has the message really gotten through to you?

In the late 1960s, some Dutch scientists conducted some research on cats that is relevant. They anesthetized the cat and implanted an electrode in the cat's brain such that when a bell was rung, a meter registered that the "sound," actually the signal to the cat's brain from the sound, reached the cat's brain. The bell was rung and the meter showed that the cat had heard the sound.

Next, a cage of mice was placed in front of the cat and the bell was rung again. The meter did not register the sound. That is, the meter did not show that the signal caused by the sound had reached the cat's brain. When the mice were taken away and the bell was rung, the meter showed that the sound had been "heard." Put the mice back and ring the bell, there was no indication of the sound being heard!

Yes, the cat was concentrating on the mice and because the mice were "more important" to the cat, it did not hear the sound. How does that happen? After all, the cat has not been physically altered when the mice are present, and yet it does not hear the sound. What happens is that in the reticular formation at the base of the cat's brain, a screening process occurs. Less important signals are screened out of existence! The cat literally does not hear the sound of the bell even though the sound exists. The sound signal never gets to the animal's midbrain and has not been heard.

The implication of this information to you as a listener should mean that when you do not want to hear the speaker, you can block her out. How many times has your mother called you when you did not really hear her? (Don't count the times that you heard but didn't want to let her know that you had heard her.) When you are thinking about something other than what the speaker is talking about, you can "tune out" the speaker and not hear a single word that is said.

The good listener has made the decision to listen and does so. She goes to class to listen and to take in all that she can. If she is not going to listen, she does not go to class.

When you walk into your classroom you ought to have made the decision that you are there to learn all that you can. Because most of your professors do not take attendance in class, don't go to class if you don't want to be there. If you "play at going to class," your body will be there but your mind won't. You may go through the motions of paying attention but when the class is over you will not have learned very much. Even your notes will not help because you really weren't listening to what the instructor was saying.

Only go to class if you are going to listen and learn. Once you have made the commitment to listen and learn in class, do everything that you can to get the message that the speaker is sending. Take in everything that is being said.

Listener 2: Summarize

For most people to get a message across they have to use a great many words. Simple concepts often require long complicated explanations. A listener can get lost in all the words. A good listener tries to reduce all the words to the ideas or concepts that the speaker is trying to communicate.

As you listen, every 10 or 15 minutes, try to summarize what the speaker has said. Pull all of the information together into an organized whole that connects with things that you already know. For instance, this entire chapter up to this point can be summarized as, "Good listening requires the listener to hear through biases and distractions to receive the idea(s) that the speaker is intending to communicate." All of the extra words and stories were added in an attempt to support that point.

When you summarize, you might keep this question in mind and try to answer it from the material that you have heard: "What is the point that the speaker is trying to get across?" "Through all of the words, through all of the examples, what is it that the speaker wants me to know?"

Listener 3:   Plus and Minus

We do not listen in a vacuum. Whenever we listen to anything, we have some background on the subject, however little. In the classroom, we rarely are in a situation in which we know absolutely nothing. Students tend to take courses on subjects that they know something about. You should use all that you already know about a subject to help you learn more from the present speaker. You have learned in other classes, from previous lectures, perhaps from reading assigned materials given to you by the current speaker, from life in general, etc. How does all of this information go together? What do you know about the subject that supports what the speaker is saying? What do you know that refutes what the speaker is saying? What did the textbook say about the subject?

Reading researchers talk about

advanced organizers and cognitive anchors. The concepts indicate that we learn best when we can tie information together and "hook" it to ideas, concepts, and knowledge that we already know. When we listen, we ought to take advantage of our prior learning to help us learn new material and to put that new knowledge into perspective. The better we can ground our knowledge into our previous learnings, the easier it will be for us to access it in the future.

Listener 4:   Question & Answer

While you are listening, you should be taking in what the instructor is saying, summarizing the main ideas that she is trying to make, and trying to connect the current information that you are hearing to your prior learnings. If you are doing all of this, you are bound to come up with questions that haven't been answered by the speaker. When you think of a question, try to answer it yourself! If you have been an active listener, you have a great deal of information at your command. Use what you know to become "a second instructor." Can you answer your own question? If you can't, is it a question that you really want to have answered? If you want the question answered, is the question one that you ought to ask in class or should you wait till after class or for the instructor's office hours?

Don't Take Lecture Notes!

You read the heading correctly. I believe you should not take lecture notes on what the speaker or instructor says in class! I come to that conclusion using three different rationales. The first has just been covered. If you are listening as I described above, listening to what the speaker is actually saying, summarizing the main ideas, connecting new information with your past knowledge, and mentally creating and answering questions, when do you have time to write down what the speaker is saying? Active listening takes just about all of your time.

An added problem in taking notes is the difficulty most of us have writing one item while we are listening to something else. Think about how you take notes. You listen to the speaker and then write down information that you received. While you are writing your notes, are you hearing what the speaker is saying? Can you listen accurately while you write? Yes, you hear something, but can you really understand the essence of what is being said while you are being concerned with things like spelling words correctly, having organized notes, and using correct grammar? People tend to turn off their hearing as they write and then turn it back on when they are ready to listen again.

The third rationale for not taking notes on what the speaker says comes from looking at the rate that people process information using our different verbal abilities or skills. How fast can you write? Most of us can write up to perhaps 20 to 25 words per minute when we need to. Some people can take shorthand and can write over 100 words per minute. However, when people take shorthand, they often do not know all of the content that is contained in their shorthand notes.

How fast do most instructors speak? The answer is about 100 to 125 words per minute for a comfortable pace. Instructors can and do often speak at rates that are above 125. Rapid speakers such as auctioneers can speak at rates above 300 words per minute. When you compare writing speed with speaking rates, you see that most people simply cannot write down everything that most speakers are presenting. You will never be able to write down everything that your instructor says.

How fast can you listen? The obvious answer is "as fast as the speaker speaks, right?" Wrong! Research on listening shows that we can listen much faster than most speakers talk. If regular speech is recorded with a tape recorder and played back using a variable-speed tape recorder, listening comprehension does not show a significant drop until about 250 words per minute. That means that without significant training, most people have the ability to "out listen" most speakers. We have the ability to take information in faster than the speaker can get it out. That assumes, of course, that the speaker starts at a point that we understand and proceeds in a logical, organized manner that takes us along step by step.

How fast do people read? Average readers read at about 200 words per minute, college students at about 350, and good readers at 500 words per minute or above. These rates suggest that we can take in information at a much faster rate through reading than we can by listening (listening rate is governed by the speaker's rate of speech, which is about 100 words per minute). Although people have preferences for reading or listening and can learn what seems to be more effectively by reading or listening, a person has to be a very poor reader in order to process more information through listening rather than through reading.

If you stop and consider the thought behind the last paragraph, you may find out that you can save yourself a great deal of time. If you actually do read over 200 words per minute, you can read twice as much in an hour than you can take in by listening for the same amount of time. Although you may enjoy sitting and letting someone else tell you information, you can learn and get more knowledge per unit of time through reading, even if you have to reread some portions of the text! Your efficiency can improve even more if you learn to use multiple reading speeds and learning techniques.

Thus far the list of educational skills and their respective rates looks like this:

Writing	20 wpm
Speaking	100 - 125 wpm
Listening	250 wpm
Reading	200 - 350+ wpm

What skill is missing from the list?

Hopefully your answer was thinking. How fast can people think? The numbers that I have seen suggest that we can think at between 400 - 800 words per minute, if we could measure thought speed. The rate of thinking for college students that shows up most frequently in articles about listening is 800 words per minute.

Now let's look at the complete list of educational skill-processing rates:

Writing	20 wpm
Speaking	100 - 125 wpm
Listening	250 wpm
Reading	200 - 350+ wpm
Thinking	400 - **800** wpm

Although there are individual differences in these rates, for the vast majority of people, the order will remain the same, with writing as the slowest of the activities and thinking the fastest.

What is the point of listing these rates? What do I want you to get from the comparison of the rates? Suppose I give you a 400-word paragraph and ask you how long it will take you to write, speak, listen to, read, and think through the paragraph; how long would it take you for each of these abilities?

Writing - 20 wpm   20 minutes
Speaking - 125 wpm 3.2 minutes
Listening - 250 wpm 1.6 minutes
Reading - 350 wpm   1.1 minutes
Thinking - 800 wpm   0.5 minutes
                     o r 3 0 seconds

Hopefully, you can see that writing is much slower than thinking.

Suppose you already had the 400-word paragraph in your head. How many times could you think through the paragraph in the amount of time that it would take you to write the paragraph one time? The answer is 40 times--20/0.5 = 40. That is, you could think the paragraph through 40 times in the amount of time that you could write it only once.

Would you know the material better if you wrote it one time or if you thought it through 40 times?

You know that anyone can lie with numbers. The same set of data can certainly be used to prove both sides of many arguments. Even so, when you compare the different learning rates that I have listed, it should be apparent that writing is very slow and that thinking is, comparatively, very fast.

I list these rates to suggest to you that working at the most efficient speed possible will help you learn more per unit of time. Yes, there are times that you must write, or listen or read, etc. However, if you have an option, you will be able to process more material by working at the fastest speed possible. In the listening situation, you cannot write down everything that the speaker is saying. You can, of course, listen and think faster than almost any speaker can talk.

The excess time that you have when you listen, the difference between the instructor's speaking rate and your thinking rate, can be an asset or a hazard. The excess time can be an asset if you use the time differential effectively. It can be a danger or a hazard if you use the time to daydream while the speaker lectures. Use the time differential between the speaker's rate of speech and your thought speed to summarize what the speaker says, to connect the current material with your past knowledge, to raise and answer questions, and to predict or anticipate what the speaker is going to say next. Only when you have done all of these activities should you be concerned about long-term retention of the material that you have learned.

Missed Classes

Occasionally you will miss some of your classes either by choice or through no fault of your own. You are still responsible for knowing the material that was covered in that class session.

I believe that it would be a good idea for you to know the names and phone numbers of at least two students in every class that you take. When you miss a class or do not understand material from that class, those students become a resource for you to draw on. You can call them to ask questions or make arrangements to copy and go over their notes.

Did you notice that I just suggested that you copy <u>and</u> go over the other student's notes? Just having the notes may not help you. Having someone talk through their notes with you will allow you to clarify points that you do not understand from their notes alone.

When you work full time and miss a meeting that your boss has called, you are still responsible for knowing what happened at the meeting. Your boss probably does not have time to go over the information that was covered at the meeting. You will, however, gain "points" (or at least, not lose them) by getting the information that was covered from a fellow employee who attended the meeting. Employers like to see their staff take the initiative or responsibility to find out what happened when they were absent.

Why not adopt behaviors in college that will prove to be useful in the world of work? Yes, it is sometimes difficult to ask others for help. It may be difficult for you to ask someone for their name and phone number. However, because none of us live in a vacuum, we need to develop interactive skills that will help us to be successful. Ask! You need information that they have and

that they will probably be willing to share with you.

Retention of Learned Material

Once you have learned what the speaker has said you can begin to be concerned about retaining what you have learned. The three basic ways to improve your ability to hold on to information that you have learned are through use, ownership, and written reminders. You can use any one of the techniques and improve your ability to remember or you can use any combination of the methods; the choice is yours.

<u>The Law of Exercise</u>

One of the oldest laws of human learning is the law of exercise. As you might expect, the law of exercise says that the more you use your knowledge, the longer it will stay with you. Ever hear the expression "Use it or lose it?" It means the same thing. Concepts, ideas, or information that you use regularly are remembered. Concepts, ideas, or information that you do not use regularly tend to be forgotten.

Did you take a foreign language when you were in high school? Did you learn it? If you took the college preparatory track in high school, you probably took classes in Spanish, French, or German. If you were like most students, however, you learned very little of the language. You heard the language in class and saw it when you did the required homework and studied for your exams. You rarely used the language at any other time.

Suppose you really wanted to learn a foreign language, what would be the "easy way" to learn that language? If you said go to a country that speaks that language and use only that language, you would be correct. In a very short period of time, you would learn a great deal of the language. As you tried to use the language, virtually everyone would become your teacher. Whenever you made a mistake, people would correct you. They would correct you out of kindness, kindness in correcting the error so that you would not make it again and embarrass yourself; they feel that you want to learn it correctly or you would not be trying to speak it. (In the United States we do not correct people when they make a mistake speaking English; that's our kindness. Of course, the person trying to learn English continues to make that mistake. Were we really being kind?) Basically it would come down to the more you used the new language, the more you would learn, and the better you would retain it.

In most of human learning, it is the same; the more you use information, the better you will be able to retain it.

1492. What happened in 1492? Columbus sailed the ocean blue, right? How many times did you go over that piece of information when you were in school? Lots, right? Can you remember the binomial theorem? You learned it, you heard it in class, you did homework problems using the theorem and you took and passed math tests with it. So, what is the theorem?

Most of us cannot remember the binomial theorem even though we knew it at one time because we do not use it regularly. The same goes for taking square roots, chemical formulas, names and dates, or other information that we do not use. This means that if you want to retain information that you learn, you have to use it somewhat regularly. Weekly or monthly reviews are needed to keep information fresh in our minds.

Using information does not have to mean sitting in a corner reviewing. You can use information when you get together with your friends, in study groups, or talking with your instructor, etc. Look at the world of work. When a group of engineers get together, what do you suppose they talk about? How about chemists, accountants, psychologists, teachers, or business people? What do they talk about? Most of them talk about their work when they are together in groups. Yes, they talk about other subjects, too, but one topic that certainly will come up in most groups is "the latest happening at work." People who like their work share it with others in their field and with people in their lives.

What about students? Students go to class and then "lock the mental box for that class" until they either study or get back to class. No fair talking about what you are learning with others; they wouldn't be interested.

Have you ever watched little kids learn something new? They get excited and run around showing everyone what they have learned. They are excited, they are pleased with themselves. The next time you are in the library, look around and see how excited your peers are with the information they are learning (the library is about as exciting as a mortuary during a funeral). If you don't care about what you are learning, you won't use it, you won't retain it, and you won't do well in that subject. Try getting something out of your study. What's in it for you? How can you use that piece of information? How does it fit with other things that you know?

Try talking about the idea with your friends or other students in the class. Talk about class material with my friends? That's crazy! Really? People who care about you like to know about things that you care about. If an idea is important, how can you show someone what it means, why it is important without "putting them down" for not knowing the idea? Try teaching an idea to a friend and then having them teach you something that they have learned. With your classmates, why not get together with some of them to talk about material that has been covered in class? How about sharing your term papers with classmates or friends? People at work share their papers and work with their colleagues. They help each

other produce better work. Why can't students help each other? (Remember, when you finish school, you will be joining the work force. Most jobs require team effort, people working together to produce a quality product. Get comfortable with sharing and working with others; you can learn a lot from them.)

Ownership

By ownership I mean that you will remember information that becomes a part of you better than you will remember isolated material that does not fit into your life. If you are able to connect the new material that you are hearing to information that you already know, you will be better able to hold on to that material for a longer period of time. In listening, ownership means that you make new information that you are receiving from the speaker become a part of yourself, part of your own personal knowledge base.

A few techniques that may help make new material become yours include the following:

Recitation

When you can recite material in your own words you are more likely to retain that information than if you memorize the material using the speaker's words. Recitation means to talk about the material out loud or silently to yourself. In some cases you may even want to write out a summary so that you can see your work.

Flash Cards

For material that is difficult for you or for material that must be learned exactly the way it is presented, such as formulas, flash cards can give you needed practice. Cards that are 3" x 5" or smaller are probably best since they are easy to carry around with you. On one side of the card, mark the key word or the main idea; on the other side write a brief summary of the information that you want to remember. Then use the cards to test yourself.

Mnemonics

To remember material in an exact order, creating a "word summary" or mnemonic summary can be very useful. Don't create hundreds of mnemonics because rote learning can cause more problems than it solves. Use mnemonics for isolated cases when your time and effort will be worth the effort. Some of the more familiar mnemonics to the American public are "FACE" (in music, the spaces in the treble clef, from the bottom up, are f, a, c, e); "Every Good Boy Does Fine" (the lines in the treble clef from the bottom up); "i before e except after c, or when it sounds like 'a' as in sleighbell and weigh"; to remember which direction to turn the clock for daylight savings time we have "spring forward and fall back"; etc.

Additional information about retention and ownership of learned material is covered in the chapter on textbook reading.

Note Taking

Earlier I said that you should not take notes on what the speaker says. I mean that. In a large number of cases, when the speaker is presenting new material, you simply cannot get it all down. Try taking the information in first, owning it, then writing down minimal notes on what you need to remember from what you have learned. Write your notes during "time outs"---when the instructor is erasing the board, answering a question that you know the answer to or when there are pauses in the lecture, etc.

In general, write as little as you can in class to help you remember the information that you want to retain. Do not write a complete sentence unless it is given to you word for word and you are required to know it verbatim. Never write a complete word when a phrase will do. Never write a phrase when a word will do. Never write a word when an abbreviation will do. And never write an abbreviation that you do not need. In essence, write as little as you can to remember the information that you want to retain. After class, either immediately after class or that evening, add additional material to your notes if you want to.

Format

You can take notes in many different formats. A few of them are listed here:

Outline

The most familiar form of note taking is probably the outline method. The method uses roman and arabic numbers and capital and small letters to show the organization of the material.

Outlining can be a useful tool. However, when you are listening to a speaker who has not organized the material using the outline method, you can easily become frustrated trying to force unorganized material into outline form.

There is a sample of outline notes on the topic of study method on the next page.

Key and Summary

The key and summary method uses the structure of the page to help you retain information. Divide your note page into three sections: make the left "margin" approximately 2 inches wide, the center section about 4 or 5 inches, and the remaining section 1 or 2 inches. In the left margin, write down a word that is the main idea or a word that summarizes the idea to be remembered. The center column is for the notes that you take, or the material that explains what the key word means. The remaining column is for a summary of the entire lecture. When the class is over, that night, or when you first sit down to study your notes, use the key words as triggers or questions for recites--oral summaries of the contents of your notes.

Key and summary notes on the SQ3R study technique would look something like the example on the next page.

Notes taken using the key and summary method can be an excellent tool for reviewing and preparing for examinations. Just cover the middle section of notes and use the keys words as test items. Read a key word and try to recite the information that you have included in center.

Graphic

Graphic notes show the interconnection of the ideas that are being presented.

In graphic notes, the main idea of the lecture is placed in a box in the center of the page. Each supporting idea or concept that connects with the main idea radiates off on lines from the central box. Details that go with each of the supporting ideas branch off the support line.

Graphic notes can be an excellent tool for people who have good visual memory. You can even enhance your notes by using colors. In the SQ3R example, each of the steps and the notes that go with it could have been written in different colors. Each page of notes would be visually different, aiding some students to remember the information through their visual memory of the structure or organization of the page.

To better understand graphic notes, study the example of graphic notes presented on the next few ages.

Study Methods

I. SQ3R (Survey, Question, Read, Recite, Review)

    A. S = Survey

        1. Read the introduction, headings, and the summary
        2. Get an overview of the chapter

    B. Q = Question

        1. Turn each heading into a question
        2. Focus on the main idea

    C. R 1 = Read

        1. Read the text material up to the next heading
        2. Find the answer to the question, the main idea

    D. R 2 = Recite

        1. In your own words, summarize the main idea
        2. Prove that you learned the material

    E. R 3 = Review

        1. When you finish a chapter or a study session, pull all of the information together
        2. Interrelate the ideas, prove that you know them

II. SQ4R (The fourth R is for 'rite)

III. OAR

Outline Notes

Study Methods

SQ3R A five-step method for studying textbooks. The steps are Survey, Question, Read, Recite, Review.

Survey Read introduction, headings, and summary to get an overview of the chapter.

Question Change each heading into a question to focus your attention on the main idea of the coming section.

Read Read the section up to the next heading. Answer the question that you asked. What is the main idea of the section?

Recite In your own words, summarize the main idea to prove that you have learned it. In essence, what is the main idea that was presented?

Review When you finish a chapter or a study session, summarize all the sections that you read, interrelate the ideas, and show that you have mastered them.

SQ4R Similar to SQ3R except for the added 'rite step after the recite. That is, after you recite, you write ('rite) out your summary of what you learned (or the answer to the question you asked in the question step).

OAR The "O" stands for overview which is similar to the survey in SQ3R and SQ4R....

Key and Summary Notes

Graphic Notes on SQ3R

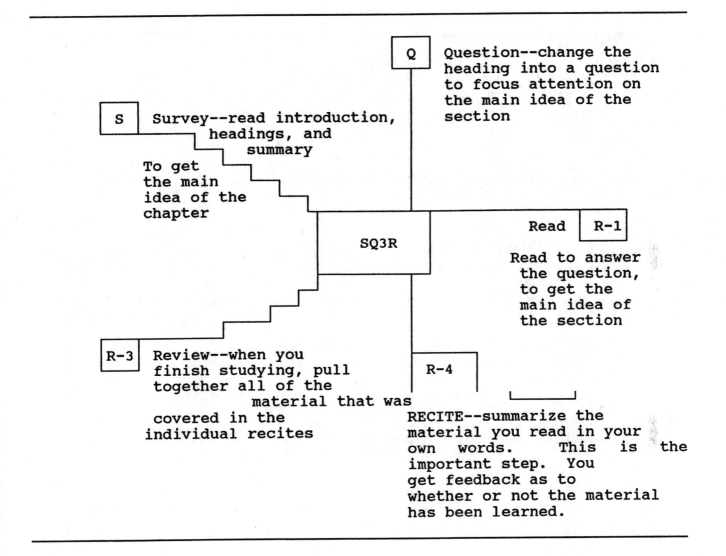

Pyramid

Branching, hierarchical or "line and staff" notes use interconnected lines to show how the material fits together. The main idea is placed at the top center of the page. Supporting ideas branch out from the main idea.

Pyramid or hierarchical notes would be good for information that has relationships that are important to know and remember. Business organizations and family trees are often shown using pyramid style notes.

Pyramid SQ3R notes might look
like this:

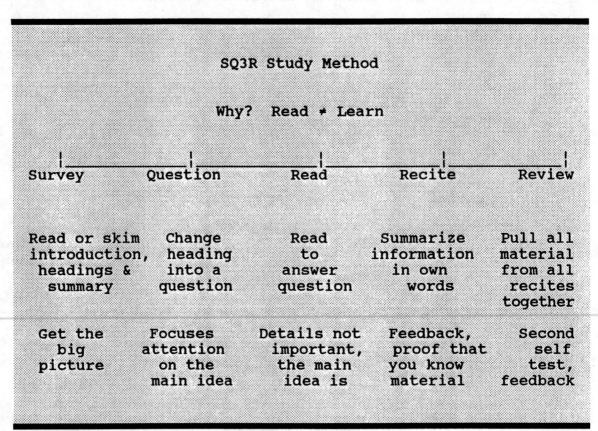

Pyramid Notes

Charts

Charts can be an excellent way of summarizing and comparing information. The columns and rows of the chart can easily show similarities and differences between concepts. If you were studying psychology, zoology, botany, or biology, for instance, you might create a chart comparing the different theories of personality or the different phyla in the animal kingdom. In essence, you would be creating information matrices that allow you to see differences and similarities.

Creating a chart will take time and require that you organize either the rows or columns in a consistent way. The benefit, of course, is that you can compact a large quantity of information into a format that will help you learn the nuances of the subject matter and more easily see similarities, contrasts, variations, and discrepancies in data matrix that you are using.

Class Preparation

Most study skills texts tell you that you should read assigned material before you go to class. The idea behind the recommendation is that you will have some knowledge of the subject matter before your instructor begins to lecture. One can, however, make a case for going to class first and reading later. You use the instructor to warm you up to the text material. Let's look at the advantages and disadvantages of each strategy.

Advantages

Reading first

You have some knowledge of the subject matter and are prepared to learn new material when you get to class.

You can have questions ready on material that you did not completely understand.

You will tend to take fewer notes because you know what material is in the textbook.

Going to class first

The instructor covers the material first, warming you up to the information that will be in the textbook.

Your reading rate will be faster because you already know some of the information that will be in the textbook.

It will take you less time to complete the reading assignment.

Disadvantages

Reading first

Each reading assignment will take you longer to complete because you are reading new information.

All of the material you will be reading will be new to you; it will be more difficult to comprehend.

You may cover material that the instructor later tells you to skip.

You may "be bored" in class if you feel that you already know what the instructor is saying.

Going to class first

Because you do not know what will be in the textbook, you will have a tendency to take more notes.

Learning lecture material will be slightly more difficult because you are not familiar with the concepts that are being covered.

Questions that you may ask in class may be answered in the textbook.

Text questions will always come after the subject has been covered in class.

Note that there are advantages and disadvantages to both reading first and going to class first. Which strategy will be best for you? You will have to decide for yourself. I have found that in some classes such as English, sociology, and psychology I could leave the reading until after class and let the instructor tell me what was important. In math, science, and accounting classes I read the text first and used class to "polish off" my knowledge.

When are _you_ ahead? When you read first or when you read after the instructor has warmed you up to the subject? Different classes probably require different strategies, so don't be surprised to find that you want to be ahead in the readings for some classes and technically behind, though by choice, in others.

Parallel Classes

When the textbook and the instructor cover the material in the same order, you have parallel instruction. Courses in the sciences, mathematics, and accounting are often parallel classes. Do you want to read the text material before or after the lecture?

Diverging Classes

Classes in which the instructor and the required readings are on the same subject area but not on the same information are diverging classes. Material that is in the readings is independent of the lecture and will not be covered in class. Upper level courses and seminars are often of this variety. Your reading for these classes can be done at any time because the information does not directly relate to the lecture sessions.

Using Your Notes

If you are going to use notes to remind yourself what you have learned, those notes will be worthless unless you review them. The best time to review your notes is in the next class session of that course. Think about your activities in class before the session begins. What do you do--talk to other students, read the paper, close your eyes and daydream? How do any of these activities help you prepare for the class session?

Reviewing before the class begins will do several things for you:

1. A review will remind you of the information that was covered in the last class session. Your instructor has organized her material such that ideas flow from one session to the next one. By reviewing just before the class begins you will be warmed up to the topic and to the logical flow of the class.

2. When you review your notes, do you always understand everything that you have written? If you review your notes before the class begins and you do not understand something, you can ask another student to clarify the point or ask a question when the instructor says "Are there any questions?" How many questions does she get? (Many instructors won't ask if there are any questions because they have learned that no one has any questions--why waste the time and effort to ask?) What better place to be when you

have a question about a lecture than in that class with the instructor?

Reviewing your notes before class is similar to the warm up you do before you compete in athletic events. In athletics, you warm up so that you will do better in your competition. Why not warm up academically before your class begins?

Supplies

As far as supplies are concerned, just be reasonable. Use whatever materials you are comfortable with. Just use your knowledge about yourself to select supplies that will help you do the job you want to do. Think about what you want to be carrying around with you and about the amount of flexibility that you want. For example, if you want to be able to reorganize pages at a later time, you will need some kind of looseleaf notebook or a folder system.

Weight may be important if you plan to carry books and supplies for several classes. Think about what you need in class before you start to carry all your books with you. In many courses, if not in most, you really do not need to bring your textbook to class with you because you do not have time to refer to it during the lecture. In other classes, such as science labs, there is material that you must have with you to work efficiently. Travel "light," bring only what you need.

Computers and typewriters are great for producing papers but

they have no place in your lecture note-taking procedure. Rewriting your notes will not help you learn the information you need. Neat notes are no substitute for poor listening skills or the lack of thinking on your part. Study your notes, edit them to make them more helpful to you, but do not rewrite them unless you have a lot of extra time to spare.

Summary

The object of this chapter has been to get you to focus your attention on learning through listening rather than having you simply go to class to take notes. Listen and learn! After you have learned, be concerned with retaining what you have learned.

Academic listening requires you to focus on the intent of the speaker. What is the message that is being presented? What do you want or need to get from the presentation? Once you have learned what the speaker has said, what do you need to do to retain the information that you acquired?

If you decide to use notes, write information that reflects what you have learned from the speaker that goes beyond what you already knew before you heard the presentation. Write to remind yourself about what you learned and want to retain for future use. Review your notes just before the next class session to clarify any points that you may not have understood and to improve your ability to listen and learn more effectively.

7 TEST-TAKING SKILLS

In most of the classes you take, your grade in the course will be determined mainly through your scores on the quizzes, tests, or examinations. The more that you know, the higher your test score will be. How much you know when you take the exam <u>is</u> important: however, how you use what you know is even more important. I will show you in this chapter how to apply whatever knowledge you have to get the highest score possible. I will review some basic information about educational measurement and then present specific techniques on how to prepare for and take different kinds of tests and examinations. In the next two chapters, I will discuss taking essay and objective examinations. Throughout, I will use the terms tests, exams, and examinations interchangeably.

Educational Measurement

Tests or examinations are measurement devices that are used to assess how well you have learned material that has been assigned to you. Tests are not designed to measure everything that you are supposed to know; they are <u>samples</u> of some of the information that you are expected to know.

Suppose you register for a class called "1,000 Words in Dutch That You Always Wanted to Know." The instructor presents the course syllabus and asks the class "How many tests do you want to have?"

The answer, of course, would be "None!" The instructor says "Okay, we'll compromise and have one exam." Is this a good solution?

This is a very poor solution. One test means that you have only one chance at your evaluation. If you do well, great. If you do poorly, you have no other way of improving your grade. When you are given a choice in the number of assessments you will have, take as many as you can get. Two exams are better than one, three are better than two, five or six would be even better. Five or six tests are a good idea? Definitely! Each test will cover less material and the total number of tests will give you many chances to show your ability. Whereas no one test will cause you to get an A in the class, no one test will cause you to fail either.

Back to the example. You have one test in this Dutch class, the "1,000 Words in Dutch That You Always Wanted to Know." How many questions do you think will be on the exam? 1,000? 500? (Even the SAT doesn't have 500 questions!) You will probably get between 50 and 100 questions on the exam. The questions will require that you know a lot of the words, but **most** of the words that were covered in the course will not be on the exam. **Most** of the words that were assigned to you, which your instructor wants you to know, will not be on the examination you will take. In all of your classes, a large percentage of the information that you are expected to know will not be on any of the course examinations. In fact, in most of your classes, most of the material that you are expected to know will not be on your quizzes or tests!

To make matters worse, the instructor can select or create questions for the test any way he wants to. Questions could come only from the lectures, only from the textbook, or in any combination that the instructor wants. In short, the instructor gets to create any course evaluation procedure that he wants.

If your instructor really can do anything on examinations that he wants to and if most of the material in your classes will not be on the course examinations, how do you know what will be on the examinations? The first alternative is that if you learn all of the material that has been assigned to you, you will be able to do well regardless of the questions that your instructor asks. The better prepared you are, the better you will do on any examination.

An alternate method of preparation would be to get a good idea of how your instructor creates test questions and to determine a strategy that will enable you to do well on tests. Old tests are probably the best method to gauge what your instructor expects of you. An old examination will show you the kinds of questions your instructor will ask. An

analysis of the exam will give an idea of where the test questions came from. It is the analysis of an old test that is important, not the specific questions that are asked. The questions can easily change; the thoughts or evaluation concerns of the instructor, however, will tend to remain the same.

Think for a minute about evaluation in the world of work. When you have a job, don't you want to know how the boss will evaluate you in determining pay raises and promotions? If your boss is concerned about staff being on time, do the people who get to work and meetings on time get the bigger raises? If so, and if you want to make more money, wouldn't you change your behavior to get to meetings and work a little bit early?

Your exam analysis is the same as assessing your boss's expectations at work. You want to know where your instructor places his emphasis just as you want to know where your boss's emphases are. Get a copy of an exam that your instructor has used previously. If questions on the old exam tend to come from the text, questions on your exam will probably come from the text. If the old exam has many calculation problems, your exam will have calculations. Note that the concern is to study the old examination to help you use your time to learn what material is most important in your instructor's opinion.

Getting an old exam to study is not difficult. Students who

have taken the course will often let you see their exams. Sometimes student organizations have "exam files." The best source of old exams is, of course, your instructor. Some instructors will make old exams available through the Reserve Room in the campus library or in their office. Most instructors will either allow you to see an old exam in class or give you sample questions that they have used in the past. Instructors know that there are copies of their old examinations around so why not ask them if you can review one?

The Name of the Game: Points-- Scoring High on Exams

An old exam is helpful to learn what material is most important to study. It is also important to know how to get the highest grade possible on the exam with the knowledge you have. In taking an exam, what you know is not as important as how you use what you know. Your knowledge is useful if it will help you to get points on the exam. The points you earn, in turn, get you your grade.

The name of the game in test taking is **points**. The more points you get on a test, the higher your grade will be. Just what the points mean is often unknown until after the exam is over.

Grading on the Curve

Most instructors do not grade on the following scale: 90-100 = A, 80-89 = B, 70-79 = C, etc. Most of your instructors use points to determine the value of each answer and then add up the points. After all the tests have been scored, they determine what the point totals mean. They create a grading scale that students refer to as "the curve." Grading on the curve means that instructors and students expect there to be relatively few A's, a fair number of B's, a lot of C's, and, hopefully, a small number of D's and F's. From the students' view, points become extremely important. The more you can get the better.

Although it is true that on tests points are important and that more is better, until you know what the total score means you really don't know anything. How would you like a test score of 95? "That sounds great, but how many points were available?" Ninety-five out of 100! Most students would jump at a score like that. However, the grade that went with the 95 was an F! That's right, an F. The instructor of a seminar course was not getting any discussion during class. It was fairly obvious that no one had read the assigned material. He gave a test to check who had done the readings. Any mistake yielded a failing grade, even 95 out of 100! (The course syllabus allowed for "pop" quizzes.)

The same semester that I saw 95 out of 100 equal an F, I saw 2 points out of 60 equal a C. The course was an advanced statistics class that had an "open book, open notes" examination. Any errors in calculation or content were severely penalized. Answers had to be totally correct to be awarded points.

The idea of all of this is to get you to attend to points on any examination. You need to know where the points are, how you can get them, and how you will lose them. Then you need to strategize to receive the maximum number of points that you can on the exam.

On an exam there is no such thing as running out of time! There is only poor time management on the part of the person taking the exam. The task before you on an examination is to get the most points you can under the rules set by your instructor. Use your time to maximize the number of points that you earn.

The point value of the questions on a test are there to tell you the importance or value of each question in the final score. The instructor is doing more than just telling you how many points there are available. Your instructor is telling you how to allot your time on the exam to maximize the points that you earn. On objective exams, the point value of each question is usually the same, so distribute your time so that you can complete the entire test. On essay exams, the instructor is telling you how much time you should be spending on each question. Hopefully, the time you spend on a question is related to the number of points that you will earn from your answer to that question.

Essay Exams

When you take an essay examination, the point value of each question should be listed either before or after the actual question. Use the information about the point value of each question to strategize how you can get the most points from your answers to the exam questions.

Suppose you are taking an essay exam that has five questions on it. Each question has the point value listed beside the item. You are told that you have an academic hour for the exam. The point values for each question are as follows:

1.	5
2.	10
3.	10
4.	25
5.	50
Total	100

What strategy would you use to get the most points from this exam? Stop and think about your strategy before you read on.

The first question you need to ask yourself is how long, in minutes, do you have for the test? You do not have 60 minutes for the test! You have 50 minutes, the amount of class time there is in an hour less 10 minutes to get to the next class. If you are not sure of the amount of time that you have for the test, raise your hand and ask the instructor. Do not assume that you have the entire class period, ask. Remember, time is a resource that you plan to use to get the most points you can for your answers.

You now know that you have 50 minutes for the exam. How

should the time be used? The point value of each question now should tell you how much time you should spend on each question. Your analysis should have produced results that look something like this:

	Points	Time for question
1.	5	2 1/2 minutes
2.	10	5 minutes
3.	10	5 minutes
4.	25	12 1/2 minutes
5.	50	25 minutes

The analysis of point value and time available in this example indicates that each point in the value of a question is worth half a minute of your time. A 10-point question should get 5 minutes of time to maximize the number of points earned, etc.

Once you know how to use your time, you can determine the order for answering the questions on the test. Many students would simply start at the beginning and work until time runs out. If you were to do that with the example above you might run into trouble. Look at the first "question"; it is worth only five points. What do you know or what can you guess about the question? (I know that there isn't a question written there! What must be true of the question that could or would be there?) The first question is worth only five points. There is a good chance that the instructor considers it to be an easy item (easy questions simply do not get many points). Besides, this is the first question on the test. How many exams

"kill" you on the first question? Not many. Instructors know that you do not like to take tests and usually start you out with a question that you can handle. They try to get you started before they try to find out how much you know.

A second strategy for the example above would be to start with the question that has the most points, the 50-point, or last, question. The rationale behind this strategy is that if you start by going after the most points and you run out of time, you will have gotten most of the points that are available to you in the allotted time.

The best strategy to use would be to start with any question you want but to budget your time in order to complete all the questions that you can handle. Analysis of the exam indicates that you should spend half of your test time on question five. Which half should it be? The first half, the last half, or somewhere in the middle? The answer is it doesn't make any difference! Just be sure that you spend half of the total time for that question! Remember, time equals points. The more time you spend on an answer, the more points you should be able to get for your answer.

Objective Exams

Multiple-choice, true-false, and matching-question tests are often referred to as objective tests because the instructor does not have to make a judgment or evaluate your answer. You must select one of the many answers that are presented in the question, and your answer is either right or wrong.

Points can be an issue on objective tests in one of two ways:

1. The point value of the questions may differ on different sections of the test. An example of this could be instructions that read "The first 25 questions are worth one (1) point each. Questions 26-50 are worth two (2) points each." In this example, you should work through the first half of the test quickly so that you can spend most of your time on the last half where most of the points are.

2. If the instructor corrects for guessing, the grading system that is used can be very important. Instructors grade objective tests by simply counting up the number of correct answers for your test score. If you took an exam with 100 multiple-choice questions that have four options each, and you knew absolutely nothing but you answered every question, your score on the exam should be 25! By chance you should get one out of four questions right by guessing. Even though you did not know any of the information, your score was 25.

If your instructor uses standard correction for guessing on the exam in the above example, your score would have been 0 (zero)! In standard correction for guessing, you get one point for

each correct answer, but you would lose one point for every three answers you got wrong. (If there had been five options per question, the correction factor would have been the loss of one point for each four incorrect answers, one less than the number of answer options.) In the example, your final score would have been +25 for the 25 correct answers and -25 for the 75 wrong answers, or 0.

When you are taking a test that your own instructor has written, and your instructor is using standard correction for guessing, guess anyway! Rarely will you ever take a test on which you know absolutely nothing. When you know something, even a very small amount, you get a higher score by guessing.

For example, on the four-option, multiple-choice test, if you could eliminate one alternative on each test question, then you would be guessing from the three alternatives that are left. By chance, you would get 33 answers correct and 67 wrong. The 67 wrong answers would convert to -22 (67 x -1/3 = -22). Your score on the exam would be 11 (33 correct answers minus the correction factor of 22).

On the same test, if you could eliminate two alternatives, you would get 50 questions right "by chance" and 50 wrong. The 50 wrong answers convert to -16 (50 x -1/3). Your exam score would be 34 (50 - 16).

Note, in the example, when you

knew nothing your score was 0. When you knew a little bit, you got 11 points. When you knew more, you received 34 points.

Do not guess on an objective exam when the penalty is equal to or more than you can earn for a correct answer. If the point value on a 100-question multiple-choice test is such that one point is earned for each correct answer and two points are deducted for each incorrect answer, you could end up with a negative score if you guess. In this case, if you know nothing and guess, you would get +25 for the 25 correct answers, but you would lose 150 points for the 75 wrong answers. Your final score would be -125 (+25 - 150).

Summary on Scoring

To summarize scoring on objective tests, guess at answers unless there is a penalty for which you lose more than you can gain by guessing. Even with the standard correction for guessing, guess. On essay exams, use your time to maximize the number of points that you earn by allocating time according to the point value of each test question.

Preparing for an Examination

All factors being equal, the more you know about the subject matter when you take an examination, the higher your test score will be regardless of the kind of test that it is. Students who know more score higher on objective tests, essay tests, teacher-made tests, professionally developed tests, fair tests, "unfair" tests, and ambiguous tests. Preparation is extremely important if you are to earn the highest grade possible for you.

Early Preparation

If you want to master your course material and do well on your course examinations, you need to devote time to your studying over a period of several days or weeks. You need to distribute your time to allow you to first learn the necessary information and, second, give time to assimilate or get comfortable with the knowledge you need for the exam. Very simply, learning that occurs over a long period of time stays with you longer than material you learn in a short period of time. Planning and time management will be very important to your overall success.

What Will the Test Cover?

I have been amazed at the number of students who never find out exactly what material the coming test will cover. Will it cover material from the lecture and the textbook? Which one will be emphasized? It makes a difference in how and what you study. For example, one of my students told about a zoology professor who told his class that 98 percent of his test questions would come from his lectures. What does that tell you about the textbook for that class? Right, it doesn't count. The instructor used the text to support the information that he presented in class.

Will the exam require that you know definitions? Will you have problems to solve? Will you need to be able to read or create graphs? Art classes often require you to identify famous works by the masters, research courses can demand that you be able to critique or design experiments, zoology and nursing exams can be situational exams with "stations" where students have to identify bones and other body parts, chemistry exams can ask you to determine what a given substance is, etc.

When you know what you are going to be held responsible for knowing, you can tailor your studying a little bit to meet the instructor's special idiosyncracies. Did you notice that I said you would tailor your studying a little bit? I hope that your primary reason for studying is that you want to know information and ideas for yourself. Yes, your instructor assigns the grade you get in the course, but your being satisfied with what you learned is most important. Therefore, when you are studying for an exam, do consider what the instructor wants you to know, but don't forget to go over the material that you want to know too.

How Much Preparation Time?

You are the only person who can figure out how much time you will need to prepare for an examination. If you have read all of the assigned material and completed all of the homework, you will not need a

great deal of time to review for the exam. If, on the other hand, you have not yet completed all of the required reading, you will need considerably more preparation time.

Once you know what the examination will cover, you can assess where you are in your test preparation and what you need to complete to be prepared for the exam at the level for which you want to be prepared. You set the standards for how well you know the material, not the instructor! You can say you want to know everything inside out and backwards, that you want to know just enough to get by with the lowest grade possible, or anywhere in between. The combination of what you want to know and what the instructor wants you to know determines the exam preparation that is to be completed.

Once you know what has to be done, you can figure out how much time it will take you to prepare for the exam. As an example, let's find the study time for your first chemistry exam. You read and mastered the material in four of the five chapters that will be covered on the exam. You need to read the fifth chapter, to review all five chapters, to review the first two lab reports that were handed in, and rework all of the homework problems to adequately prepare for the coming exam. You figure that you will need 4 hours to read the last chapter, 1 or 2 hours to review each chapter, half an hour to study each lab report, and 5 or 6 hours for going over all the homework problems. That means that you need from 15 to 21 hours of preparation time (4 hours to read, 5 to 10 hours to review the five chapters, 1 hour for the labs, and 5 or 6 hours for the homework problems).

When you estimate study time, can you estimate your preparation time accurately? Or rather, when you estimate study time, <u>do you estimate accurately</u>? No. You probably underestimate most of the time. (Who wants to suffer more than they have to?) Because most of us underestimate how long it will take us to study, add on some extra study time to make sure that you are not surprised by not having enough preparation time. If you usually come close in your study estimates, add 10% to your total. If you usually misjudge by a lot, add 20% to your total. In the last example, if we add 20% to the total, 21 hours, we get a "grand total" of 25 hours of study needed to prepare for the chemistry exam.

Although it took some time to figure out how much time you need to get ready for the exam, you now have all the bad news: how much study time you need-- no surprises later. The total preparation time for your chemistry exam is 25 hours.

Twenty-five hours of exam study for one exam? Yes, 25 hours, that is the number of preparation hours that you need for this examination. It could be more for some classes, it will be less in most of your

classes. You do not have to study all of the time--just 25 hours. No guessing--25 hours.

In summary, to be efficient in your examination preparation, you need to know what you have to read and study before you begin work. Once you know what you need to do, you need to know how much time the work will take you. For each exam preparation activity, such as reading two chapters, compute the number of hours you will need to complete that activity at the level of competency that you wish to have. Lastly, total the time you need for all of the activities related to preparing for that exam.

Budgeting Your Time

Now that you know how much time you will need to get ready for the exam, all you have to do is find that amount of study time!

Let's suppose you computed the number of hours you would need to prepare for the chemistry exam one week before the actual examination. With seven days to prepare, you need a little less than four hours of study each day to reach your goal. Where will the time come from?

If you have a fairly regular schedule each week, you can review your typical week and make adjustments in how you will spend your time. If your days and weeks vary a great deal, you will need to make preparation for the exam a priority each day. In either case, you will probably need to move other activities around to make room for the extra study time that you need.

Even if you plan four hours for chemistry each day, "things" often happen that disrupt even the best plan. Remember Murphy's Law? If anything can go wrong, it will, at the least convenient time. When we apply Murphy's Law to exam preparation, try to protect yourself from the unexpected. If you leave your studying to the last minute, something is bound to go wrong. If, on the other hand, you get ahead in your exam preparation, Murphy never seems to show up to bother you.

In the chemistry exam example, instead of studying four hours each day, put in five or six hours on the first two days. With the extra study hours you will be a little ahead so that if something should go wrong, it will be easier for you to get back on track.

The idea of budgeting your preparation time is to "guarantee" sufficient time to complete all the studying that you need. At the same time, you want to be sure that you will have time for other things like meeting with friends, working, sleeping, etc. The sooner you can determine the preparation time you need, the easier it will be to control your time and anxiety.

Preparing for Midterms & Finals

During exam time students are often pressed for time. Even if you try to keep up with all of your studies, somehow exam time always seems to mean that you still need more study time. Preparing for final exams can be an especially taxing time.

There just isn't enough time to do everything that you want to do. Suppose it is three weeks before your final exams and you are trying to get everything under control. What kinds of things do you need or want to do before or during exam preparation? Some fairly common activities you would probably want or need to consider are

> work
> sleep
> class
> transportation time
>   (getting to and from
>   work and school)
> eating
> personal hygiene time
> TV time
> partying
> time with your friends
> family time
> recreation time
> laundry and housework time
> and, oh yes, studying.

To get control of your time, how much time do you need or want for each activity? (Let's assume you have three weeks before final exam week and that there is a full week for the finals.)

work	60 hours (15 hours/week)
sleep	224 hours (8 hours/night x 28 days)
class	45 hours (15 hours/week)
travel	40 hours (10 hours/week)
eating	56 hours (2 hours/day)

personal hygiene	28 hours (1 hour/day)
TV time	48 hours or more (12 hours/week)
partying	as much as possible (120 hours)
friends	as much as possible (120 hours)
family	?
recreation	?
church/ religion	?
home chores	12 hours
studying	90 hours (20 hours/week plus 10 hours for exam preparation for each of 5 classes)
Total	933 hours

The total of 933 hours for all of the items that I have listed still does not contain any time for recreation, family or miscellaneous activities. The 933 hours that are listed exceed the 672 hours that are available during the four weeks (168 x 4 = 672) by 261 hours. That is, you have 261 more "scheduled" hours than are actually possible. Something, or rather, several things, will have to go.

Before you decide on what things you have to or are going to get rid of, stop and think about your priorities for the four weeks in question. Which activities are most important to you? If you are concerned about getting the most out of the semester, learning, and grades, then attending class and studying have to be your priorities. Note, you decide on what your priorities are going to be. Don't just assume that school comes first; in many cases studying won't be the student's number one priority! So, decide for yourself which activities are most important to you during your finals preparation time.

Once you know your priorities, you can reexamine the other items on your list and try to keep as many as possible in a "reduced" form.

Making and Finding Time

Even though you only have 168 hours available to you each week, some of that time can be stretched, reshaped, or exchanged to give you what appears to be more time. Time can be stretched if you can find ways to make it do two or more things for you concurrently. Going to the library with some of your friends and studying in the same general area can meet some of your social needs (you are together) while getting some studying completed. Afterwards you can get together for some coffee, etc. In a way, you work first then reward yourself with social activities. Similarly, other activities might be restructured so that two or more of your activities can be done at the same time. Examples include studying at work or at meals, having meals with friends, reciting while driving or doing laundry or

132

housework, studying while relaxing in a hot bath, etc.

Reshaping your time could mean that you change when you do things. You still use the same number of hours, you just rearrange your
schedule for a while as your priorities shift. For example, you might get up an hour or two earlier each day and get some studying done before the rest of your activities begin. This way your exam preparation has the priority position in your day. Instead of studying at night, you spend your evening hours unwinding with friends. Commuters might stay on campus to study instead of going home for dinner and studying afterwards. Work hours might be moved and/or reduced to provide a more efficient schedule during finals.
Meal times might be moved to give you more study or work time. Whatever changes you make should be aimed at getting you better or more study hours from a temporary change in your regular schedule.

Time exchange literally means moving blocks of time or commitments around within a day, week, month, or other period of time. If work hours need to be reduced, why not talk to your boss and see if you can reduce your hours now and make them up (you may need the money) at a later time? If you plan early enough, you might "bank" some work time before exam week (put in extra work hours before the exam period) so that you do not lose any pay.

With friends you might trade

not seeing them during finals for going off on a weekend trip together after all the exams have been completed. Friends should or can be a great help to you if you are really pressed for time.

Think about the word friend for a minute. What does the word friend mean? Yes, it means people you hang around, people you spend time with. More than that, it means people you care about, people who care about you. People who care about you will do things to help you if they can. Real friends will look out for you and warn you of impending danger. Real friends will ask you why you aren't studying when they know or think you should be studying. Real friends will miss you when they can't see you because you need the time to study; they will give up seeing you because they know that is best for you.

Trading or exchanging time can be done with most of your activities except, perhaps, sleep. Time is needed now for study. The other activity or activities will have to wait. Just be sure to tell or consult the other people who will be affected by your schedule changes when you are making your plans.

Cramming

When I talk to students about preparing for examinations, the first topic of concern is usually cramming. When you run out of time or haven't planned for or made enough time to study for an exam, does it pay to cram? Many teachers and most study skills books will tell you not to cram. They tell you that you won't learn the material. The truth is, cramming <u>does</u> work. Students know it works. Studies on cramming show that students who cram do better on exams than students who did not put in any time studying. That is, if two groups of students are given a test on material that only one group has studied, the group that crams does better than the group that was not given time to study. Last minute study is better than not studying at all.

The problem with cramming has to do with long-term retention of the information that is studied. Cramming gets the information in for a short period of time. However, when you equate study time and compare long-term retention of cramming with distributed, or "spread out," studying, distributed study is better. In a way, it all comes down to whether you are interested in learning material or getting grades. If your emphasis is on grades, cramming can be effective for you. When you are interested in learning material and retaining information for a longer period of time, spread your study time out over several days, a week, or longer.

If you plan to cram, or if you run out of preparation time and you have to cram, cram effectively. Yes, there are things that you can do, as well as things that you should not do, to get the most out of last minute studying. For an example, let's assume that you

need 15 hours of study to adequately prepare for an exam and that you left all of the studying until the last minute. You plan to pull an "all nighter" to get all the studying completed.

The "Don'ts"

There are two major don'ts to avoid during your cramming session--don't eat any big meals and don't cat nap. Eating a big meal will fill you up and cause you to want to go to sleep. You can't afford to be sleepy; eat small meals and keep yourself a little on the hungry side. Easily digested proteins are probably best. For some, that can mean lots of pasta. (Oh my, the calories! The pasta doesn't have the calories; it's what you put on the pasta that has most of the calories.)

The second don't is don't cat nap, don't lie down for "just a minute." If you lie down and close your eyes for that little minute, you and I both know that you will wake up after the exam is over! Rip Van Winkle you're not. Lying down to rest may be necessary, but in this case, it is probably also an avoidance technique that you are trying to use to avoid studying. Besides, it is socially acceptable to be a poor, hard-working student, stressed out, needing sleep. You'll get lots of attention, you'll get your sleep, and you'll fail your exam. No naps!

The "Do's"

The critical problems with

long-term study are (1) staying awake and studying effectively and (2) retaining the information that you learn and need to have available for the examination. If both of these issues can be solved, you can make your study time effective.

The typical responses to the question "What can you do to stay awake?" usually involve some kind of drugs. Answers that I have heard include drinking coffee, tea, or soda for the caffeine; taking NoDoz, bennies, amphetamines, or speed; taking an antihistamine or allergy medicine; etc. True, most of these drugs will keep you awake. The problem is that they do not increase your learning ability, they lower it. Your study becomes less effective with these drugs.

Consider coffee, for example. There is evidence that says that a little bit of coffee, half a cup for most people, will increase effectiveness. However, you can lose effectiveness by drinking too much coffee, tea, or caffeinated-soda. That is, when you exceed the amount of caffeine that improves your performance, the extra caffeine actually becomes debilitating. It lowers your efficiency or performance.

You do not have to use drugs to stay awake and increase your learning effectiveness. If you want to stay awake, two very simple solutions are available to you. First, use cold water. Wash your face in cold water, take a cold shower, or wash your hair in cold water! Try taking a cold shower and going to sleep right after the shower. If you were sleepy and turned on the shower, cold water only, would you actually have to get in the shower to wake up? If you were really, really tired and got into that cold shower, how long would you have to stay in before studying began looking pretty good (or at least a better alternative than standing [shivering] in a cold shower)? A side benefit to using cold showers is that the longer you study, the cleaner you'll be!

The second technique I recommend for staying awake and alert is physical exercise. I defy you to jump rope for two minutes and then go to sleep. Try jumping jacks for two minutes and then try to sleep. You can't do it. When I suggest exercise to keep you awake, don't overexercise or you will defeat the point of exercising. This exercise is for keeping you awake and alert, not for getting you in good physical condition. Jogging for an hour will certainly wake you up, but it will also make you tired and exhausted. Exercise enough to get the blood flowing, to remind your body that although it may be beyond your normal hour for going to sleep, this time you are not going to sleep, you are going to work.

To be efficient at studying, you need to take breaks. Think of your mind as a container of information. If you continue to pour new information into that container, you will overfill it. Continuous studying does bring in new information. However, at some point you will start to overload the circuits. Too much material will come in and you will not be able to use all of the information that you are getting. The "excess" will be wasted.

Remember Steven Wheeler? He was the management expert that proved to the business world that giving employees breaks would make them more effective. When you study you can be more effective by pacing yourself---study, break, study, break, etc.---to keep your mind from getting confused by all of the information you are trying to learn.

Effective cramming uses all of the techniques that have been discussed in this book but uses them in a condensed fashion. The learner must intend to learn, he must be alert, information must get into his head and there must be a constant check to evaluate whether he knows the information at the level at which it needs to be known. Study in small chunks, master the material, and stop. Study in small chunks, master the material, and stop. Study in small....

Anticipate Test Questions

Most college teachers have never been taught how to create good tests and good test questions. Their training is in their academic discipline. Instructors create tests that resemble the tests they received as students. In a way, most instructors are amateurs when it comes to test construction. They create

questions the same way you would, from previous test-taking experience. That means that you should be able to create test questions that are likely to be on your course examinations.

Try an example or two. I remember one student who was taking chemistry and studied chemistry over 20 hours a week. He received a very low score on his first chemistry exam, one that did not seem to reflect all the work that he had done. When I asked him how he prepared for the exam, he indicated that he had studied definitions of terms used in the course. "Why?" I asked. "Because the instructor never asked us for definitions," was his reply. Because class sessions had been spent going through "chemistry problems," wouldn't it have been more logical to expect problems on the exam?

When you are studying problems in an accounting, science or mathematics class, such as $2 + 2 = ?$, is it really so difficult to predict that your instructor might give you a problem that looks like this ($? + 2 = 4$) or this ($2 + ? = 4$)? If you have been studying several different kinds of equations, can't you predict that the instructor might ask you to use two or more of these equations at the same time? In literature and theater classes you will be asked about characters and plots; history classes will ask you to explain events that led up to an incident of great significance, etc.

Old exams, of course, should give you an idea of the kind of questions that your instructor has asked in the past. Use those sample questions to create problems on your own. Remember, your questions do not have to be perfect. You are simply going to use the questions to prepare for your instructor's test. If previous classes have had essay questions, you will have essays. If there were calculation problems on the old test, you will have calculation problems.

If you have been given questions that will be on the exam to take home and study, it is usually a good idea to prepare actual answers before taking the test. Although you might not want to write out your answer, you should at least outline your basic response to each question. You could skip writing or outlining your answers, but most of the other students won't. They'll have an advantage over you when it comes to producing written answers on the real examination. In addition, rehearsing your answers before the test will save you time during the examination.

Test Anxiety

Many students report that they receive lower grades than they ought to because of being anxious either while they were taking the exam or when they were preparing for the exam. Anxiety before the exam prevents you from studying efficiently. Anxiety during the exam interferes with showing what you know. Getting anxiety under control is therefore important if you are to be a successful student.

Anxiety is our reaction to thoughts that we have or to events in our lives. It is a natural reaction to a situation that we perceive as being threatening. Our reactions to threatening situations could easily be either anxiety or fear. Fear is our response to a dangerous situation where running away or fighting would or could be appropriate. Anxiety, on the other hand, occurs when running away or fighting would not be suitable or when the threat comes from an intangible or imagined source. Running away during an exam would not be an appropriate action to the threat caused by the exam, so instead of running away we get anxious.

Anxiety can affect us by causing physical reactions such as high blood pressure or through poor performance such as ineffective studying. Whatever your anxiety-induced reactions are, they can be changed. You learned your present response, so you can learn new responses.

The best way to deal with anxiety is not to get anxious in the first place! However, because anxiety is an emotional reaction and comes from both good and bad situations, you would have to learn to be pretty mellow not to get anxious at some time in your life.

Did you notice that I said that anxiety comes from both the

good and bad things in life? If you get engaged, you might be anxious for a while. When you walk into a test and you are not prepared, you are likely to get anxious too.

Anxiety is not all bad. Facilitating anxiety helps us do better, it facilitates, or aids, our performance. When you take a test you need to have some degree of anxiety to do well. If you were to take a test that did not count, that would not be graded, or even looked at, would you do your very best on it? Probably not. On the other hand, you can have too much anxiety, and because of that anxiety you will not do as well as you could. That is debilitating anxiety. It blocks or hinders your performance.

Most students do not have any problems "getting up" for a test. They get slightly anxious and use that anxiety, facilitating anxiety, to do well on the exam. If you find that you are not getting motivated or "up" for your exams, try thinking about the implications or consequences of doing poorly on the exam. Don't make a monster of the exam, just try to be honest with yourself about the negative implications and thoughts that you will have if you don't do well. If thinking about your lack of motivation or concern about your performance in school doesn't help you correct the situation, you probably ought to see a counselor or an advisor to reconsider why you are in college.

Debilitating anxiety is the problem anxiety for most of us. It is the kind of anxiety that blocks us from doing well. We are most familiar with this kind of anxiety or tension in sports, particularly in championship games. Have you ever heard an announcer say something like "They're not playing their kind of game. They've got to settle down and play their kind of game"? The announcer is talking about the players being "up-tight", not playing the kind of game that they are really capable of.

I remember a little of the NCAA basketball game between The University of North Carolina and Georgetown University. Patrick Ewing of Georgetown scored the first eight points of the game but the score was Georgetown 4, North Carolina 4. Impossible? Not true, it did happen. Ewing scored for Georgetown. At the opposite end of the court he tried to block a shot and was charged with goaltending---two points for North Carolina. He scored another two points for Georgetown and then was charged with a second goaltending call when he tried to block another shot by North Carolina. Each goaltending foul resulted in two points for North Carolina. Ewing had scored four points for Georgetown and his two goaltending fouls had given North Carolina four points.

Patrick Ewing was probably the best college player in the country that year. Why did he give North Carolina so many points? The tension caused by the game had him playing too hard, he tried too hard and made mistakes. Coach Thompson called time out to settle the team down and to get Ewing and the rest of the team to play the kind of game they were capable of.

Debilitating anxiety can be controlled in a number of different ways. The time out in the last example can be one of your techniques. Here is another example of using a time out or mental escape to reduce tension.

Years ago, I had myself connected to a biofeedback machine. Electric wires were connected to both my forehead and my fingers. My body temperature at both places was monitored. Tension would raise the temperature at my forehead and lower it at my finger tips. I was asked to make the needle on the gauge go down. I was assured that just by controlling my thoughts I could make the needle go down. I tried. The needle went up. I tried harder and the needle shot up. I tried breathing slowly, and the needle stopped going up as fast but it still moved up. I got to the point where I could hold the needle steady, but I couldn't make the needle go down. The instructor started talking to me about biofeedback and about the experiments that were being conducted in the lab. After a minute or two he asked me to look at the needle. It was back down to the bottom of its arc. It immediately started to move up again. I finally learned to mentally escape thoughts about controlling the needle and made the needle go

down. Trying to make the needle go down caused tension, which raised the temperature at my forehead and raised the needle. Relaxation decreased tension and reduced the differences between the two points.

Deep Breathing

When you get anxious, stop and take several slow, deep breaths. Try using your elementary school physical education training. Slowly inhale and exhale saying "In goes the good air, out goes the bad air." By laughing, slowing yourself down, and breathing deeply, your anxiety should diminish.

Fantasy

Another technique for getting anxiety under control is the use of fantasy. In your mind, escape to a fantasy world, you know, the place you have in your daydreams where everything is just the way you want it to be. While you are in fantasyland, you will not be thinking about the test or whatever else was bothering you, and your anxiety will decrease.

ABC Theory

Another technique for controlling anxiety is the use of what I call ABC theory. A psychologist named Albert Ellis created a theory in psychology that is called rationale emotive theory. Ellis believes that many, if not all, of our emotions are controlled by our thoughts. If we can control our thoughts, we can control our emotions.

As an example, let's consider taking or studying for a test. Using the ABC theory, "A" is the test, and "C" is anxiety. Graphically it would look like this:

```
A                        C

Test  ----------->   Anxiety
```

You have a test and get anxious. Does the test cause the anxiety? No, says Ellis. The test or the idea of taking the test causes us to produce a stream of thoughts, and the thoughts cause the anxiety. In the graph, A is still the test and C is the reaction to B. B is the thought flow that we create when we think of the test. For example

```
A ------>  B ------>   C

Test   I didn't study   Anxiety
       enough, I'm
       going to fail
       this test. If
       I fail, my
       parents will
       kill me. I'll
       fail the course
       and maybe I'll
       even fail out
       of college.
```

Ellis calls A the antecedent, B the stream of thoughts, and C the consequence, or outcome. Note, it is the thoughts that are generated that end up causing the anxiety.

The thoughts that are present have some basis in reality. However, anxiety gets generated when the basic information or situation is entangled with half truths and faulty reasoning. Look at some of the thoughts in the last example. Would your parents really kill you if you were to fail an exam? They might get upset or angry or disappointed but it would end there. Would failing one exam mean that you would fail the course? Rarely is it one exam that causes a student to fail a course; it is the total score on all graded assignments that give you the final grade.

Some of the components of the ABC model can be changed. The A, the test, is probably a given. I say probably a given because you could decide not to take the test and try to get a make-up exam instead (more on that later). If you are going to take the test, the test, the A, becomes a given. B is not a given. Your thoughts about the test can be changed. If you change your thoughts, you will change the outcome, the C.

Think of your mind as a tape recorder. The recorder is running. It is saying "You are dumb and stupid. You are dumb and stupid. You are dumb and stupid." You don't like being thought of as being stupid. You worry about the exam and get anxious. What do you suppose the solution is?

Yes, stop the tape recorder, stop the message. Next, get rid of the old tape and create a new one. The new tape might say something like "I did poorly on the last test because I did not complete all of the homework problems. I got them all done this time. I don't like taking tests, but I can get good grades when I have done all the work. I have done all the work this time. I can get a decent grade on this exam, etc." The new thought pattern will create a new consequence, a different outcome, one without anxiety, or at least a reaction with less anxiety.

Remember when you were little and learned to read? Do you remember reading the story about the little train engine? The little engine had to pull a long line of railroad cars over a mountain. He made it over the mountain, in part, by saying "I think I can, I think I can, I think I can."

We can also see the use of a "positive attitude" in sports. Haven't you heard sports announcers say things like "I wonder which team will show up this time," "Nobody seems to want to win this one," or "The coach really has the team up for this one"? Even in professional sports, announcers talk about any team being good enough to beat any other team on any given day, if one team is up for the game and the other isn't. Most sports are physical, mental, and psychological. Winning teams think they can win.

However, just because you have a positive attitude does not mean that you are going to win. Try turning that one around. If you have a negative attitude, if you say "I can't win," do you have any real chance of winning? Similarly, it is difficult to make a case for having a negative attitude

help you when you are taking a test. The positive attitude by itself, without knowledge of the subject matter, will not get you a high grade on an exam. A positive attitude with knowledge is a hard combination to beat.

If you get anxious on examinations and that anxiety is debilitating, try identifying the statements that you are saying to yourself that are causing the anxiety. Stop the negative comments by inserting positive statements in their place. By changing the self talk, the B, you will get a new C, a different consequence that should help you do better on your exams.

Systematic Relaxation

Physiologically we cannot be both anxious and relaxed at the same time. Systematic relaxation uses that incompatibility to reduce anxiety. If you can teach yourself or make yourself relax when you are anxious, you will no longer be anxious. You won't be anxious because it is physically impossible to be both anxious and relaxed at the same time. Confused? Try the idea out before you throw it out.

Take one of your arms and make a tight fist, so tight that your entire arm from your fist to your shoulder is one mass of muscles pulling against one another. (Don't hurt yourself by "pulling" a muscle!) Hold the fist tight for 20 seconds or so. Then slowly relax the arm. Let your arm come to rest on your lap, desk, or whatever.

Don't move it, just let it rest for 20 or 30 seconds. Now, slowly make a fist again, hold it for 20 seconds, and slowly let the arm rest again.

When the fist is tight, you have stress or tension (anxiety). Note how it feels. When the arm is resting, it is relaxing from the work that it just completed.

After you have <u>slowly</u> completed the exercise with one arm, do the same procedure with the other arm (fist, relax, fist, relax).

After both arms have been done, work on your legs. With one leg, point your toes toward the floor and try to raise your heel up through your foot. (Your foot doesn't work that way; your leg will become a mass of muscles pulling against each other just as your arms did before. Be careful not to pull a muscle by trying too hard.) Hold the tension for 20 seconds, and then relax the leg for 20 seconds. Repeat the sequence again with that leg and then do it twice with the other leg. Remember to work slowly.

Next tighten your stomach muscles and hold that for 20 seconds before you relax for 20 seconds. Repeat the process a second time.

Puff your chest out and hold it for 20 seconds, and then relax for 20 seconds. Again, repeat the sequence a second time.

Take your chin and force it down to your chest, and hold that position for 20 seconds.

Relax for 20 seconds and repeat the sequence.

Each time you have created stress or tension and then you relaxed. If you go through the entire sequence slowly and concentrate on how the tension and relaxation each feel, you will have "escaped" from the anxious state you were in when you started. By focusing on the relaxation exercise, you "forgot" to stay anxious!

Once you have physically relaxed, you can mentally relax by thinking about a pleasant "fantasyland" that you have in your dreams or in your mind. Hopefully, you have had an experience or a dream that is <u>perfect</u> for you. Mentally go there for a little while and enjoy the fantasy. Relax and breath slowly and deeply.

By doing the physical exercises and mental imagery, you relaxed. By definition, you will no longer be anxious! You taught yourself to relax so that you could better deal with the situation, test, and so forth.

Once you have taught yourself to relax, you can shorten the procedure by doing only the mental escape. During an exam, if you begin to get anxious, stop what you are doing, escape to your fantasyland, and calm down. After you have calmed down, return to the test.

"I don't have time to fantasize during a test. I need the time to finish the test." True, except, if you are getting excessively anxious, you are going to lose a lot of points simply because you are panicking. You will misread questions, answer questions that you haven't been asked, make clerical or mathematical mistakes, etc. You will not be at your best and your work will show it. Why not slow down and get under control?

Anxiety Control Summary

The title of the musical Stop the World I Want to Get Off sums it up pretty well. When you get anxious, stop what you are doing and get yourself under control. Unless you are under control, you will not be able to adequately show what you know. If the techniques that I have covered are not enough to help you get anxiety under control, I urge you to talk to a counselor or your adviser about what you can do or who you can see to manage your anxiety. Remember, if you learned to be anxious during tests, you can learn not to be anxious during tests!

Staying Healthy

As you prepare for exams, the last thing that you want to happen is to get sick just before or during the exam. Make-up examinations are usually available if you do get sick when the exam is given, but they are usually more difficult than the regular exam. If you get sick before the exam, miss your study time, but recover in time to take the test, it may be difficult to prove that you were sick or difficult to get a make-up exam. At any rate, getting sick or run down is to be avoided if at all possible.

Preventive measures ought to be taken to keep you in good health while you prepare for your exams. Basically, you need to eat right, get enough sleep, and exercise properly. Students often tell me that they didn't have enough time to eat or shop for food while they were preparing for their exams. Others report gaining weight because they eat too much. Just try to keep a regular eating pattern that includes at least three meals spaced out throughout the day. Make sure you are getting the basic nutrition that you need to stay healthy.

Sleep often gets put aside during exam week. "I don't have time to sleep" is a cry I hear. If you cheat too much on sleep you will create health problems by being worn out. Your body will not have the energy reserve to fight off colds, flus, mononucleosis, etc. Even during the pressure of getting ready for and taking final exams, you need good "deep" sleep, the kind of sleep where your body can relax and recharge itself for the next day. Pace yourself to allow adequate rest and sleep.

Exercise can be an excellent way to break up your study sessions and help you stay healthy. The pressure from exams can cause stress and tension. Exercise can be a good way to offset the negative impact of that stress. While you are exercising you can forget about the examinations and rejuvenate yourself. If you have been studying for a long time, your body has been stationary, inactive, and lethargic. You will also overload your brain circuits. Get your blood flowing with a bit of exercise, then get back to your studies again. You will be much more effective.

Taking Your Exams

Even with adequate preparation it is possible to do poorly on an examination by not using good exam skills on exam day or during the exam. It all starts by getting off to a good start. Unless the exam is given at a very early hour, try to keep your normal morning routine. Get up, wash, get dressed, and have something to eat more or less the way you usually do. Study or review a little if you want to but don't try learning everything in the few hours before the test that you should have learned throughout the course.

Be Early

It may seem basic, but get to the exam on time or slightly early. How many times have you seen other students coming in to an exam 5 or 10 minutes late? The loss of the 5 or 10 minutes really isn't all that much. The problem comes from the student's attempt to make up for lost time. They hurry through the directions and read the questions hastily. Often they get lower test scores simply because they didn't read the question correctly or made "stupid mistakes." You will probably feel pressured even if you are prepared and on time, so why create a problem that you don't need?

Remember Murphy's Law?

Anything that can go wrong will, when it is least convenient. During exam time, cars don't start; they run out of gas or run into other cars. Alarm clocks malfunction and refuse to go off, power outages occur, calendars don't have exams scheduled, etc. Give yourself a little extra time getting to the examination room just in case you encounter problems. (Do remember to check where the exam will be given; it may not be in your regular classroom!)

Instructions Are Important

Listen to your instructor whenever he says anything! Obviously the basic instructions for the test are important. Be sure that you attend to what your instructor is saying and not to what you want him to say. During the exam, when another student asks a question, listen to the answer. Instructors often say more than they intend to when they answer questions. When they attempt to clarify the question that is being asked, they can suggest material to be included or excluded in the answer. If they rephrase a question, they may have changed it in a way that suggests what they want in the answer. If your instructor is going to help you out with part of the answer, or give you details about what he wants, why not use the added information that he has provided to improve your answer?

One of the courses I took as an undergraduate was a graduate course in the History of Experimental Psychology. Each week we had at least one assigned chapter to read from the textbook and a book written by a famous psychologist such as Freud. For the midterm exam we were responsible for six books and seven or eight chapters of the textbook. When the instructor passed out the exam, we were surprised to find just a simple list of 25 names and words. There were no instructions on the page, just the 25 words. We were instructed to read over the list. Then the instructor asked us to read the list a second and third time. (Boy, did we get anxious! All we wanted to do was get on with the test.)

Next, the instructor told us "Do not identify these terms! Tell why each person or concept is important to the history of experimental psychology. I repeat, you do not have to identify the terms. Does everyone understand?" We all shook our heads up and down. The instructor repeated the instructions a second time. (We were getting frustrated and annoyed.) He then repeated the instructions a third time. Finally, he turned us loose on the exam. Needless to say, we dove in and started writing as soon as we could.

The next week, we got our exams back. First the instructor announced that over 60% of the class had failed the exam! This was a class of approximately 35 graduate students in psychology and 60% or more failed the midterm. The class looked bewildered. We were stunned. Most of those who failed received a score of

0 (zero)! After the papers were returned to us, the instructor lectured us on the importance of following directions on an examination. He said, "My instructions were to indicate why each of the concepts, terms, or people were important to the history of experimental psychology. Most of you just identified each term. No points were awarded if you simply provided an identification without an explanation of why or how the term was important to the development of the field." In short, most students hadn't answered the instructor's questions.

When you are taking an examination, read your professor's instructions, listen to your instructor when he gives verbal instructions or answers student questions, and then answer the questions the way you have been instructed to.

I will cover specific information about how to actually take a test in the chapters on taking essay and objective examinations.

Before You Turn In the Exam

Hopefully, you will have monitored your time during the exam so that you have a few minutes left before your test paper must be turned in. Use that time to check over your answer sheet or test booklet. Did you answer all of the questions that you could? Did you follow the directions that you were given? If you had to complete calculations, did you show your work? Is your writing legible? Does your paper look neat and professional? Correct any careless errors, edit your answers if necessary, and show your instructor that you can produce quality work.

After the Exam

You have not used all of your exam skills until you have reviewed your corrected answer sheet. Did your instructor grade your answer sheet correctly? Instructors are human. They make mistakes. Even computerized answer sheets can have inaccurate grading! Carefully go over the answer sheet to make sure that all of your answers were corrected and that you got all the points you should have.

Check Your Answers

Begin by reviewing your answers. Look at the answers that you got correct. If you were in doubt about some of these answers, take a minute to review the answers and pat yourself on the back for getting them correct.

Look over the answers you got wrong. Why did you miss each question? (Don't say, "Because I had the wrong answer," that doesn't help you learn how to do better on the next exam.) Did you miss questions from the text or from lectures? Did you read the question correctly? Did you understand the question before you answered it? Did you make careless errors?

Once you can explain which questions you missed, can you begin to look at why you did

not know the correct answer? If you missed questions from the textbook, did you read all of the assigned material? If not, you ought to do all of the reading before the next test. If you thought you knew the material pretty well but earned a low test score, raise your preparation standards as you get ready for the next test.

Did you mostly miss questions from the lecture? Did you go to all class sessions? Did you get notes for the sessions that you missed? If you did not understand points that the instructor made but were afraid to ask questions, couldn't you have done better if you talked to the instructor before or after class or during office hours to get clarification of material that you didn't understand?

If you misread questions, why not slow down next time and mark up the test questions to help you stay on topic? Many students circle the key word of the question to keep them focused on the central point of the test question.

If you didn't understand a question because you didn't know a word that was used in the question, how about asking the instructor to explain the question using other words? I remember asking students to "explain SQ3R and give a rationale for each of the steps of the method." Most students got the explanation of SQ3R correct but did not answer the second part of the question. Later I found out that most of the students did not understand the word "rationale," but no one asked what it meant! If you don't understand your instructions or a question, ask your instructor to clarify what he means.

Your analysis of your test paper should tell you what caused most of your errors. Once you know why you missed each question, you should be able to see a logical way of improving your performance on the next exam. If you cannot understand why you missed a question, see your instructor during his office hours.

Finally, were your answers graded correctly? Was partial credit available, and did you get points for answers that were only partially correct? Your instructors are human, they make mistakes. If you think that an answer wasn't graded properly, see your instructor. (More than once I have missed grading an entire page of answers. I know of one department that stopped using computer-scored answer sheets because the error rate was above 5 percent; 5 percent of the answers were graded wrong!) If computer answer sheets were used, did the scanner pick up all of your answers? If you are in a large class, more than one person corrected the answers. Different people award points differently. If you suspect that you should have had more points for an answer, see your instructor.

If your answer sheet has been graded improperly, you are the only person who will be able to catch the mistake. You will be the only person who will lose points and earn a lower grade because of the error. Check the grading on your exams.

Check Your Points!

After you have reviewed all of your answers and you are sure that the exam has been graded correctly, check to see that you received all the points that you should in your final score. Add up all the points! "But the instructor has already put my score on the front of the exam." True, but remember your instructor is human and human beings make mistakes. With exam scores the error might give you more points than you really earned or less. Murphy, of course (remember Murphy's Law?), says that you won't get more points, you'll get fewer than you should.

In helping students with their test-taking skills, I noticed that students with low test scores often had scoring errors on their test papers. Usually the error resulted in the student's receiving a lower score on the exam because the points had been added incorrectly. Good students never seemed to have these arithmetic errors.

Once I noticed that poor students did not appear to check their test scores for accuracy, I decided to experiment with students in my study skills class to see if students with low test scores would catch scoring errors. I created a "magic task" that would give students extra points toward their course grade. (The old Groucho Marx TV show had the "magic word," that is, if a contestant said the magic word, he would win a prize.) If students in my class did the magic task, they would earn the bonus points that would count toward their grade. Of course, they did not know what the task was, though they were assured that the task was obvious, one that they should do if they were good students.

On the first class examination, after correcting the answer sheets, I subtracted one, two or three points from the earned total score and put the false test score on the answer sheet. (I thought that the more points a student lost, the more likely it would be for them to see the error.) All points for all questions were written on the answer sheet, only the total test score was wrong. Answer sheets were returned to the students. Two weeks later, of the 102 students who took the exam, a little over 30 students returned their test papers saying that they had found an error in the scoring. Only 1/3 of the students found the error!

At the end of the semester, I checked to see which students had found the scoring error. Every student who earned an A in the course found the error. All but one student who earned a B found the error. No student who failed the class (over 20 students failed) found the arithmetic error! The number of points lost because of the scoring error did not seem to make any difference in who turned in their test paper for correction.

Good students check over their exam papers to see that they received all the points they should have! Good students learn from their test errors so that their test scores more closely show how much they really know.

Adjust Your Study Strategy

When you have gone over your exams and discovered why you missed questions, you can examine your study techniques and strategy and make adjustments if necessary. Each type of error you made on your exams should suggest to you some logical thing to do to eliminate most of the problems. Missing questions from lectures says that you need to concentrate more on effective listening techniques, that you need to improve your ability to create notes that will help you to retain information better and/or that you need to learn the content of your notes better. Missing questions from your textbook suggests that you need to learn more from the text, perhaps by using SQ3R or raising the level of knowledge you want to learn from your books.

If, after you analyze your exams, you do not have a good idea about what you need to do to improve your learning and your test score, talk to either your instructor or a learning specialist on campus. Even without your test analysis, your instructor ought to be able to make a few practical suggestions to you about how you can learn more in his class. Your campus Counseling Center should be able to help you find a study skills

148

specialist on campus if there is one.

Your returned test paper needs to be used to help you perform better if you want to. Successful people, successful students, learn from their mistakes. Take the time to learn from yours.

Summary

Before you take a test in any of your courses be sure you know what the examination will cover. If you are not clear about what you should study, talk with your instructor. Once you know what the exam will cover, try to figure out how much study time you will need to adequately prepare for the exam. How will you have to adjust your regular schedule to get enough time to complete your study?

When you take an exam, go for points. Learn to determine where you will earn points on each exam as well as how you will lose points. Then devise a plan of action that will get you the most points in the time that you have available on the exam.

After you get your corrected examination paper back, go over it to make certain that you have been graded fairly and to learn from the mistakes that you made. Figure out why you didn't know an answer during the test and alter your future studying to see that you do not make that same mistake again.

8 ESSAY EXAMINATIONS

Essay examinations generally require the test taker to compose a written response to test questions. They are sometimes referred to as subjective examinations because when different instructors correct the test answers they can, and usually do, come up with different scores for the same test answer. That means that the evaluation is subjective, or it is up to the individual who is scoring the exam. The difference in scoring can be as little as a few points, the difference between, say, a B and a B-, or as much as five grades, one evaluator giving a test answer an A while another assigns the answer an F. The grading on essay tests is based on both the content or knowledge shown in the answers given <u>and</u> on the quality of the writing and thinking that has been displayed in the answer. Objective exams, however, will consistently receive the same score regardless of who scores them. The instructor's answer key provides all the information that the scorer needs to correct the test.

To score high on an essay exam, you need to focus your attention on knowing the content that will be covered, learning what your instructors expect in a complete answer, and improving your ability to present information in a coherent and logical manner. Improving your skills in any of these three areas will enhance your essay exam scores.

Know the Material to be Covered

Nothing helps you improve your essay exam score more than knowing the content that you will be tested on. In a multiple-choice examination, you know that the answer is there in front of you. All you have to do is recognize the right answer. With essay exams, you <u>create</u> the answer! You must know the information and have it available to you in order to write the answer. You need to know the content better, in more depth, than you would for an objective exam.

SQ3R becomes an excellent study tool for getting prepared for an essay exam. When you study using SQ3R, you create questions and answer them as you work through your text. You learn the information and use it. In the Recite step, you receive feedback that tells you whether you know the information that you have been studying at the level at which you need to know it.

In an essay exam, not only must you know the ideas and concepts that have been assigned but you must also be able to interrelate those ideas when you formulate your answer. In an objective exam, you might be asked to give the year in which "Columbus discovered America." In an essay exam, you would be asked why Columbus did what he did. You would have to know much more, be able to bring that information out of your memory, and be able to write a logical, coherent answer to the question. (By the way,

Columbus did not discover America. He was just one of the first Europeans to reach North America.)

When you prepare for an essay exam, it is usually a good idea to study from general ideas to specifics, from broad main ideas down to the details that support them. Essay exam questions will not ask you about minor details that have been covered in the course; rather, they will focus on major points, or the main ideas. Yes, you will need to know details to be able to write complete answers, but the details can be lacking and you could still receive a high grade if you can get to the major concepts that your instructor expects in a good answer. In short, when you are preparing for essay exams, don't concentrate on the details. Focus your attention on the essence of what the author and your instructor have been telling you. For each section of material from the text and from your lectures ask yourself "What was the point being made?" or "What was the essence of what the author or my instructor said?"

Your Instructor's Expections

Students often complain to me about not knowing what their instructors want in a complete answer. That is understandable, especially because different instructors will be expecting different levels of knowledge for the same grade. Why guess about what your instructor expects of you? Ask her to give you a sample question that she might have on a test. Then ask her to provide an A or a complete answer to that question so that you can get a feel for her expectations.

Try looking at it this way. When you have a job, you usually want to know what the boss expects of you. If the boss asks you to write a report for the Better Business Bureau, it would be helpful to have some idea of what she means or wants in that report. If the report is an annual affair, there should be a copy of last year's article that you can use as a guide to produce this year's report. It would also be a good idea to get your boss's impression or evaluation of last year's work so that you can create a better report or more closely approximate your boss's expectations. If there hasn't been a report before, wouldn't it be a good idea to get a general impression of what she is thinking of or would like to see in the report before you begin work?

Getting a handle on how you will be evaluated is normal behavior in the work place. In college, why shouldn't you know about the evaluation you will be receiving in your classes? If you find it difficult to ask for this information during class, see your instructor during her office hours. When you talk with her, make it clear that you are looking for guidance in how to study for the class and how you will be evaluated, and not that you are looking to be given the actual test questions that you will be asked on the examination.

Create Your Own Test Questions!

Several times in this text I have told you that the vast majority of college instructors have never taken a course in how to prepare good tests. They create test questions almost the way that you would. Yes, they know more about the subject matter and they have more experience with tests, but they really haven't been trained in good educational measurement techniques. That means that you ought to be able to create some test questions that will approximate questions that your instructor might ask you.

By creating your own test questions you do several things. First, you get yourself involved in your own learning. The more involved you are with your own learning and education, the more you will learn.

Second, by asking and answering questions while you study, you will get feedback as to how well you know the material that you are studying. If you have difficulty with your own questions, there is a good chance that you will have difficulty with your instructor's questions. Use the feedback you get from answering your questions to alter your studying.

Finally, as you try to answer your questions, you ought to be getting some feedback on how well you are putting together your answers. From the "tone" or "sense" of your answers, do you get the feeling that you know what you are talking about? If not, shouldn't you put more time into learning more of the information that will be covered on the exam?

The Rule of Three

One of the easiest ways that I have found to focus student attention on some of the mechanics of taking exams I call the Rule of Three. It states that every exam is written or will be corrected at 3:00 in the morning. Crazy? I don't think so. Try thinking it through.

You are an instructor. What part of your job do you like least? The answer probably has something to do with paperwork. What part of your paperwork do you like least? A likely answer is "writing or correcting tests"! (You don't like to take tests, and instructors don't like to write or correct them!)

Now think of yourself and your work habits. If you are employed, you very likely have several different things to do on that job. What happens to the tasks that are assigned to you that you don't like to do? Yes, they get left till last. (You may just luck out and not have to do them, right?)

Look what happens when we put the ideas in the last two paragraphs together. Instructors have jobs with tasks that they don't like to do. They, too, tend to put off working on those tasks they do not like. Because writing or correcting tests is distasteful or unpleasant, it means that an instructor often waits until the last minute to write or correct her examinations. The last minute, as far as I am concerned, is 3:00 in the morning the day of the test or the day that corrected exams are due back to the students.

Now apply the Rule of Three to essay exams. The rule doesn't help that much with guessing what will be on the exam. However, try thinking about what happens if you take an essay exam that you <u>know</u> will be corrected at 3:00 in the morning.

Seriously now, stop reading and think about the things that you can do with your essay test answers, other than content, that will affect the grade that you receive on your exam paper. More specifically, what six things can you do with your answers to essay test questions, other than the content or information, that will improve your test results?

Now, stop and apply the Rule of Three to answer the question. Your wording may be different from mine, but did you come up with the following ideas?

1. <u>Brevity</u>. Short answers are better than long answers if the content is the same. At 3:00 in the morning, your instructor does not want to wade through a lot of material to find the correct answer for the question. "BS," boring stuff, will not get you higher grades on an examination. Your instructor has been trained in the course content and knows what should be included in a correct answer. When you decide to wing it, she will

recognize the unnecessary material.

One trick that some students have developed in answering essay exams is to write out the instructor's test question on their answer sheet. How many points do you earn for rewriting the instructor's question? None, right? Other students choose to paraphrase the question before they answer it. How many points do you get for paraphrasing the question? Right again, none. Still others rewrite or use the question to lead in to their answer. How many points do they earn for that?

I have noticed that better students tend to produce shorter answers. Why might that be true? Because better students know the subject matter; they know the information that is needed for a good answer. Poorer students do not seem to know what is needed for a good answer so they try to pack in everything that they know about the subject whether it relates to the question they were asked or not. Try looking over your essay answers. Why or when are your answers long? When you don't know the answer, right?

An answer to an essay question does need to be complete and to cover the assigned question but it should not contain material that is not needed. Keep your answers short and to the point.

2. <u>Neatness</u>. Good students produce answers that look like they were written by a professional writer. If the student has had to erase, she

makes neat and complete erasures. The paper looks as if it were a report that someone might give to her boss at work.

Often, when instructors look at an essay answer they can tell the gender of the writer without even reading the answer. Neat answers tend to come from women, whereas messy answers tend to come from men. Men seem to favor taking tests or writing their answers with a number 2 (soft) pencil that smudges easily. When the paper is read by the instructor, there are answers that have been "blackened" or crossed out so dark that no one can see what was written; erasures have left messes, sometimes with wrinkled or ripped paper; blunt pencils were used so that letters cannot be read easily; etc. Overstated? Perhaps a little bit, but not much. Male students just do not seem to attend to what their work looks like.

Try looking at the situation from the instructor's point of view. You pick up a paper, take one look at it, and say, "This looks horrible." What grade do you "psychologically" put on the paper without even reading it, an A or an F? Suppose the paper really does look horrible, one of the worst that you have ever seen. What do you do? You can read it with that psychological F in your mind or you can put the paper at the bottom of the stack. If you put the paper at the bottom of the stack, have you forgotten about it? No! Are you looking forward to reading that paper? Again, no.

In your mind, what is happening to the grade of that horrible looking paper even though you aren't even reading it? The grade, or the grade that you think the student will get, is going further down, F- or worse.

Switch gears for a minute. When you are going on an important job interview, why do you make a special effort to look good? Because first impressions are important, and you want to make a good first impression. When you go out on a first date with someone you like a lot, why do you try to look your best? To make a good impression, of course.

If first impressions are that important in landing a job and when you are going out on a first date, they should also be important when you are trying to show an instructor that you are a good student. You are trying to make a good impression with your instructor.

It is 3:00 in the morning and Dr. Smith is reading 87 essay test answers. How do you suppose she feels? She picks up a neat paper that has been beautifully written in ink and that has no crossed out answers or corrections. Won't she look forward to reading that paper?

We are talking about psychological warfare with test papers. What kind of impression do you want your instructor to start out with when she reads your test answers?

3. <u>Organization</u>. One of the

biggest criticisms that I hear about essay test answers and student papers in general is that often a paper looks like the information provided was just tossed around in practically any order, as long as it got down onto the page. The attitude of the writer seems to be "You're so smart, here's what I know, find what you want!" The student then proceeds to throw in everything, including the infamous kitchen sink.

Instructors are not impressed with what I call "garbage pailing," dumping in miscellaneous junk just to fill a page. College-level instructors want you to start at some reasonable point that I'll call A and to proceed to point Z in some kind of logical order, taking the instructor along with you each step of the way. Where you start isn't important. Writing the information in such a way that another person can easily follow your logic flow is.

Some students like to provide an outline as a component of their answer. Others provide lists to organize multiple parts of their answer. Still others number the parts of their answers or section off their answer with "bullets" or dashes in front of each different segment. The idea is to show the instructor visually or through composition of your answer that you really know what you are talking about.

4. <u>Grammar</u>. On an essay exam you are trying to impress your instructor with your knowledge and expertise. What happens at 3:00 in the morning when your instructor is reading your answer and she "trips" over a major grammatical error? Think about it for a minute. The instructor is sitting there comfortably going over your answer when the grammatical error stops her from going on. She stops reading (she knows that something is wrong) and backtracks; she reads at least part of your answer a second time, trying to figure out what you are saying.

Note what the grammatical error has done. First, it stopped the almost "automatic pilot" reading that your instructor was probably doing (remember it's 3:00 in the morning). Second, you have focused your instructor's attention on the notion that something is wrong; just what is wrong may not be known immediately. Third, you made the instructor back up and reread, this time looking for something that "must" be wrong.

When you are looking at anything for errors or mistakes, don't you tend to find more of them? When instructors focus their attention on finding something wrong, believe me, they can and will find something wrong.

Notice, I have not focused my attention on the error itself, but rather I have concentrated on what happens because of the error. The grammatical error causes a closer examination of your work, which in turn leads to finding errors that reduce your grade. Don't draw attention to your work through mechanical errors; just concentrate on getting all the points that you can.

If your mechanical skills are weak, avoid writing complex sentences. Don't try to be funny or cute if you cannot punctuate your writing correctly. Don't try to make your answer "interesting" or "different" if it means that you will lose points because of a grammatical error. Let your instructor be bored in peace. Write simple sentences. (If your writing skills are weak, I would, however, urge you to work on improving those skills by taking all of the writing courses, or classes that require writing, that you can.)

5. <u>Spelling</u>. In your essay answer you are trying to prove how brilliant you are (or, at least, that you know the information needed to answer the question). What does a spelling error tell your instructor? No, not that you are stupid, just that you cannot spell a word correctly, right? Wrong! Unfortunately, "society" or your instructor's educational upbringing takes over once she spots a spelling error. Your instructor learned that spelling errors are associated with "dumb" students. Even though many brilliant people cannot spell well, your spelling error has put you into the dummy category. Down goes your grade.

No, that logic really isn't correct. However, it is the way that an instructor could think when she sees a spelling error. Learn to spell the words that you will need for your exam. If there are technical words and concepts that your instructor will expect you to know and that you are likely to need on your examination, learn to spell them and use them correctly in a sentence.

If you must use a word in your essay answer and you are unsure of its spelling, put "sp" in parentheses (sp) after the word. The (sp) tells the instructor that you know that the word is spelled wrong! Now what does your instructor think of you? She thinks that you at least know that the word is spelled wrong. But please, do not put (sp) after (sp) every (sp) word (sp) just (sp) to ensure (sp) that you catch every possible mistake.

6. <u>Answer the Instructor's Question</u>. I leave this idea until last because almost all student groups that I have asked to create the "six things that you can do to improve an essay answer other than content" miss this concept. **The single, most important concept to keep in mind when answering an essay question is to answer the question that your instructor asked!** You can do everything correctly, study and learn all the assigned material over a period of time, and earn a low grade on the examination if you do not answer your instructor's question. (In the last chapter, I gave the example of graduate students identifying terms instead of describing why each was important. It is a true story. Brilliant students failed an exam simply because they did not answer the question that the instructor

had asked!)

When you answer an essay question, it is not necessary to write down everything that you know about the subject matter. You only need to provide the information needed to answer the question. The question "What did Harper's Ferry have to do with the Civil War?" does not ask you to tell everything that you know about the Civil War. It doesn't even require you to know where Harper's Ferry is! All the instructor wants you to do is show how the events that occurred at Harper's Ferry were related to the Civil War. Answer your instructor's question, not the question you think you were asked.

Applying the Rule of Three

When you sit down to take an essay examination, keep this general idea in mind: your task is to answer the instructor's questions as briefly and neatly as you can in an organized manner while avoiding grammatical and spelling errors. More specifically, you should do the following when you are about to answer an essay question:

1. Read the question! Don't just glance at the question and start writing; actually read the question word for word.

2. Read the question that your instructor asked. Many times when students are taking an examination, they read the question and immediately start writing their answer. Unfortunately, many times they are not answering the question that they were asked. First you read the question, then you reread the question with the idea of finding out what your instructor has <u>really</u> asked, not what you want your instructor to have asked. (We tend to change test questions to be what we want them to be.)

3. Think about your answer to the question. Get your thoughts organized so that you will be able to convince your instructor that you know what you are talking about. Some students like to create an outline of the points or information that they want to include in their answer, to help them remember their thoughts. The outline need not be a "formal" outline, just words or thoughts that will trigger the content that you want to include. In some instances, the outline could become part of the answer you give to your instructor. If you write an outline, keep it brief and to the point so that you do not use too much valuable time.

Keep two points in mind as you put your answer together. First, your instructor will be concerned with the content of your answer, that is, the information that you provide. Second, your reasoning and organization also will be important, that is, how you support your main point.

As you organize your answer, remember that the first part of your answer is most important. The first several sentences that you write set up expectations in the grader's mind. If it sounds as though you know what you are talking about, the grader presumes that the rest of the answer will be of the same quality. However, a poor beginning with an excellent summary at the end will rarely receive a high grade because the grader has already mentally assigned a low grade before she gets to your excellent finish. Try to make a strong opening that convinces your instructor that you really do know what you are talking about.

4. After you have mentally created your answer, read the question again to see that you have mentally answered the question that the instructor asked you. Haven't you ever written an essay answer only to discover that there was a lot of information in your answer that either wasn't needed or that didn't answer the question? That's when you erase or cross out your answer and still try to get an answer completed before time runs out. Writing is very slow when compared with mental processing time. You lose a tremendous amount of time when you write information that you do not need. Think through your answer, Step 3, and then check to see if your answer really answered the instructor's question. If it does, then proceed to Step 5.

5. Write your <u>organized</u> answer as <u>neatly</u> and <u>concisely</u> as you can while avoiding <u>grammatical</u> and <u>spelling</u> errors. Remember the six aspects of an essay answer that will affect the grade your answer receives at 3:00 in the morning? They are neatness, brevity,

organization, lack of grammatical and spelling errors, and, most important, answering the instructor's question. All of these points have been addressed when you use this five-step process in answering essay questions.

When you finish writing your answer, be sure to proofread your writing before you turn in your answer sheet. If you need to, and have the time, you can add a little to an answer or edit slightly to improve your final answer.

"Read the question, reread the question, think about the answer, read the question a third time, and then write the answer. That all takes a lot of time. I'll never be able to finish the test on time!" Not true. By using what I call "brain speed," you can actually produce better, shorter answers and save time.

When I took my doctoral comprehensive exam, we had 12 hours of essay test questions spread out over two days. Each day we had two 3-hour test sessions with an hour off for lunch. Questions were given to us in sealed brown envelopes. When most students received their envelope, they tore it open, read for a minute or two, and started writing. I watched other students furiously writing as much as they could in the three hours that were available. I, too, ripped open my envelope. I read the questions four or five times, almost memorizing them. Then I got up and walked over to the exit, leaned against the door frame, lit my pipe, and smoked for almost half an hour. I returned to my place, wrote my answers, and was the first one out of the testing room for three out of the four testing sessions.

Needless to say, the proctors kept an eye on me; they couldn't decide whether what I was doing was legal or not. Still, they left me alone. What was I doing while I was propped up against the door? Thinking, of course. I was thinking of the things that I wanted to say, how the faculty would evaluate each answer, what "they" wanted me to say, how to show as much as I could while writing as little as possible, etc. When I wrote my answers, all but one was written on two pages (one side each of two pages, not both sides) of a standard "blue book." I had condensed my answers to an amount that I could comfortably write in the time allotted.

The essence of my idea is that you should think before you write your answer! First make sure you know what the test question is, then construct an acceptable answer in your head, and, finally, write the answer to the question that you were asked.

Once you have completed writing and proofreading your answers, turn in your answer sheet and leave the room. Try not to create a disturbance as you leave. Save any discussions of the test and correct answers until you are out of range of the students who are still taking the test (you don't want to disturb others while they

work, and you certainly don't want to help them earn higher grades because it will lower your "relative," or curved, score).

After the Test

After the test you may want to look up information that you included in an answer to reassure yourself that your answer was correct. If not, try to relax. There is nothing that you can do after the test that will affect the grade that you receive. The exception occurs when you know of an error in the test that may affect the grading. In that case, see the instructor.

When your instructor returns your graded answer sheet make time to go over the corrected answers as soon as possible. You need to feel good about the answers that were correct and to find out why you lost points on the answers that did not receive full credit. As you learn more about what your instructor expects in an answer, you can tailor your study procedures to accommodate the feedback that you have been given on the exam.

Analyze Your Errors

When you receive your corrected test paper; go over it carefully to learn from the feedback that your instructor has given you. Look at the answers that received full credit and read them over to see just how complete they were; think about any questions that you had when you were writing your answers and how you solved them. Read over the answers that did not earn full credit, and see if you can understand why your answer did not get all of the points that were available. If your instructor has written comments, do you understand what your instructor has said?

After you have tried to analyze your answers, if you do not completely understand why they are not correct or why you lost credit on your answers, you should do the following:

1.   Reread the test questions to see if you fully understand the questions that you were asked. When you are sure that you understood the questions, reread your answers to see if you can understand where you went wrong.

2.   Review the relevant material in both your textbook and your lecture notes. Can you see what information is missing in your answers?

3.   Review your answers with a classmate. Perhaps she will be able to show you what information is missing. If she had correct answers to questions that you missed, will she let you review her answers so that you can compare the two and learn more about what your instructor wanted in your answers?

Talk With Your Instructor

If, after analyzing your answers, you still do not understand why you lost points, see your instructor during her office hours. Make sure that the focus of the session is on what you should have done to have had more complete answers to the questions that you were asked and on how you can improve your studying for her class. Do not get into a fight over your grade. The grading of essay answers is subjective, and your instructor can usually explain why you lost points. Your concern needs to be with how you can better meet your instructor's expectations on the next examination.

Summary

Before you begin to answer an essay question, be sure that you know the question that your instructor asked you. Read each question at least twice. After you have thought about and organized your answer, reread the question before you begin writing your final answer. Write a neat, short, organized answer without spelling or grammatical errors. Finally, review your graded exam paper to learn what you did that was wrong and how you can improve your essay examination skills.

9 OBJECTIVE EXAMINATIONS

Multiple-choice, matching, and true--false tests are often called objective exams. They are objective because given an answer key, any two instructors correcting the same exam should give that test paper the same score. Each answer is either correct or not correct based on the answer key. Essay examinations are called subjective exams because different instructors scoring an answer sheet can, and often do, assign different grades based on their "subjective" opinion of the answer. The test scorer uses independent judgment as to the quality of each answer.

From the student's view, objective exams can and should be easier because the correct answer to every question is on the test page. Your instructor gives you all the answers! Of course, he gives you lots of wrong answers too. All you have to do is pick out the correct answer from all of the wrong alternatives that are given. The problem, of course, is knowing which of the alternatives that you have been given is most correct.

To improve your scores on objective exams learn the course material better, learn to read and analyze test questions better and/or improve your test-taking skills.

In this chapter, I will focus on showing you how to read and analyze objective test questions and answers. I will also show you how to score higher on objective examinations by knowing and using good test-taking skills and, at the same time, teach you some of the "tricks" of test taking. However, none of the techniques and skills that I cover will help you improve your test scores more than you can by mastering the material that will be included on the examinations you take.

Generally speaking, the more you know, the higher your test scores will be. The exam-taking skills that I present will add additional points to your test scores. Put another way, <u>nothing succeeds in improving your test scores more than knowing the information on which you will be evaluated</u>.

That means that you need to know what each test will cover and that you plan your time to learn as much of the assigned material as you can before the test. For more details on test preparation, review that section of the chapter on examinations.

Before going into the serious techniques about how to score higher on objective exams, let's try a light-hearted approach, one that is easy to learn and fun to apply. (Who said that learning had to be painful?)

The Rule of Three

In the last chapter, I said that the Rule of Three was "Every test was written or will be corrected at 3:00 in the morning." The idea behind the statement is that because instructors dislike writing and correcting tests, they often leave writing or correcting tests until the last minute. With essay tests I tried to show you how to avoid disturbing or perturbing the instructor with grammatical and spelling errors or messy, wordy answers when you "know" that your exam paper will be corrected at 3:00 in the morning. The idea is to avoid making test-taking errors.

With objective exams, the Rule of Three can also be helpful. This time, however, your instructor has made test construction errors that you can use to select the correct answer. Two factors combine on an examination to create a condition from which a test-taking student can benefit:

(1) your instructor has not been trained to write good objective test questions, and

(2) at 3:00 in the morning, few people are at their intellectual and psychological best; they are bound to make mistakes.

With these two thoughts in mind, try answering the following hypothetical test. The test contains eight questions, each with four multiple-choice alternatives.

Despite the fact that you cannot read and understand any of the test questions, if you have good test-taking skills, you should be able to answer every one of these questions correctly. Every test question has one and only one correct answer.

Hint: Look at Question 4.

"Wait a minute," you say, "there is nothing written there!"

True, but why complicate your task with a bunch of words that you may not understand!

Remember, there is a correct answer to Question 4 just as there is a correct answer to each of the other seven questions.

Stop complaining and get to work on the test!

Make-believe Examination

This examination has been designed to test your skills in taking objective tests. Even though you cannot understand the questions you should be able to get every item correct by using test taking skills. Circle the letter which precedes the best answer to each question.

1. When you are bletting, be sure that the clough is securely fastened to the
    a. oval blettum   b. dontrom
    c. bulem   d. grandula

2. Kones frequently smitt with phanies because
    a. no foshers are present
    b. the stoph usually wothers the stimer
    c. all of the stophs and borths zentil
    d. the borth never flins the kot

3. In New York City, the loctal rundles with an
    a. tenthman   b. mormonian
    c. orkian   d. cattos

4. a.   b.   c.   d.

5. Which of the following are the causes of arth noralia?
    a. the hopens linvered the frentals and the vorlex donned
    b. the keggses latted in setlum
    c. most vortlows met with the frentals
    d. pectals maloused in the crabel

6. Sebbelton will be true when
    a. lambtoms wander with sheptoms
    b. sheptoms fram, if the brudgles rezzel with the trector
    c. bardnards haylip the strawler
    d. pitchman forker with slow grassels

7. When the stoph wothers the stimer
    a. alternate simmers neble on the young libbles
    b. the main keppel will drem the pong
    c. kones usually smitt with phanies
    d. carpman vent with doseman and fil

8. Which (is, are) always present at frondon time?
    a. ewloos and ramptons   b. ramptons and bodders
    c. ramptons and leves   d. ramptons

Test Review

Did you really try to answer every question on the test? Did you think to question about how much time you should take for the test or how the test would be scored? Whenever you take a test you need to know some basic information to earn the best score possible for you under the conditions that are given. How a test will be scored can significantly affect your test score. If you do not remember why, review the section on grading in the chapter on general examination skills. To score high on an exam you also need to know how much time you will have to take the test so that you can budget your time to earn as many points as you can.

Now, let's review the correct answers to the Make-Believe Examination to see how much you know about scoring high on objective exams. I'll begin the review of the correct answers with the question that should be the easiest for you to understand. Then, I'll go through the rest of the questions in order.

Question 3

Question 3 is the easiest to explain. The correct answer to Question 3 is c, <u>orkian</u>. Read the question carefully: "In New York City, the loctal rundles with <u>an</u>." What do you know about the article <u>an</u>? Right, the next word must begin with a vowel. The only answer that begins with a vowel is <u>orkian</u>. <u>Orkian</u> is the only answer that is grammatically

correct!

"Now wait a minute," you say, "it can't be that easy." True, most of the time instructors will not give away answers, but sometimes they do so unknowingly. Remember the Rule of Three? Let's use it to understand what happened with this question.

At 3:00 in the morning your instructor was writing this test. Usually an instructor will write the stem of the question, the first part of the question first---"In New York City, the loctal rundles with an." Once the stem of the question has been written, the correct answer is written next to one of the option letters a, b, c, or d. In this instance your instructor wrote the correct answer next to letter c. Because professors know and use standard English grammar, the instructor knows that each answer must begin with a vowel. "Then why didn't each answer in this question begin with a vowel?" Probably because your instructor got interrupted while he was writing the question; perhaps he got up to get a cup of coffee. When he came back to the test, he saw that he needed three more answers, so he wrote them.

Fortunately for you, he did exactly what most students do when they finish their writing---nothing. He did not proofread the question that he wrote! If he had gone over the question he had just written, he would have caught the error and corrected it. (If the question had read "In New York

City the loctal rundles with [a, an]" the clue to the correct answer would have been eliminated.)

Remember, most instructors have never been trained in test construction techniques. They make test construction errors that can help you get the correct answer without knowing the material, if you are sensitive to their mistakes. Even those who have been trained in test writing make some of these mistakes.

Question 1

The correct answer to the first question is a, oval blettum. There are three different reasons for oval blettum being correct. I discuss one of those rationales later for a question that more clearly demonstrates the point.

The first explanation of why oval blettum is correct relates to the word bletting. The instructor used the same root, blett, in both the stem of the question and in the word blettum in answer a. At times it is difficult for an instructor to find a different word to convey an idea that he has used in the stem of the question.

Perhaps another example will help you see the connection. Suppose you write a test question that reads "The purpose of a plow is to_____." How many good alternative answers can you come up with that avoid using the word plow?

Oval blettum is correct because the word blett tips you off to

the correct answer. Within the test question, your instructor provided information that could have been used to help you find the answer.

The second reason why oval blettum is correct is because it is the different answer, it has two words instead of only one. Different answers have a tendency to show up as being correct more often than they should statistically. When you have an answer that is obviously different, be careful. See if the different answer is a "filler," or a "junk," answer, that is, the last alternative that the instructor could think of for the question and therefore likely to be wrong, or is the different answer correct? (Different answers being correct is the weakest of the guessing techniques that I cover. However, if nothing else works, try it.)

Test makers tend to write the correct answer first, the near correct or the next best answer second, and then try to find one or more alternative answers that might be seen as being possible by students who do not know the material well. When the test writer "runs out of gas," he is likely to come up with responses that will help you get a question right. If his different answer is junk, cross it out and get to work finding the correct answer out of the remaining three alternatives.

Question 2

The answer to question 2 is b for at least two different

reasons. First, b is the different answer because of the word usually. All of the other alternatives use the absolute terms all, never and no. How many things can you say all, always, no, none, or never about and be correct? Watch out for those terms when you study. If you see something in your textbook that says that something is always or never true, mark it because it is likely to become a test question. On tests, watch for absolute words, because they can tip you off to the correct answer.

The second reason that b is correct is because of the relationship between the word frequently in the question and usually in answer b. They go together and often can be used interchangeably. Each implies some degree of latitude in something.

Question 5

The correct answer to Question 5 is a, for two different reasons. First, a is the different answer. It is different because it is the only plural answer. Read the stem of the question again: "Which of the following are the causes of arth noralia?" Are is plural and requires two or more parts in the answer. Although the other answers contain words that are plurals--keggses, vortlows, frentals, and pectals---each of those answers is singular.

In the chapter on essay exams, I told you that instructors expect you to use standard English grammar. You are in college now. You have a right to expect that your instructors will also use standard English grammar when they write their tests and assignments. Watch out for grammatical cues that will point you to, or away from, a specific answer. At 3:00 in the morning it is easy for an instructor to miss some of these errors that can help you out.

Question 6

Question 6 is the best guessing technique question on this test. The correct answer is b for three different reasons.

First, b is the different answer; it has a comma in it. In Question 1, two words made the answer different. Watch out for different answers. On this test, the different answer is correct at least six times.

The second reason that b is correct is that the answer is both general and specific at the same time. Statement b is a conditional statement that says that certain conditions must also occur, "when...if." The correct answer to a multiple-choice question must be both broad enough to be the correct answer and narrow enough to be the only correct answer. Conditional statements help meet these specifications. The conditional statement takes the broad first part of the answer and narrows it with the conditional statement. That is, the first part of the answer is limited to not all cases, but only to those under the conditions specified in the second part of the statement.

The third reason that b is correct is probably the simplest, yet the single best guessing technique for multiple-choice guessing that there is---b is the longest answer! "It can't be that simple!" Yes, it can. When you have to guess on a multiple-choice question and you don't have anything to go on, the longest answer will be correct over one third of the time!

A number of years ago I collected multiple-choice tests and answer keys from all of the freshman and sophomore courses that were offered during our summer school. I had collected a large number of test-taking techniques that supposedly improved test scores when guessing was necessary. Each technique was written on a card. A student was given the stack of test papers from over 50 different classes and was told to answer all questions that he could using only the technique written on the card. Of all the techniques we tried, only one technique consistently got scores above chance (25% correct). The longest answer was correct a little over one third (35%) of the time! The best score that we were able to achieve by using the longest answer was 91%, and that was without reading any of the answers.

The longer the longest answer is compared with the next longest answer, the greater the probability that the longest answer is correct! Look back at Question 1. The longest answer is a. It is just a little bit longer than the other answers. On the basis of the answer being only slightly longer, a is only likely to be correct. In Question 6, answer b is much longer than any other answer. There is a high probability that b is the correct answer.

Why is the longest answer correct? Most people say it is because it takes more words to make the right answer totally correct. The correct answer needs clarifying words, conditional phrases, etc., to make the answer broad enough and yet narrow enough to be the only correct answer.

I can't argue with that rationale, but I can give you a much better explanation for the longest answer being correct.

Remember the Rule of Three? Tests are written at 3:00 in the morning! Usually an instructor writes the stem of the question first and then the correct answer. He needs three wrong answers. At 3:00 in the morning will he really take the time to write long, wrong answers? He wants to get finished as fast as he can; that means short, wrong answers! (If you were the instructor, would you take the time to write long, wrong answers?)

On this test, four of the correct answers are the longest alternative. The longest answer error is difficult to avoid. It is your best multiple-choice test-guessing technique.

Question 7

Do you like birthday presents? Do you like gifts in general? If so, then you should love Question 7. The correct answer to the question is c.

Look back at Question 2. Question 7 is simply Question 2 written in reverse. That is, Question 2 gave you the correct answer to Question 7! It should have been a "gift" answer for you.

Yes, sometimes instructors provide information in a question that you can use to get another question correct. When I was a freshman, I took basic chemistry. We were told that we had to memorize the Periodic Table, that is, the table that lists all of the chemical elements by group. Sure enough, on the first exam, the second question was "Reproduce the Periodic Table." The answer page was blank, so we didn't even have the numbered columns to help us. I started to answer the question but soon realized that I had made a mistake somewhere because one of the columns wouldn't come out with the correct number of elements. I stopped work and went on to the other questions. The last question was something like "Compute the atomic weight of the following compound." The chemical formula for the compound was given along with the Atomic Weight Table needed for the calculation. If you know a little about chemistry, then you may know that when the instructor gave us the Atomic Weight Table, he also gave us the Periodic Table. He had answered his own question! Only a few students out of a class of over 600 got the question right despite the fact that the instructor had given us the entire correct answer.

Be on your toes when you are taking a test. If you see something that relates to another question, your instructor just may have helped you out. Remember, at 3:00 in the morning your instructor isn't likely to proofread his questions and catch "question duplication" or "give-away information" (material in one question that helps you get other questions correct).

Question 8

Which word in the stem of Question 8 is the keyword, or the tip-off word? The answer is <u>always</u>. Now read the question again, "Which (is, are) <u>always</u> present...?" The answer is <u>ramptons</u>, answer d. Look at the four possible answers. <u>Ramptons</u> is part of every answer. Therefore, <u>ramptons</u> must be part of the correct answer. By adding the word always to our consideration, would you bet on one thing being present every time or two things? Because absolutes do not happen all that often, you would be ahead betting on one item occurring each and every time. Therefore, the correct answer has to be <u>ramptons</u>; it is always part of the answer.

Note that answer d is the different answer. This time it is the only singular answer. Answer d is also different because it is the shortest answer. Watch out for different answers.

Question 4

Now let's go back to Question 4. Even though there wasn't any material for you to read in this question, you should have been able to determine that d was the correct answer to the question. Look at the question. If you assume that there really is a correct answer, there must be some clue to finding it. You have nothing to go on except the letters a, b, c, and d. It must have something to do with those letters! Now, look at the correct answers to the test:

1. a
2. b
3. c
4. ?
5. a
6. b
7. c
8. d

Why would an instructor use a pattern on his answer sheet? To make his work correcting the answer sheets easier, of course! If you find a pattern in the answers, use it. Be careful, though. Some instructors like to play games. An instructor could give you a pattern like the one above and then change it just a little. Instead of the correct answer being in the pattern after, say, 15 questions, he puts the next best answer in the pattern. If you simply use the pattern "blindly," you get the first 15 correct, and then fail the test because the pattern changed and you missed it.

I remember taking a frustrating exam in my undergraduate course in Psychological Tests and Measurements. One of the first "rules" that we learned was never to use a pattern in your answer. If an instructor wants a true measure on how much his students know, a pattern that makes correction easy will defeat the goal if some students get high scores because they detected the pattern. (An easy point to remember, right?)

Our first test was a multiple-choice exam. Each question had four possible answers: a, b, c, and d. Every so often I had 3 or 4 a, b or c answers in a row. It looked strange, but it could happen. After everyone had turned in the answer sheets, the instructor gave us the correct answers: 5 a's followed by 10 b's, followed by 10 c's, and ending with 15 d's in a row! We could have killed him. Can't you picture us taking the test? Two a's in a row, then 3. The next answer can't be a, right? Wrong!

Here is one more example of using patterns to get the correct answers on an exam. If you get an answer sheet that looks strange, be especially careful about your answers. This example occurred in a graduate class I took. Each question had four answers as usual. However, the letters in front of the answers weren't a,b, etc. Instead, the letters changed on each question. The first question had l, m, n, and o for answers, etc. No answer sheet was provided, we just circled the letter preceding the correct answer on the test

```
 1  2  3  4  5  6  7  8  9 10 11 12 13 14 15 16 17 18 19 20 21 22 23

 L  B  P  Q  W  A  G  R  H     P  R  L  A  S  A  K  C  A  G  A  N  O  X
 M  C  Q  R  X  B  H  S  I     Q  S  M  B  T  B  L  D  B  H  B  O  P  Y
 N  D  R  S  Y  C  I  T  J     R  T  N  C  U  C  M  E  C  I  C  P  Q  Z
 O  E  S  T  Z  D  J  U  K     S  U  O  D  V  D  N  F  D  J  D  Q  R  A
```

If your answer sheet looks strange, be careful!

```
 1  2  3  4  5  6  7  8  9 10 11 12 13 14 15 16 17 18 19 20 21 22 23

 L  B  P  Q  W  A  G  R  H     P  R  L  A  S  A  K  C  A  G  A  N  O  X
 M  C  Q  R  X  B  H  S  I     Q  S  M  B  T  B  L  D  B  H  B  O  P  Y
 N  D  R  S  Y  C  I  T  J     R  T  N  C  U  C  M  E  C  I  C  P  Q  Z
 O  E  S  T  Z  D  J  U  K     S  U  O  D  V  D  N  F  D  J  D  Q  R  A
```

The answers were "MERRY CHRISTMAS AND A HAPPY NEW YEAR"!

itself. If we had had an answer sheet, it could have looked something like the first answer sheet.

As you can see, each question has four answers, but instead of using the usual a, b, c, d letters in front of each answer, different letters were used. All we had to do was to answer the questions as usual, marking the correct answer!

The correct answers to the test turned out to be a pattern.

The instructor had intended to give us a present for the Christmas holiday, but the gift backfired. He put a message to us in the pattern of correct answers. Regretfully, only a few of the students found the message in the pattern of correct answers, "MERRY CHRISTMAS AND A HAPPY NEW YEAR." At the spring semester the instructor used "ENJOY YOUR SUMMER VACATION" as the hidden message.

Watch out for patterns. They do occur sometimes at the college level. However, they do not occur all that often.

Summary

When you are taking an objective test, watch out for the standard instructor errors of test construction such as the longest answer being correct; grammatical structure that points to, or eliminates, an answer; information within a question or a test that can be useful in answering questions; and the possible use of patterns in the answer key. All of these "irregularities" can help you get more answers correct on a test.

Use Your Knowledge First

Now let's get back to learning how to score higher on multiple-choice examinations by using good test-taking strategies.

Whenever you take any test, remember to read and listen to the instructions that you are given. Objective tests are no exception. First read the instructions. Also, remember to read each question and answer critically so that you answer the question that your instructor asked you and not the question you wish the instructor had asked. If you normally rush through your tests and lose a lot of points for careless mistakes, try using your finger as a pointer as you read each question and answer to slow you down and keep you focused on the words that are actually on the page.

Once you know what you are supposed to do on the test, work through the exam as rapidly as you can, answering all the questions that you can on the basis of what you know. Try not to get stuck on any item for very long. When you have test questions that are difficult for you, or questions that you can't answer, mark or circle the question so that you can easily get back to it, and go on to the next question. Use your knowledge to answer all of the questions that you can.

As you work through the test the first time, try to keep in mind that most of the test questions have been written for "Joe and Jane Average." That is, most instructors do not write their questions for people like Einstein and Marilyn Vos Savant (both are classified as geniuses). Instructors write their questions to see if most of their students have learned the material that has been assigned. Don't begin working through your test looking for trick questions or trick answers. Just use your knowledge to get as many answers correct as you can.

After you have worked through the exam the first time, you will have done at least three things. First of all, you will have answered at least one question correctly so you know that you won't get a zero on the test! Hopefully you got more than one question right and you learned that you do know some of the material. Second, because you probably answered more than one question correctly, your confidence should have started to move in a positive direction; after all, you do have some, hopefully most, of the questions answered correctly. Third, you have identified problem questions that you need to concentrate or work on. You have used your time efficiently by getting the "easy" questions out of the way in a minimum amount of time.

Keep in mind that most instructors find it difficult to predict how well students will be able to answer a new question. If I have used a question before, I have some information available to me about how hard that question is. When I write a test, I usually try to start out with questions that aren't too difficult. Other instructors seem to do the same thing. We know that you don't like to take tests and that you may be worried or "stressed out" about the test. We try to start you out with questions that will build up your confidence before we ask the more difficult questions.

As an instructor finishes writing an exam, he has often used up most of his "pet" questions. Many times a few more questions are needed to get to an even number of questions such as 40 or 50. That's when question duplication occurs; that's when some easy test items are tossed in just to complete the exam. When you answer exam questions on the basis of your knowledge and leave the rest for later, you will have gotten all or most of the easy items right, including the toss-in questions at the end of the test.

Now comes the work of objective test taking.

Rewrite the Test Question

Once you have used your knowledge to answer all the questions that you can, it is time to go back to the items that you couldn't answer the first time through the test. One of the easiest techniques for analyzing multiple-choice test questions is to change the format of the question into true--false questions.

Let's look at Question 3 on the Make-Believe Exam we used before. The original question looked like this:

In New York City, the loctal rundles with an

    a.   tenthman
    b.   mormonian
    c.   orkian
    d.   cattos

When you rewrite the question into four true--false questions, you simply repeat the stem of the question, or the first part of the question, with each of the answers that you were given in the question.

The revised question would look something like this:

a. In New York City, the loctal rundles with an tenthman.

b. In New York City, the loctal rundles with an mormonian.

c. In New York City, the loctal rundles with an orkian.

d. In New York City, the loctal rundles with an cattos.

As you read each of these statements, try to determine whether it is true or false. In this case, you would have found the first answer to be awkward or grammatically incorrect. Hopefully the same thing would have happened with items b and d. Although you may not be able to understand c, the answer does flow, and it is grammatically correct. Your mental answer sheet for this analysis might look something like this:

a. In New York City, the loctal rundles with an tenthman.

False?   Grammatically incorrect.

b. In New York City, the loctal rundles with an mormonian.

False?   Grammatically incorrect.

c. In New York City, the loctal rundles with an orkian.

True? The only answer that is grammatically correct.

d. In New York City, the loctal rundles with an cattos.

False?   Grammatically incorrect.

Only one of these revised statements looks as if it is correct. If your thought processes have been right, you should have the correct answer to the original test question. Mark your answer sheet and go on to the next problem question.

Mark Key Words

Another way of focusing your attention on critical material when you analyze a test question is to mark key words in the stem of the question. Once you have highlighted these words, think about them. What do you know about either the words or the concepts in the question that can help you to determine the correct answer?

In your tests, all of the words that are used should make sense to you. If you have a word that you don't understand, be sure to get it clarified by the instructor. (Remember the example from my class when no one knew what the word rationale meant?) Most tests are not intended to be vocabulary tests aimed at checking how many words you know. So ask. At worst, your instructor will say "That's a word you should know from the assigned material."

Back to "key words." Once you have the key words or the main idea of the question identified, stop and think about all that you know that relates to the key word(s) that you marked. What did the instructor say in class about it? Was there anything in the text that might be of help now? Hopefully, as you start thinking about the subject, you will bring up into current memory material that will help you answer the test question. If so, use that information to answer the question and move on to the next question. If you still do not have a single answer that you think is correct, move on to your next strategy for uncovering the correct answer.

Reason

Hopefully, your knowledge or one of the techniques discussed above will have helped you to begin narrowing down the number of alternative answers from four, to three, and maybe even to two. If your knowledge and your item analysis haven't gotten you to the correct answer, try comparing the alternative answers that you have left. Reason through the alternative answers and see if you can come up with the correct answer.

Years ago I took an accounting class that had multiple-choice examinations. The exams were difficult because the instructor would anticipate most of the errors students could make on an accounting problem, and he would include all of the incorrectly calculated answers as the alternate answers in his multiple-choice questions. If you weren't sure whether to include an item in your calculations, both possible answers would be there. You had to know what you were doing to get the correct answer.

One question was especially difficult. The instructor had a list of five statements. The question asked which of the statements was correct. I read through the statements and knew that three of the answers were correct and that one was wrong. The fifth statement made no sense, but it contained several accounting terms that I knew that I didn't fully understand.

After reading and studying that alternative four or five times, I knew that I wouldn't be able to comprehend the problem statement, so I tried my exam skills.

This is the question:

Given the following statements-

1.   The Allowance for Depreciation account is a contra asset account which should have a debit balance after adjustment.

2.   Under depreciation accounting, intangible assets are assumed to have no salvage value.

3.   While the journal is maintained in chronological order, the ledger accounts are posted in the reverse of chronological order; that is, the last transaction journalized is always the first transaction posted to the ledger.

4. In a compound entry, three or more accounts are affected.

5.   Closing entries are journalized, but they are not posted.

Which of the above statements are _true_?

    a. 1, 3, 5

    b. 1, 3, 4, 5

    c. 2, 3, 5

    d. 1, 2, 4, 5

    e. 1, 2, 3

I knew that Statements 1, 3, and 5 were correct. I also knew that Statement 4 was definitely wrong. Rather than just guessing, I decided to see if I could solve the question using the limited information that I had on hand. I found that

a. 1, 3, 5   Possible.

b. 1, 3, 4, 5   Wrong because Statement 4 is wrong.

c. 2, 3, 5   Wrong because Statement 1 is correct and not there.

d. 1, 2, 4, 5   Wrong because Statement 4 is wrong.

e. 1, 2, 3   Wrong because Statement 5 is correct and not there.

The only possible correct answer is letter a. I was able to reason down to the correct answer without knowing all of the information that should have been needed to answer the question.

Often, you will be able to come up with the correct answer simply because your instructor did not think ahead to all of the possible errors that could be made in attempting to answer his test questions. Use the knowledge you have to reason through the alternatives; sometimes you'll come up with the winner.

Guess

When your knowledge runs out, if your analyses do not produce a single correct answer, and if you cannot reason down to the correct answer, try guessing. Don't just guess! Use your knowledge about guessing to help you make the best possible guess under the circumstances you are in.

It's Either B or C

In four-answer multiple-choice test questions, all of the answers are not equally probable. That is, a, b, c, and d do not have the same probability of being correct on a test. In theory, each of those answers should be correct 25 percent of the time. In reality, answers b and c are the correct answer more than 25 percent of the time, whereas a and d are correct less than 25 percent of the time. That means that if you can eliminate either b or c, the other is your best guess. If b is eliminated, then c is correct; if c is eliminated b is your best guess.

When you have a five-answer multiple choice question, your guessing technique changes significantly. Now c is the most popular position for the correct answer. When we analyzed the correct responses on multiple-choice questions with five choices, c was used by instructors significantly more than either b or d and answers a and e were not used as often as they should have been if all answers are supposed to have an equal chance of being correct.

All of the Above and None of the Above

The multiple-choice answers "all of the above" and "none of the above" can be legitimate or good multiple-choice answers. However, many times instructors will use "all of the above" and "none of the above" to stretch the number of credible alternative answers on their test questions. When this happens or when an instructor makes a logical error in creating the question, you might be able to benefit from his error.

A simple group of answers might look something like this (the question isn't important; just use the answers):

    a. Cat

    b. Horse

    c. Dog

    d. None of the above

    e. All of the above

Regardless of the question, answer e cannot be the correct answer. For e to be correct, a must be correct, b must be correct, c must be correct, and d must be correct. Read answer d. It says "None of the above," meaning that answers a, b, and c must all be wrong before answer d can be right. The first three answers just can't be right and wrong at the same time. Therefore, answer e can never be correct as this set of answers is written. The instructor has made a logical or test construction error.

(If you find this error on a test, do not tell your instructor about it during class. See him during office hours so that he is not publicly embarrassed by his mistake. Fight for the point on the question only when it will make a difference in your final course grade!)

The correct way that all of the answers in the sample should have been written is

    a. Cat

    b. Horse

    c. Dog

    d. All of the above

    e. None of the above

Now all of the answers could be correct. You have to know the material to get the correct answer.

Instructor Bias

There will be times when you will have used all of your knowledge and all of your test-taking skills and you still will not be able to come up with what you hope is the correct answer. Don't despair, there may still be a chance to beat the odds.

Try counting the number of times that each answer has been used on the test and use that information to get the best possible guess. That is, count the number of times you used answer a, b, etc. on the test, then guess. Try this example. You have a question, perhaps Question 33, that you can't answer on an exam that has 80 questions. You might end up with a summary that looks something like this:

    a. used 9 times

    b. used 15 times

    c. used 15 times

    d. used 40 times

That is, on your test you have marked 9 a answers, 15 b answers, etc. Now, what is your best guess for Question 33?

The correct answer is <u>not</u> a. Very few instructors go through their answers to get a particular number of a, b, c and d answers. They have better uses of their time. However, instructors do have biases that may affect where they put the correct answer. In the sample answer "analysis," the instructor has a bias. He doesn't like "position" a; in this example, he doesn't put the correct answer in the first possible answer spot (if the first answer is correct, you, the student, won't have to read all the answers that he created).

This instructor likes d answers. Look at the number of correct d answers; there are <u>40</u>. Over 50 percent of the answers you marked are answer d. Earlier I told you that a and d were not popular alternatives---we may never know why. Yet this instructor is using alternative d for the correct answer just over 50 percent of the time. That is an instructor bias. In this case, your best guess would be answer d. No other guessing technique, not even the length of the answer, will be correct more than 50 percent of the time.

Note, the instructor bias could be toward one letter (in the sample, toward answer d) or away from or bias against putting the correct answer in a certain place (against putting the correct answer in the a position in the sample). Whatever the case, if you find out that an instructor has a bias as to where he puts (or doesn't put) the correct answer, use it to help you get the question correct.

Changing Answers

While you were working on Question 33 in the section above, you reread Question 34 and were thinking about changing your answer. Should you change your answer or not?

The answer is, that depends. Generally you will be ahead if you change your answer! "But I thought that you shouldn't change your answer." That's what a lot of people say: "Don't change your answer because first impressions are usually correct."

Stop and think about that last statement for a minute. Are your first impressions really correct most of the time? You meet someone for the first time. Are your first impressions about the person correct after you get to know him over a period of time? Very often the answer is "no." Sometimes we end up liking a person we were turned off to when we first met him. Other times we learn to dislike someone who gave us a good first impression. If our first impressions about people aren't always correct, why should our first impressions about test answers be much better?

When you go to change an answer on a multiple-choice test, three things can happen:

- you can go from a wrong answer to the right answer,

- you can go from the right answer to a wrong answer, and

- you can go from one wrong answer to another wrong answer.

When students change answers, about 50 percent of the time they go from a wrong answer to the correct answer.

The basic rule for changing answers is, don't change answers unless you know something when you go to make the change that you didn't know when you first answered the question. Perhaps you marked an answer and then, as you worked on other questions, you remembered something that makes you realize that you answered an earlier question wrong. Go ahead and change your answer. If, however, you are thinking about changing an answer because you have too many c answers, or you have several b answers in a row, etc., leave your first answer alone.

Because there are individual differences in most things in life, there have to be individual differences in whether you should change your answers or not. Some people get more correct by changing answers, whereas others lose by changing answers. You ought to know what is right for you. Most students, however, simply don't know if they score higher or lower by changing answers.

When you change answers on a test, mark the answer sheet in some way so that you will remember which answers you changed. When you get your test paper back, find out whether you got more answers correct by changing your answers or by staying with your first choice. When you have recorded this information from several tests in different classes, you should have a good idea of whether _you_ should change an answer or not. You will have collected information that tells you whether you get more points or lose them when _you_ change an answer.

The Longest Answer

Although there are a number of different guessing techniques, remember that the best single method of guessing is to select the longest answer. Sometimes other factors will cause another answer to be correct, but generally speaking, the longest answer is your best guess.

Test Analysis Work Sheet

To help you learn about the kinds of errors you make on objective examinations, create a test analysis work sheet to help you examine how well you performed on your examinations. Create vertical columns to analyze the kinds of information you want to know about the questions you missed. Headings for the columns could include lecture (for questions that came from class lectures), textbook, articles (for items that came from outside reading such as research articles that might have been on reserve at the library), negative question (for questions like "Which of the following was NOT a reason for...."), changed answer, computation question, computation error, clerical error, misread the question, I thought I knew it, guessed, etc. As you are able to pinpoint a specific type of error you make, create a simple heading to describe that error.

When you have an exam on which you scored lower than you either expected or wanted to, go over the exam using your test analysis work sheet. The idea is to find a pattern to the questions that you have missed. For example, if you regularly miss definition questions, when you study be sure that you really know what the terms used in that class mean. If you misread questions, were the errors caused by working too fast when you took the test? If so, even though there is a time limit on the test, slow down as you read (perhaps you can use your finger as a pointer when you read). Read the question word by word so that you understand what the instructor has written.

"That's a lot of work for one exam! The stupid thing is over. Can't I just forget the exam and just work harder?" Sure you can. You can put in more time, get a tutor, join a study group, and lots more. But how do you know where to focus your attention? Will working harder on all aspects of the class improve your learning and test performance? Probably, but why not learn from your past mistakes? You will gain more with less effort.

Try looking at the way you will work or have worked in an office. Your boss has given you an assignment to write the weekly report on sales receipts. He wants the report by 10:30 each Monday morning so that he can review it before he meets with his management staff. The first week you are responsible for the report; information from two departments is missing and you don't complete the report until after 1:00. Is your boss pleased with your performance-- after all, you got all of the information that he wanted? The answer, I hope, is no. "But I didn't have the information I needed to write the report" you say. "That's your responsibility; next week be sure you have it" is a possible response that you will get.

If you don't do something to secure the information you need from the two delinquent departments, you are sure to anger your boss. What you do and how you do it is up to you. However, if you concentrate your efforts at working hard on the other responsibilities that you have, you can be the best employee that the company ever had, and you'll still end up in trouble if that weekly report isn't completed on time.

At work we use the feedback that we get from our bosses to be better employees (or just to stay out of trouble). Use your analysis of your test results to focus your attention on your weaknesses. Your instructor, through the corrected answer sheet, has provided you with information that you can use to improve your studying in the future. Use it!

Getting the Test

"Analyzing a test to learn from your mistakes sounds great, but all I get back is the graded answer sheet" or "But all I get for feedback is a test score from a list my instructor posts outside his office!" When you don't have the test questions you can't get detailed feedback that will tell you the kind of mistakes you made. You won't be able to correct your mistakes.

The only acceptable solution is to see your instructor during office hours to ask to review your test. (I obviously do not see not reviewing your test as an acceptable solution.) If you sound like you are really interested in improving as a student, most instructors will allow you to see the test and your graded answer sheet. If you sound like you are there to fight over your grade, you may not be allowed to see the test.

Suppose you have created a personal test analysis sheet and bring it with you when you go in to see your instructor. What will his reaction be to your request to review your test when you show him your work sheet? If you were the instructor, wouldn't you be impressed by a student who came to see you with a work sheet that has been designed to help diagnose the kinds of errors the student made on your test?

"Dr. Smith, I'd like to go over my exam to see what kinds of mistakes I made." What would your response be?

Many instructors will let you go over an exam but they won't let you copy down questions. When they see you with paper and pencil in hand, they may think that you want to write down the questions. If that comes up, just show him your work sheet so that he can see that you are there to work and learn. Serious students who look and act as though they are there to learn, rather than arguing for a certain grade, tend to get more assistance than those who appear to be "grade grubbers."

Computerized Answer Sheets

Sooner or later most students run up against computerized answer sheets, particularly if they are in a large lecture class. The major concerns with these answer sheets are to be sure that your answers are corrected and that the grading is accurate. "But the computer will score the answer sheets. What's the problem?"

Basically, there are two problems. The first is in

getting your answers scored. Computer answer sheets are scanned by an optical scanning device and then scored. If your marks on the answer sheet are not dark enough and large enough for the scanner to pick up, the computer will think that you did not answer the question and will mark the answer as blank and therefore wrong. Often your instructor will post the computer printout that shows both the responses for every question and the total score for each student. When you take the test, be sure that you have answered every question. When you check for your score on the exam, see if any of your answers were wrong because no answer was recorded. If you have answers that are wrong because the answers weren't recorded, see your instructor about getting your answer sheet hand scored.

I remember one student who received a D on his computer-scored test. I asked him for the answer sheet for the test. When I looked at the answer sheet, I noticed that his answers seemed to be very light. I asked him what kind of pencil he had used on the test. He showed me his "number 2" pencils. They were marked 2H (the H means hard). The student was an architecture major, and that was the kind of pencil he had to use in his drawings. When I reminded him that he should have used a soft number 2 pencil so that the graphite or mark on the answer sheet would have been darker, he looked surprised, but understood immediately. I kept his answer sheet but sent him back to his instructor to see

if he could get his answers hand scored. He came back very dejected with a "no" for an answer. I then called the instructor and explained that (1) I was the one who had discovered the difficulty, (2) I had personally kept possession of the answer sheet so that no question could be raised about the student having changed the answers on the test paper, and (3) the student reported that 16 of his answers were scored with no answer recorded, whereas the paper I had in my hands had every question answered. The instructor agreed to hand score the test. The student got 12 of the 16 supposedly blank answers correct. His grade went from D to B.

Be sure your answers on a computer-scored answer sheet are dark enough to be recorded!

The second problem with computer scoring is that computer-scored test results are not always accurate. I know of one department that stopped having their answer sheets computer scored when they found out that the computer-scoring error rate was above 5 percent. That is, for every 100 answers scored, 5 would be scored wrong. Because you are the only one who loses if your answers are graded incorrectly, get in the habit of checking your answers to make certain the grade you get is the one you earned.

A variation of the computer-scoring error is the hand-scoring error that occurs when an answer key or mask is used to correct papers. An answer key is often folded so that the correct answers can be laid next to the answers on the test paper for scoring. If the answer key slips off by one question, the test score will be wrong. If a mask is created, the same problem can occur. (With masks, holes are punched out for the correct responses to each question on the answer sheet. The mask is put over the test paper and the answers that show through the mask are the correct ones. Correct answers are simply totalled and written on the test paper.) Again the problem that can occur is that the mask slips when it is held over the answer sheet, and a wrong test score is the result.

Because it is your test score, check to be certain that your paper has been corrected properly!

Matching Questions

Back in elementary school you probably liked to see matching questions. You had two columns of words, and you had to draw a line between the words in the two columns to create the best possible match.

In college, matching questions can be, and often are, extremely difficult. Be careful. Look at the format of a typical matching test question in the next column:

Choose the best match for each of the following items:

1.	vvvvv	A	aaaaa
2.	wwwww	B	bbbbb
3.	xxxxx	C	ccccc
4.	yyyyy	D	ddddd
5.	zzzzz	E	eeeee

The actual questions and answers are not important. What _is_ important is what can happen on this type of test question. The correct answers to this question could have been

1. A

2. A

3. A

4. A

5. A

That is, A is the best match for all five questions.

The correct answers to the question could also have been

1. A, B, C, D, E

2. B, E

3. A, C, E

4. D

5. B, C

That is, there can be more than one correct answer for each

question.

The correct answers could even have been

1. A, B, C, D, E

2. B, E

3.

4. D

5.

That is, there is no good match for questions 3 and 5.

When you take a matching test, be sure to check the following:

1. whether an answer can be used more than once,

2. if there is more than one correct answer to a question, and

3. if there is a correct answer for every question that is in the set of questions.

By the way, using all of the possible alternatives that I just listed can be a very good way of assessing whether students really know the information at the level an instructor expects. However, when you are taking a matching test, you can easily feel tricked if you haven't thought of the possible problems you can encounter.

Summary

When taking any test, knowledge of the subject matter is essential. However, because of human errors in test construction, it is often possible to better your test score by improving your test-taking ability. On objective tests, first use your knowledge to locate the correct answers to as many questions as possible. If your knowledge isn't sufficient, try to reason through the alternative answers by creating true--false questions out of each multiple-choice alternative; does one statement end up true while the others are false? Try to think about the main concept in the question. What do you know about it? What did your instructor stress about it in class? In essence, can you bring up any more information about the subject matter from your memory that will help you find the correct answer?

Your last alternative in answering an objective test question should be guessing. Your best pure guess is the length of the alternative answers; the best guess is the longest answer that is given.

Remember, your aim in taking a test is to score as high on it as you possibly can. In most cases, that means that you answer every question even if you have to guess. Blank answers are never correct, so use your test-taking skills to gain as many points as you can by answering every question.

10 CAMPUS RESOURCES

When you arrive on campus, you will be in an entirely new environment. The people you will meet, the instructors you will have, and the buildings you will take classes in are all new to you. In many ways, your campus will be a maze that you will need to learn if you want to get the most out of college.

Keep in mind that the college is there <u>to serve you</u>. The faculty and staff are there to help you get the best education that you can. Even the rules and regulations that you encounter along the way are there to help you get an education that is equivalent to or better than students have received at your college in the past.

Unfortunately, not everyone on your campus remembers that you are the reason that they have their job. They may not be all that helpful to you or be able to answer questions for you. You will have to become your own advocate and learn how to use the agencies on your campus when you need help.

I am not going to review the kinds of services that you will be able to find on your college campus because your college catalog and student handbook have specific information about agencies on your campus that I could not possibly be aware of. If you do not have both of these documents, I urge you to get them as soon as possible so that you can refer to them when you need help.

In many ways, your campus is a small city that has most of the services that you need to enable you to earn a college degree. However, when you are in a bind and need information, you will have to get used to the idea of working independently to get the assistance that you need. Services are there; you just have to find them. Once you get to the office that you need, the staff person that you talk with should be able to help you get the information that you want. If you cannot get the help you need from that person, ask for a referral to a more appropriate agency.

Colleges Are Bureaucracies

When people talk about college, they rarely indicate that college is really a collection of people and agencies who work together in an institution of higher education. Although that statement may be obvious to you, it has tremendous implications to you as a person who can benefit from using the services that your college offers. Because colleges are bureaucracies, and bureaucracies have many independent components, not everyone who "should" know something will actually be able to help you. Rather than getting frustrated, and perhaps angry, blame it all on Murphy (Murphy's Law---if anything can possibly go wrong, it will), and try another person, another question, or another agency.

The point to remember is that

most campuses have agencies and staff to help you with just about any problem or concern that you can have about getting through your college education. The majority of the time, they can probably help you with just about any problem at all, whether it is related to college or not. No, they won't be able to solve all your problems for you. They will just be able to help you help yourself, to assist you in developing a variety of strategies that you could use to resolve your problems.

Ask

The "help you help yourself" in the previous paragraph is really important. You need to stay in charge of your life; to stay in control. If you are going to college right after you have finished high school, your parents and your school system have watched out for you for most of your life. In college, you have to take responsibility for your education and all other aspects of your life. If you are going to college after you have been out of school for a number of years, you have already been taking responsibility for your life. In either case, to help you help yourself, create a support system or network to assist you in learning all that you can about your campus and the opportunities that are available there for you.

While you are going to school, you will have some problems with something---getting classes, understanding some concept, dealing with personal concerns, etc. Having problems is to be expected. What you do to resolve your problems is what is really important.

When you have a problem, concern, or question, you need to be comfortable with asking for help. In high school, teachers might have noticed that you looked troubled and said something to you or referred you to a counselor. In college, you'll be on your own. Most instructors will not know you well enough to realize that something is wrong. You will be treated as an adult and be expected to look out for yourself.

Many students tell me that they are afraid to ask for help because their question may be dumb or stupid. My response is "The only stupid question that I can think of is the one you do not ask!" If you do not understand something, you need to get it clarified---before your instructor asks you that question on an exam or before the problem gets any bigger! You are in college to learn. If you are having problems that are interfering with your learning, or if you do not understand something, ask---ask for help, ask for clarification; just ask!

Who Do You Ask?

Ask any teacher, staff member, or student. Ask the person you feel most comfortable with. Use your head, of course. If you have a question about a concept that you don't understand in class, don't ask a student who misses class all the time! Talk with your instructor before or after class or during her office hours, ask your teaching assistant, or ask a student who asks good questions in class. Just ask the most competent person who is available to you. Ask!

Assertiveness

Being assertive means standing up for yourself and your rights. Assertiveness and assertive come from the word assert which means to promote, or to state with assurance. To assert yourself means that you have confidence in yourself or in your viewpoint and that you will work toward your own best interests. Assertiveness means that you have the ability to express your thoughts, your needs, and your feelings to others without impinging on their rights.

Being assertive does not mean being obnoxious, aggressive, or insensitive to others. It does mean that you value yourself and that you are willing to defend yourself and your rights when you feel that either has been violated or infringed upon.

Being assertive on campus means that you will stand up for yourself, your work, and your views. When you feel that you have been mistreated or evaluated incorrectly, you will speak up for yourself and ask to be treated as others have been treated. For instance, if your history graduate assistant gave D's and F's to everyone in your section when other graders were assigning their students A's and B's, you are being assertive if you go to your professor and ask to have your examination regraded, or if you organize a small group of students to make the same request.

On college campuses, as with life in general, you need to look out for your own best interests at least part of the time. If you have a problem, need information, or feel that you have not been treated fairly, think of all the alternative strategies that you have for dealing with your concern. If you need assistance in working out your problem, what is the best campus agency for helping you with that issue? Once you have identified your best strategy, assert yourself, and implement it to the best of your ability.

Networking

Networking means creating and using a system of people and agencies to help you. In the business world, one form of networking has often been called the "old boys' network." Recently, women have been creating a women's network. In each case, individuals can get support, get information about jobs, use contacts to get ahead or to land contracts, and keep up to date on the latest business news through a network of people.

The idea of networking in college is basically the same. Juniors and seniors in your major know a great deal about the courses, faculty, and requirements of your department. Faculty and staff at your school know each other and the kinds of resources that are available to you if you need help. Campus employers can be both on-the-job supervisors and mentors to their employees.

Create your own personal support system to help you get the most you can from your college. Do not use only one source of information---it may be biased. Use several of your resources to gather information, then make the best decision that you can using all of the opinions that you have gathered. For example, Sam may say that Dr. Jones is a great history instructor, she really knows her subject matter---Sam got an A in her class. However, when you talk with other students, you find out that Dr. Jones is disorganized in class, she is often late for her lectures, her examination questions seem like they were meant for graduate students, and she has a reputation for being hard on nonhistory majors who take her classes. Given all of your information, you can decide whether or not you want to take the class based on what you want to learn and what you have learned about Dr. Jones.

Academic Advisors

One of the first people that I would recommend for your network would be your academic advisor. She knows the requirements for your degree, something about some of the faculty members who will instruct you, and where to go on campus for assistance. Remember, however, your advisor will not really be a member of your network if you do not see

her! That means that you have to see her more than at just the required times that relate to a specific semester's enrollment. For advising appointments, it would also be a good idea to have studied your degree requirements and have a tentative schedule worked out before you get together with your advisor. If you are not comfortable with your assigned advisor, you usually have the option to select another if someone is available.

Student Organizations

I highly recommend that you join the student organization in your college major. I am particularly interested in getting you to use the advanced students in your department as guides or resources to success in your program. Ask these students questions like "Who is the best (or worst) instructor that you have had, and why?" "What is the best course that you have taken in the department and why do you rate it so highly?" You can also ask questions about the required sequence of courses, support classes that others have found useful, alternate ways of meeting departmental or college requirements, and who else you can talk to about a class or agency. When you are getting recommendations on classes, faculty, or jobs, remember to ask why each student recommended the class she did. The answers to the above questions will tell you a great deal of information that you can use to make up your own mind.

For ethnic minorities, women, and returning students, I highly recommend your being in contact with both student and campus organizations that are concerned with issues in those areas. Student organizations will have their own support network already established so that you can take advantage of the knowledge of those who came to campus before you. Campus support agencies will know of specific help that is available through the college and can assist you if you should have problems with faculty, staff, students, agencies, or regulations on campus. Both student organizations and campus agencies will know about faculty and staff who may be of special help to you and should be able to recommend classes and faculty members to take or, in some cases, to avoid.

For example, until recently there were very few women students in the fields of engineering and physics. A woman taking an advanced physics course could very well be the only woman in that class. A student group for women science students or women engineering students could provide both support and future classmates for other advanced courses. The group should also be able to give you information about empathic faculty, tutoring or self-help sessions.

Significant Others

Your network can also include people in your living arrangement (home, apartment, or residence hall), workplace, recreational activities, and special interest clubs---in essence, people who are important to you. Include faculty members whom you liked or learned a great deal from--- just drop in during their office hours to chat or ask questions. Chaplains, other religious leaders, and religious groups that are important to you should also be included in your personal network. Your employer and coworkers could also be incorporated in your network. Just about anyone from any group that you are interested in can be part of your personal team.

The Team Approach

Remember, when you get out of college and have a job, you will be part of a team. Very, very few adult workers function in isolation from other people. People work in teams to get their jobs done. When a problem arises, an employee will talk to her coworkers, her boss, her family, or her friends to get suggestions or help.

Recently, industry has been adopting the quality circle approach to improve its profits and the caliber of its products. Quality circles are groups of workers getting together to solve problems. In college you can create the same kind of support team to help you learn and experience all that you can or want.

Use the Network Work Sheet to list the members of your personal support team. As you study you team, are there any people or areas of expertise that you need to add to your network to make it stronger? You might want to share this work sheet with one or two of the members of your team to get their impression of your support team.

Name	Relationship/ Expertise
_____	
_____	
_____	
_____	
_____	
_____	

My Support Team

Campus Agencies

The mission of every college or university is basically the same---to help you improve your knowledge, skills and, in general, your education. Each college or university has its own structure or organizational pattern. However, most schools will have a variety of agencies designed to help you with specific problems or concerns. When you have a problem, use your campus catalog, your student handbook, your schedule of classes, or your support network to get to the office or agency that you need.

The most obvious way to find an office, of course, is to ask someone where it is. Just ask any faculty member, staff member, or student---they should be able to refer you to the right place even if you do not know the correct name of the agency. I will describe a few offices and why they can be important to you. The names of these offices on your campus may not be the same that I use, but they or their functions probably exist on your campus.

Academic Advisement

Academic advisors are there to help you select classes that will meet your campus degree requirements as well as to facilitate your formal education. Advisors will not usually select classes for you. Instead, they will help you choose the best courses from among the options that you have. This means that you have to have done some thinking about what you want from your education and what skills and competencies you need to learn for the academic goals that you have before you go to see your advisor.

Student Organizations

Many student organizations have offices on campus. Your

student handbook should give you specific information about each organization, its office location, and the name of the chief officers of the group. Those who participate in campus activities tend to be good resources because they are involved on campus.

The most important student organization for you will be the student group in your academic major. Third- and fourth-year students in that group can be a major source of information about campus resources and campus life in general.

Chaplains

Campus religious leaders are there for both religious and personal support. You can consider them ombudsman, that is, people who can help you with a wide variety of problems, from roommate hassles to relationship difficulties, financial concerns, and a wide variety of personal emergencies. Although finding a chaplain of your own religious persuasion may be your preference, I have never known any campus religious leader to refuse to help a student because of her religious beliefs. Chaplains who have been on campus for several years have learned a great deal about campus support agencies that they will share with you.

Human Relations/Equity Office

Discrimination on campus may take many different forms, from outright refusal to allow you to belong to an organization to much less subtle incidents such as not calling on you in class. No college will tolerate discrimination that is based on race, gender, marital status, nationality, political beliefs, religion, or age. If you get the feeling that you are not being treated as other students are and you think that you are a victim of discrimination, consult with a staff member of the human relations office.

Libraries

Everyone thinks about libraries as a place to study or as the place to go when you have a term paper to do. Libraries can also be a source of information on just about any topic of interest or concern to you. Suppose you are worried about how you will pay for the rest of your college education. You can, of course, go to the Financial Aid Office and apply for scholarships and grants. At the library, you will also find information about these funding sources. You can research alternative ways that other students have paid for their college education. There are articles about students who have started their own companies, unusual employment opportunities, stories about uncommon funding sources that other students have used successfully, and more.

Regardless of the cataloging system that your library uses, the best way to get information from a library is to consult with the reference librarian. She will know the library shortcuts to getting answers to questions that you may have. Ask her for help.

192

Other Campus Agencies

There are a wide variety of support agencies on your campus. A short list of those that have not been mentioned would include

Admissions/Registrations

Bursar/Cashiers Office

Career/Placement Center

Counseling Center

Commuter Services

Dining/Food Service

Disability Support Services

Financial Aid

Health Center

Housing/Residence Halls

Judicial Office

Legal Aid Office

Learning Skills Center

Minority Student Center

Orientation Office

Parking Office

Recreation Department

Returning Students Center

Student Activities Office

Student Publications Office

Student Union

Veterans Office

For specific information about these agencies on your campus, consult your student handbook or your college catalog.

Remember, all of these agencies, and others, are there to help you with your education or with living arrangements that you need to complete your degree. You are paying for the services that are offered. If you need the services that are offered by these offices, I urge you to make contact with them and ask for the help that you need.

Summary

The faculty, staff, and agencies at your college are there to serve you and to help you get the kind of education that you want. For you to get the most out of the services that are available to you at your campus, you need to be assertive and ask for help when you need it.

Create your own support network or team to help you master the maze of your college. As members of your team, include your academic advisor, faculty whose classes you have enjoyed, members of the student organization in your departmental major, and other significant people in your life such as your religious leader, your boss, and members of your family. Use your advisement team's advice to maximize what you get out of your college experience.

11 LEARN TO USE THE SYSTEM

A chapter about using the system in college in a study skills book might seem to be misplaced or unusual. It is. I am including this chapter so that you will have a better idea about how things happen in college and what you can do to get individual treatment, if you need it, to get through what I call "The Maze of College." Special treatment could involve such things as getting more time for tests, substituting courses in your degree program, appealing grades or policy decisions, getting special parking, taking sequential courses at the same time, etc. Topics in this chapter include

Advising
Calculation of grade point
    averages
Financial Aid
Unusual grades---I, W, NG, P/F,
    Audit
Academic honors
Credits versus quarter hours
Professorial ranks
Academic warning and
    dismissal
Departments and colleges
Sexual harassment
Discrimination
Security
The Student Right-To-Know and
    Campus Security Act

All of this information is part of the maze of college that you will be negotiating to earn your degree.

Grade Point Averages (GPA)

Why include the calculation of grade point averages, or GPAs, in a study skills book?

Because of the importance that people place on knowing your GPA! The fact that grade point averages do not accurately predict success on the job or success in life is not well known. However, the general public, and even people in education, tends to believe that the higher your grade point average, the more capable you are. For decades the field of higher education has been trying to prove that college makes a difference in people's lives. Very few studies can show that the four or more years that students spend in college make a significant difference in a person's life other than financially. College doesn't appreciably change our values, our political affiliation, or our basic beliefs. Average college students are just about as successful in life as those who were superior students in college.

Then why all the emphasis on grade point averages? I don't really know. I suppose it is because grade point averages are quantitative; they look as if they are measuring something important. Whatever the reason, grade point averages are used a lot of different ways, and, generally, the higher your GPA, the easier it is to get special treatment, job interviews, etc. Grade point average is also used for admission to graduate and professional school, for entry to selective or competitive majors, to determine whether you graduate or not, for academic status (honors, warning, and dismissal), and for earning and maintaining scholarships and grants.

The Four-Point System

Most colleges are on the four-point system. That is, when you calculate a grade point average, the highest grade, A, is worth four quality points per credit. (In the three-point system, the calculations are the same except an A is worth only three points. If you have a two-point system, an A is worth two points.) Quality points are only useful in the calculation of grade point average. The quality points for the grades in the four-point system are

A = 4 quality points per credit

B = 3 quality points per credit

C = 2 quality points per credit

D = 1 quality point per credit

F = 0 quality points per credit

Sample Grade Point Calculation

Subject	Credits	Grade	Quality points
English	3	B (3)	9
Math	4	C (2)	8
Tennis	1	D (1)	1
Chemistry	4	A (4)	16
Sociology	3	F (0)	0
Totals	15 credits		34 quality points

To get the grade point average, divide the total number of quality points by the number of credits that were attempted in which the grades of A, B, C, D, or F were earned.

$$\frac{34 \text{ quality points}}{15 \text{ credits attempted}} = 2.266 \text{ grade point average}$$

Note the effect of the F on the grade point average. The three-credit course that was failed added no quality points to the numerator (the upper part of the fraction), but it added three points to the denominator (the lower number of the fraction), thus reducing the final grade point average.

Unusual Grades

In addition to the five letter grades that are normally used in the calculation of grade point average, other grades exist. In most colleges, these grades do not calculate into your grade point average. However, your school may be an exception, so find out what your school's policy is. The unusual grades (I don't know what else to call them) include

Audit	Audit, no credit
I	Incomplete
NG or NGR	No Grade or No Grade Reported
P/F	Pass/Fail
S/U or S/F	Satisfactory/ Unsatisfactory or Satisfactory/ Fail
W	Withdraw

N/A   Not Applicable

X/F   Failure--Academic
                Dishonesty

Audit

When you audit a class you receive neither credit for the class nor a grade that will be used in the calculation of your grade point average. Usually that means that you do not have to attend class or complete any of the work that is normally assigned in that class. You take the class because you want to learn about the subject but do not want to do all the work that is assigned by the instructor.

Students audit classes for many different reasons including the following:

1. They want to learn about the subject but do not want to do all the work that is assigned or take the course examinations.

2. When a course is very difficult, some students audit the class the first time and then take it for credit after they have learned some of the material. They also get a good look at one of the course instructors and can decide whether they want to take him when they register for the class the next time.

3. Some people take all or most of their classes for audit simply because they are interested in improving their formal education but they do not want to get a college degree or be involved with

being graded by an instructor.

4. Auditing a class means that you have reserved a space in that class and that the class will be listed on your academic transcript. When you apply for a job or for graduate or professional school, people will want to see your academic transcript. They will see that you have audited classes, that you have learned things that go beyond the regular classes that you have taken.

Depending on the policy of your college, audited classes may cost you the same as regular grade option classes or, if you are a full-time student, they may be free. If you want to broaden your education but simply do not want to be pressured by course examinations, auditing a class may be a desirable option for you.

Incomplete

When you registered for your classes, you may have signed up for more work than you can handle. If, during the semester, you see that you will not be able to complete all the work that is required for a class in the time that is available to you, see the instructor of that class and ask for additional time to complete the assigned work. Incompletes have to be requested by the student. That is, instructors usually do not give you an I if you just stop going to class. They need to hear from you; to know that you want to complete the work but that you need additional time.

Just because you ask for an I does not mean that an instructor has to give it to you. Campus policy usually demands that you have a passing grade in the class and that you have completed at least half of the assigned work before your instructor can give you an I. Check your campus's policy to see what rules apply to you.

If you do get an I, remember that it is your responsibility to complete the work for the class. Your instructor has no obligation to remind you to get the work done. On some campuses, the I becomes a terminal I that cannot be completed after a certain period of time. On others, the I changes to an F after a set period of time. Still others have Incomplete Grade Contracts that your instructor fills out and both of you sign. A contract usually gives the completion date that you and your instructor have agreed to, the assignments to be completed, the grade that you will receive in the course if you complete the work, and the grade you will receive if you do not complete the rest of the specified work.

The most unusual story I have about I's is about a student who was getting B's and C's in all his classes. The student wanted to go to a professional school, medical school I think, and knew that his semester grades would hurt his chances for admission. He talked to all five of his instructors and was given I's in all five of his classes. Although it took him over a year to get all the work done, he earned A's in all five classes. His grade point average for that semester was a perfect 4.0!

If you find that you are running out of time and need an I, check your campus policy on I's before you talk to your instructor. Think about the amount of extra time that you need before your appointment. Ask him for an extension to a specific completion date. He'll know that you have given the matter some thought before seeing him and be more inclined to give you the I.

No Grade Reported

A no grade, NG, can mean at least two different things:

1. No grade was assigned to you because you did not complete any work in the course.

2. Your instructor did not get your grades in on time.

3. The instructor's grade sheet or electronic grade submission "got lost," misfiled or delayed in transmission.

If you get an NG, check with your instructor to find out what it means on your campus.

A few years ago I heard about a group of graduating seniors who had received an NG in a required course they needed to graduate. The problem wasn't discovered until several of these students showed up at the Dean's Office because their scheduled graduation had been denied. The instructor was called but he wasn't available. The department had no report of grades. Finally someone realized that the instructor left the country on a one-year sabbatical without turning in his grades. All the seniors who had expected to graduate were being denied graduation because a required class hadn't been completed! (The story does have a happy ending. The Dean assigned passing grades to everyone who was scheduled to graduate. When the instructor returned, grade changes were made to reflect the actual grade that the students had earned.)

Pass/Fail (P/F)

Many colleges allow you to choose your grading option for your classes from among the regular grade option (A through F), pass/fail, and audit. A few campuses only use the pass/fail option. A pass may mean that you had a grade of D or higher or a C or higher, depending on your campus policy. If your campus uses the regular grade option, the grade of P probably does not calculate into your grade point average. However, if you fail a pass/fail course, the F may calculate into your GPA.

Many students take classes pass/fail when they take non-required courses that are either difficult or in areas in which they lack an adequate academic background. The pass/fail option allows students to experiment with new subject areas without endangering their grade point average.

Although the pass/fail is a grade option that I highly

recommend, check on the specific rules about the option that are applicable on your campus before you use it.

Satisfactory/Fail (S/F)

The S/F grade option usually means that you do not have an option for how you are to be graded. Only the satisfactory/ fail or satisfactory/ unsatisfactory grade option is available to you. The S or satisfactory grade probably does not calculate into your GPA. The F, on the other hand, may go into your grade point average. Check on your campus to find out what the rule is.

Withdraw (W)

At times students enroll in more classes than they can realistically complete with satisfactory grades. Many campuses allow you to withdraw from a class with a grade of W 6, 8 or 10 weeks into the semester. The W does not affect your grade point average. If you have too much academic work to do and you know that you will not be able to get it all done with acceptable grades, see if you can use the W option. Note, however, that some campuses have a limit to the number of classes that you can withdraw from in a given semester.

The W differs from the I in that the W is a terminal or final grade. Therefore, before you drop a class, think about whether you could possibly complete the class if your instructor would allow you more time. If you could complete the class, consider requesting an I. If not, take the W and use your time and energy to successfully finish your other classes.

N/A

Some students who have earned a low grade in a course take an equivalent course at another school and then transfer the credits back to their own school. When they do, the low grade that was earned originally is still used in the grade point calculation even though the student successfully completed the course at another school. When you change majors, some of the courses that you took earlier may not be relevant to your new major. If the grades that you received in those classes were low, they continue to lower your grade point average. In these cases, many colleges mark the original grade n/a, not applicable. The n/a removes the original grade from the grade point calculation. The original grades, however, remain on your transcript. Low grades may also be declared not applicable if you have not attended college for more than five or ten years.

XF

If you are found guilty of cheating or some other form of academic dishonesty, your instructor, department, or college can award you an administrative grade such as XF that indicates that you received the grade because of academic dishonesty. The grade is administrative because it was not an evaluation of your performance in the class but rather the result of some judicial action. The F, however, may be used in the calculation of your grade point average. Note, the judicial results are then a part of your academic record.

Grade Changes

If you receive a grade in a class that is lower than you expected, check with your instructor to see if the grade is correct. Grades are usually correct. However, because your instructor is human, he may have made a mistake in either the calculation of your grade or in reporting the grade that you earned. If an error has been made, or if your instructor allows you to do some extra work to raise your grade, he can submit a grade change form to assign you a different grade. Because there usually is a time limit within which an instructor must make the grade change, if you see a possible mistake in your grades, see your instructor as soon as you can.

Appealing Your Grade

The grades that you receive in your classes usually cannot be appealed to a higher authority unless you can show that your grade was "arbitrary or capricious," that is, that you weren't graded fairly. Needless to say, it is very difficult to get a department head or dean to change your grade. (Some colleges have an appeal board that reviews grade appeals.) If you think you were graded unfairly, check to see what your campus's policy is on appealing grades. If you are concerned about your grade or whether the grading method is allowed under the grade appeal policy, first talk with your instructor. If you are not satisfied with his response, appeal the decision to the proper authority, usually the Department Chair or the College Dean.

Repeat Policy

Repeating a class that you have taken can affect your grade point average if you earn a different grade the second time that you take a class. How much your GPA will be affected depends on your school's repeat policy. Some schools average the two grades that you receive when you repeat a class, whereas others use the higher grade when you repeat a class. Before you repeat a class, find out what your school's policy is and how retaking a class will affect your grade point average.

Using Grade Point Information

Now that I have shown you the basic information about grades and grade point average calculation, let's see how you can use this information as you set up your strategy for the semester. The first fairly obvious point is that grades from courses in your major are usually more important to you than those from other classes. When you apply for a job, interviewers will often ask you what your grade point average is and what your GPA was in your major. Although each class may carry the same number of credits and therefore have the same effect on your overall GPA, courses in your major should normally get more attention.

Courses that have a higher number of credits have a greater effect on your grade point average than classes with fewer credits. Give classes with more credits extra study time to ensure a decent grade in the class.

At the end of the semester, when you are short of time, think about the effect each grade in each course will have on you. A four-credit A and a four-credit F will significantly affect your grade point average. If you have a class with six or more credits, make sure that you earn at least a B in the course; C's or lower could ruin your grade point average.

When you have taken on too much academic work, can you use an I instead of a W to reduce your workload? If you need to take a W, which class should you take it in? Remember, if you get a W in a required class, you will have to take it over again. If you must drop a difficult class that you will have to take again, do you have time to continue going to that class after you withdraw from it? Just going to the class should help you learn more, thus giving yourself a better chance next time.

Academic Honors

Most colleges have a variety of academic honors that they award for excellent academic work. Some of the most common include the Dean's List, summa cum laude, magna cum laude, and cum laude. These academic distinctions are based on your grade point average. The Dean's List is an honor that can be earned each semester. The others are honors that are earned at graduation. Your college catalog will have the specific information you will need to see if you qualify for these honors.

In addition to academic honors, most college campuses have honor societies. For details about the academic honors societies on your campus, check your college catalog or contact your Dean or Academic Provost's Office.

My concern about academic honors is to help you get the most out of your college experience. When you apply for a job or for graduate or professional school, academic honors may help you get the edge on your competition. You may be able to use time management strategies and efficient study skills to gain these honors. On the other hand, you may be able to use the idea of academic honors to motivate yourself to do better in your classes.

Remember, pure academic ability is only one part of earning academic honors. The most important part of earning academic honors is having good study skills and making time to do the necessary studying to learn the information and skills needed to earn your grades.

Academic Warning/Dismissal

The reverse of academic honors is dismissal from college because your work is not up to the level demanded by your faculty. In general, colleges warn you if you are not performing adequately. They use the terms academic warning or academic probation to give you time, usually one semester, to improve your academic work. That decision, and the decision to dismiss, will usually be based on your grade point average.

If you should end up on probation or warning, I urge you to contact your academic advisor to get his advice on what strategy to pursue to improve your status. Although the common sense notion of "work harder" may be applicable in some instances, knowing how your college's policies work and selecting appropriate courses are also part of most solutions.

Academic dismissal means that you are no longer able to take classes at the college. Your grade point average was too low and the college thinks that you will not be able to do college-level work in its classes.

Students get dismissed for a wide variety of reasons. Whereas some people may not have the ability to do college-level work, most of those that I have met who were dismissed could have handled the academic work. The two major causes of their academic dismissal were

1. Not getting sufficient studying done to pass their

examinations.

2. Circumstances beyond their control such as being sick for several weeks, a death in the family, an automobile accident, or being sent out of town by an employer.

Regardless of why you were dismissed, there is a procedure for getting reinstated into your college. Usually there is a petition to a reinstatement board to be completed. Questions that you must answer on the petition include your explanation for the problems that you had that led to your dismissal and what you have done or are planning to do to ensure adequate academic performance if you are reinstated. Most reinstatement boards want to see that you have learned from your dismissal and that you are taking some action---such as working with a counselor, advisor, or instructor---to become a better student.

If you are dismissed, do not be surprised if your college requires that you sit out a semester before they will allow you to return to classes. The time out from classes is aimed at allowing you time to consider your priorities and perhaps to learn some additional skills that will help you to work more successfully when you return to classes.

If you are dismissed, talk to an academic counselor, an advisor, or a learning skills specialist and develop a plan of action that will overcome the problems that you have had with performing at acceptable levels in your classes.

Credits vs. Quarter Hours

A credit means that you have been in class for one hour each week. Because most college classes meet for about three hours each week, most courses are worth three credits.

Some colleges, however, have a different system that uses the quarter hour. A quarter hour is equal to two thirds of a credit hour. If you take a class for three quarter hours and then transfer to a college that uses the credit hour system, your three quarter hours will equal only two credit hours (3 quarter hours x 2/3 = 2 credit hours).

Professorial Ranks

In the academic world, all instructors are not the same. The terms teacher, professor, Ph.D., lecturer, instructor, and teaching assistant (TA) have meanings that students usually do not understand.

Teacher

Teacher usually refers to an educator in elementary, middle, junior high, or senior high school. In most instances educators on college campuses are not referred to as teachers but rather as instructors or professors.

Professor

In college, the word professor carries at least two different meanings:

1. A general reference to the person who is in charge of the class, e.g., "My professor lectured about...."

2. The actual academic rank or status of the person (e.g., "My instructor is a full Professor.").

In the first case, professor is a casual, all-encompassing term meaning instructor. The formal term professor is more difficult to explain.

Professor is the highest of three professorial ranks that begin with assistant professor. An assistant professor is often someone who has recently completed his Ph.D. and is relatively new to teaching in higher education. Assistant professors usually have from five to seven years to either get promoted, permanently assigned to the rank of assistant professor, or terminated from the college. (The five- to seven-year period comes from the old apprenticeship that tradesmen such as carpenters and bakers were required to have before they were admitted to their guild or trade.)

After the rank of assistant professor comes the associate professor. Out of every 10 assistant professors, only about three or four will be promoted to associate professor. At universities, this promotion is heavily based on the assistant professor's research and grant productivity. Some people refer to the process as "publish or perish," meaning that if an assistant professor does not get his research work published in academic journals, he will not keep his job. At two- and four-year colleges, the promotion will be based on the assistant professor's teaching ability and his involvement in departmental or college committee work. In either case, the promotion is to the rank of Associate Professor.

As I mentioned before, the highest rank in the professorial system is professor. Only about one out of three associate professors will be promoted to professor. A professor has shown strong academic credentials for years. He is well respected by his academic peers. He is an authority in his field.

Instructor/Lecturer

Exact meanings for these two words are difficult to pin down. An instructor is often someone who is still working on his graduate education. Instructors can also be educators who do not have the graduate degrees that are needed for the professorial ranks.

Lecturers have the greatest variance in academic background. A lecturer could be someone who does not have any graduate work and perhaps even lacks an undergraduate degree. At the other extreme, a lecturer could be someone who has a Ph.D. and holds professorial rank at another college but is visiting or instructing at your school for some limited period of time.

Teaching Assistants

Teaching assistants, or TAs, are usually graduate students who have a job assisting an instructor or department with college-level teaching. Other teaching assistants have completed their graduate work but have taken on a job of helping the main instructor with the work of the classes--- grading papers and tests, and so forth. Sometimes a teaching assistant will be in charge of the class, whereas other times he is part of a team. Whatever the case, someone has responsibility for supervising his work. That is, the TA may be new to college teaching, but he usually has experienced faculty members available to assist him.

In addition to the term TA you may also see the term graduate assistant, or GA. A graduate assistant is basically the same as a teaching assistant. He is a graduate student who is working on his graduate degree while holding a job---his graduate assistantship. Teaching assistants are usually assigned to classroom responsibilities, whereas graduate assistants or research assistants have assignments outside of the regular classroom.

Departments and Colleges

The faculty members on your campus are grouped together in units that are usually called departments. The faculty in each department will come from all of the academic ranks that I have discussed. They are headed by a Department Chair who is responsible for the administration of the unit. The Department Chair can, in unusual circumstances, alter departmental requirements. For instance, if the department requires that you take a statistics class within the department, for a very good reason, the Chair might allow you to take an equal or more difficult course in another department or college. He usually will not actually change your grade in a course. Your grade is your instructor's responsibility. However, what the Department Chair can do about an instructor's grade is to discuss the problem with the instructor pointing out problems or issues that might be involved. He can recommend that the instructor reconsider your grade, but rarely will he actually change a grade.

Academic departments are grouped together in colleges that are headed by a Dean. The Dean is the chief administrator of the college and is responsible for everything that goes on in each of his departments. Problems that cannot be settled at the departmental level can be brought to the Dean's attention. Deans can also make changes in degree requirements if the situation warrants it.

When I was an undergraduate, I was required to take a calculus course. I asked my Dean to allow me to substitute a graduate class in statistics in place of the calculus course--- I was planning to go to graduate school, and the statistics course would clearly be useful. The calculus class, though easier, did not seem to be as practical to me. The Dean allowed the substitution.

Using the System

A bureaucracy is created to organize people and functions into an efficient system. A bureaucracy has rules, regulations, and procedures that have been established to take care of normal conditions in a relatively efficient manner. No one in the system has to think about what to do or how to do it. Procedures have already been established to deal with everyday concerns. Your campus is a bureaucracy that has been established to help you learn and get a college degree with a minimum of difficulty. Requirements have been established, classes are available, assignments have been made, before your arrival on campus.

The difficulty with a bureaucracy is that whenever something that is different comes along, it isn't always clear what should be done. The typical first response is often "But that's the way you have to do it." Some people call the procedure "stonewalling"; the system puts up a stone wall to stop attempts to get around normal procedure or policy.

If you need an exception to some policy or regulation, don't be afraid to challenge the system. The school, the system, is there to serve you. Gather information about the policy that you want to change so that you understand the intent of the policy. Next, gather together your thoughts and reasons for wanting an exception in a logical, coherent argument. Then start at the most logical place that comes to mind for dealing with your issue. Remember, however, to start at the bottom of the bureaucracy. A standard response to usual requests will often be "Have you spoken to....?" If you haven't spoken to that person or someone from that office, you'll be sent there to begin the appeal process.

The point to remember when you are dealing with "the system" is that everyone in the bureaucracy has a boss. The person you talk to first has a boss. His boss has a boss and that boss has a boss, and so forth. Just appeal your way up the ladder.

Let's say that you are in a major that requires a foreign language but you want to learn a language that your school doesn't offer. Talk to your advisor about how you should go about getting a waiver to take your foreign language classes at a different school. He will know what procedure you need to follow or he will be able to find out what the policy is.

When you make requests of the system, be sure that you keep a list of the people and offices that you talked with. If you are tracking down something on the telephone, write down the phone numbers, the offices that you call, and the names of the people that you talk with. When someone asks you why you are asking them your question, you can specify who referred you. Even if the referral is wrong, you have shown that you are responsible.

Remember to be pleasant yet assertive when you are dealing with people in the system. I remember working with one student who was very difficult to talk with. Some people would probably call him obnoxious. He had made his demands to several different people but no one would help him. Normally helpful people would not even refer him to the appropriate place to deal with his problem. His manner turned people against him.

If you need to fight the system, do so after you have gotten control of yourself and the situation. Most people in the service professions like to be helpful. Their job is to help you. Help them help you by "staying cool," even if the decision goes against you. Just remember to ask where and to whom you can appeal their decision.

Advising

Advisors are there to help you select courses that will meet your campus degree requirements. For an advisor to help you, you need to have done some thinking about what you want and need from your education. Perhaps a brief look at a "how not to do it" example will help. I was working with a student who seemed to have almost no motivation to study for any of his classes. When I asked him about his classes, I found out that he had four introductory lecture classes, the smallest of which was about 200

students, and English 101. None of the classes were particularly interesting to him. When I asked him why he took them, he said "My advisor said they would meet the general requirements." Selecting other classes that could have been of greater interest to him had never crossed his mind.

Before you see your advisor, think about yourself---your academic strengths and weaknesses, your work habits, the amount of time that you are willing to devote to your college education that semester, what you want from your college experiences, etc. Use that information to select classes that will meet both your needs and your degree requirements. Use your advisor to verify your choices or for advice on specific questions that you have come up with.

If you have located classes at another college that you want to build into your degree program, if independent study or an internship are of interest, if studying abroad sounds like an idea that you would like to pursue, ask your advisor how you can implement each idea. I know many academic advisors. They enjoy working with students who are involved in getting the best education they can. The hard cases for advisors are the students who come in and say "Tell me what to take."

Help yourself use your advisor to the fullest; think about what you want from your program and about the skills and knowledge that will help you get the most from your classes before you meet with him.

Financing College

Financing your education can be much more than simply getting money to pay for tuition and fees. Financial aid can have at least two different meanings that you can build into your college experience. The first, of course, is locating funds to pay for college. The second is the peripheral knowledge and skills that you can learn from your work that you use to finance part of your education.

Your campus Financial Aid Office will have most of the information that you will need to apply for federal aid. The basic form used by that office will also be used for scholarships and loan programs. They also have information about computer search companies that may be able to locate funding sources for you.

Other sources of financial aid can sometimes be created. Some students have found partial funding through state political representatives such as state delegates and senators. Others have found or created funding by contacting local fraternal and business organizations. Students have created small businesses to fund their education. Still others have gone to work for firms that have educational support programs that pay for college courses.

A personal work/study program can be created to earn a living while paying for part or all of your education. Think about the kinds of skills that you want to gain from having a job, and blend your employment with a four-, five- or six-year educational training program. For example, suppose you want to learn skills that will help you get a management position in a large corporation. If you take a job as a bank teller, you will

1. Get paid for working and can use some of your earnings to pay for college.

2. Have access to a training program that may include some funding for at least work-related classes.

3. Learn interpersonal skills from working directly with the public.

4. Get bonded and have extensive experience in working with large amounts of money.

Other work/study/learn possibilities include science majors and engineering students taking specialized positions with technical firms, art students looking for jobs at museums, music majors at concert halls, education majors at schools as substitute teachers or aides, and so forth. Many students even take full-time positions in practically any capacity at colleges and universities where tuition assistance may come as part of employment; they work full time and go to college part time.

Creativity is the key to creating a personal college finance program that combines earning money with work experience that will help you after you graduate. Strategize with your financial aid counselor to create the best possible program or plan for you.

Discrimination on Campus

In the best of all worlds, everyone would be treated equally and fairly. Unfortunately, that is not the case. Women and racial minorities are often discriminated against. Cases of reverse discrimination are also beginning to show up.

If something occurs to you on campus that leads you to believe that you have been treated differently because of your sex, race, religion, age, political beliefs, or marital status, there is an office on your campus to help you. The office may be called a Human Relations or Equity Office. In almost all cases, your concern will be handled confidentially, with no action being taken until you thoroughly understand the options that you have and what you would like to see done.

Confidentiality is important. If you bring a complaint against someone, there is a chance that they will retaliate by giving you a low grade, etc. The counselor in the Human Relations Office will listen to your complaint and let you know if the offense qualifies as d i s c r i m i n a t i o n. Confidentiality means that your contact with the office will not be made public unless or until you allow action to be taken.

Just because you may feel that you have been treated unfairly does not mean that you have been discriminated against. I remember one student coming to see me about a problem he was having with his instructor. He felt that the instructor was discriminating again him because of his race. After we talked for a while and the student explained a variety of situations that occurred in class, he began to realize that the instructor was not discriminating against him; the instructor was insensitive to all of the students in the class!

If you feel that you have been discriminated against, contact the appropriate office on your campus. Remember, your contact will be kept confidential until you decide to have some action taken because of the incident. Few institutions of higher education in this country will tolerate discrimination on their campuses. Your action will help eliminate unfair treatment of both yourself and others. Also, talking with someone will help you feel more in control and may give you options that you had not considered.

Sexual Harassment on Campus

As with discrimination on campus, sexual harassment also will not be tolerated on most campuses. Basically, sexual harassment means that unwanted sexual advances, comments, jokes, and contact have not been stopped after someone, usually a woman, has made it clear that the behavior is not desired or appreciated.

In the ideal world, the place to begin if you are being sexually harassed is with the person who is making you uncomfortable. You need to let that person know that his "attention" is not wanted and that future incidents will be reported. Ideally, the unwanted behavior stops, and that is the end of it.

In the real world, however, you may have difficulty in getting the message across. If the perpetrator is in a powerful position compared with yours, such as your boss or a faculty member, you may feel that you, your grades, or your job may suffer if you confront him. In that case, your best strategy will be to go to the Human Relations Office to talk with a staff member there. Your contact with that office should be confidential, but do remember to ask about confidentiality before you get into specifics and names. (Confidentiality means that your name will not be released, that is, your identity will not be revealed unless you allow it.)

Specific action by the Human Relations Office, such as calling the offender, will not be made without your expressed consent. The staff member should clarify your charges, explain to you the various actions that can be taken, and summarize the likely outcome of each alternative. For instance, suppose you feel that the incident was important to report but that you just wanted the offender notified that the incident was reported and that no other action would be taken.

In effect, a confidential file on the offender would be opened with the incident recorded. Should other incidents involving that same person be reported in the future, a case history would have been established. If several incidents occur over time, more serious action will probably be taken.

I read of one case in which an African American student reported an instructor for telling her that she would never be successful in her field because African Americans and women just weren't successful in that area. When the student reported the incident, all she wanted was to have that kind of behavior stopped. When the instructor was confronted, however, his comments about his intentions made the situation even worse. Eventually, the college terminated his contract, not because of the specific situation alone, but because of the likelihood that it would occur again.

Personal and Property Security

Personal and property security in a study skills text is extremely unusual. I include it because of the number of times that I have seen students' academic program disrupted because of thefts or threats to their personal well-being. If you keep yourself and your property safe, you can concentrate on your academic work.

<u>Property Security</u>

Colleges are an almost perfect

place to commit theft. Rooms and offices are often left open because of the trusting or naive nature of people on college campuses. Unknown persons walking a hall in a residence hall, fraternity, sorority, or even an office are often not questioned regardless of how out of place they may look simply because of the diverse people, dress, and behavior that are seen on campus on a regular basis.

Most campus theft is "open door theft." That is, the thief simply walked into the room through an open or unlocked door and stole what he wanted. Frequently, property is taken from public areas such as libraries, classrooms, and dining halls where students leave their belongings (books, purses, and bookbags) while they are tending to other things. Many times a person has been seen hanging around before the theft, but no one thought of reporting him.

One case that was reported in our campus paper seemed particularly appropriate for a college campus. Three men were seen beside the side of a residence hall along a busy walkway. One man stood while the second climbed onto his shoulders. The third climbed up over the other two, entered the open window, handed down the components of a stereo system, and then climbed back down. The three carried away their loot. No one reported the incident until the owner called the police several hours later to report the stereo system missing. Several witnesses came forward and explained what had happened. The crooks were never caught.

Textbooks and knapsacks are often the target for campus thieves. Don't leave them unattended, they'll disappear. Similarly, cars will disappear if you do not lock them. If you leave valuables in view when you go to class, you are inviting trouble. If you bring a bike to campus, be sure that you have a good lock and that you know how to secure your bike properly.

Security on campus should be the same that you would use going to any city. Keep your valuables locked up; lock your door when you leave; walk on lighted pathways; avoid walking by yourself when it is late at night; engrave your name and an identification number (your driver's license is one of the best to use) on large, valuable items; and don't carry large amounts of cash.

Don't lend your room or residence hall key to others or leave it in your mailbox. Also, don't give your PIN (personal identification number) from your bank account or your telephone credit card information to anyone. Other students may get your codes or keys and use them.

I recently heard about a student who had thousands of dollars of telephone calls charged to his account by a student who had learned his credit card number. Another student had money taken from his bank account by someone who learned his PIN.

You don't have to become paranoid to protect yourself and your property; you just have to use your head. Don't help dishonest people rip you off because you did not use reasonable security.

If you are concerned about property security on your campus, or would like to engrave some identification on your possessions, contact your campus police to learn how to protect your belongings.

Personal Security

In most instances, personal assaults on college campuses are much lower than in most other areas of the country. Robberies, murders, and physical assaults are uncommon on college campuses, though they do occur. The one notable exception to fewer threats to your physical person while on campus is probably date rape. Statistics on date rape suggest that about one in four women report that they were forced into unwanted sexual activity at least once in their lives. Women must learn to avoid situations in which they can become victims---being alone with dates too early in the relationship, drinking too much, not having your own available transportation, giving mixed messages, etc.

Men must learn that when a woman says "no," they had better take it as a "no" because increasing numbers of women are reporting offenders to either local or campus police. It is increasingly important for both men and women to communicate clearly with their partners, especially when sexual intimacy is involved. (For additional information concerning personal security on your campus, talk with a representative of your campus police.)

The Student Right-To-Know and Campus Security Act

This federal law states that students, parents, employees, and applicants to institutions of higher education have the right to know the crime statistics for every college campus in the country. More specifically, the federal Crime Awareness and Campus Security Act of 1990 which is part of the Student Right-To-Know and Security Act requires that "beginning September 1, 1992, and each year there after..." institutions of higher education that receive aid from the United States government "publish, and distribute, through appropriate publications or mailings, to all current students and employees, and to any applicant for enrollment or employment upon request, an annual security report containing at least:

1. Statistics concerning the occurrence on campus, during the most recent school year, and during the two preceding school years for which data are available, of the following criminal offenses reported to campus security authorities or local police agencies:

    (i) murder;

    (ii) rape;

(iii) robbery;

(iv) aggravated assault;

(v) burglary

(vi) motor vehicle theft.

2. Statistics concerning the number of arrests for the following crimes occurring on campus:

(i) liquor law violations;

(ii) drug abuse violations;

(iii) weapons possessions.

If you are concerned about your safety on campus and want to know what your campus crime rate is, just ask your campus admissions office or police department for the information. Your campus must make this information available to you.

Summary

In this chapter I provided some basic information about important parts of the academic community. I discussed college grades and the calculation of grade point average to help you understand one of the basic concepts on which you will be evaluated both on campus and when you are applying for employment. I presented instructor ranks so that you can understand the academic status of the people who are teaching and advising you. I provided information about discrimination, sexual harassment, and security to help you remember that though you will be dealing with good people in a fairly protected environment, things can go wrong, and you may have to protect yourself.

Use the system to both protect yourself and to get the best education that you can from your experiences at college.

12 EARNING CREDITS AND DEGREES

When colleges were first started in this country, degree requirements consisted of demonstrating to the rector, or the chief administrator of the college, that you had mastered all of the information that your faculty expected you to know. If the college rector felt that you had earned a degree, he would grant it to you. If, however, you hadn't learned enough, or if you had violated a college rule or gotten into difficulty with one of the staff, you could be dismissed.

When you went to another college, you would have to start again from the beginning. If you didn't like the school or faculty and decided to leave that school and went to another college, you also started all over again. For example, if you went to William and Mary for three years and then left to go to Harvard, at Harvard you would start again from the beginning, almost as if you had never been to college before.

Credits didn't exist, only college degrees existed. You completed your entire degree at just one school. When the rector felt that you had learned enough, you earned your college degree. Even if you had been in school for five or six years, if the rector felt that you had not learned enough, he could decide that you would not get a degree regardless of how hard you had worked or what other college faculty said. You either earned a college degree or you left without it, without any credentials that you could take to another college.

About 100 years ago, higher education created the Carnegie Unit, which you know as the credit. A credit refers to the number of hours of classroom instruction that you have. One credit means that a class meets for one hour a week for a semester. Now when you change colleges, your classes may transfer with you. When you finally collect between 120 and 128 credits in the right subjects, you probably have earned a college degree.

College degrees today are broken down into requirements that usually include general school requirements, a major, possibly a minor, and elective courses that you decide to take.

Accreditation

In many, if not most, countries, education is coordinated and controlled by the national government. The national Department of Education controls the content and the quality of elementary and secondary schools as well as higher education. In this country, the founders separated public education from the central government. When higher education began in this country, the federal government was also kept from gaining control. Community boards of trustees controlled each college.

Without a central governing body, colleges had no way of

knowing the quality of higher education throughout the country. To establish quality control, accreditation agencies were created to evaluate the caliber of each college. Colleges and universities voluntarily belong to their regional accreditation board. (The country is divided into six accreditation regions.) Every five years, the quality of every member college is reviewed by an accreditation team. Input on the excellence of that college and its programs are sought from students, faculty, staff, administrators, graduates, community employers, and other institutions of higher education.

Most colleges are accredited. However, new schools and those schools that have either been denied accreditation or never applied for accreditation can present problems for students. I recently worked with a student who had supposedly completed almost two years of college course work. When she attempted to transfer those credits, she found that none of the credits would transfer to her new school because the original college had not been accredited.

If you are intending to earn a bachelor's degree, be sure that the college you are attending is accredited---they'll give you that information in the first few pages of their catalog. If you cannot find accreditation information, ask about it at any campus office.

If you have taken courses from a school that you later discover is not accredited, do not despair. You may be able to use the information that you learned in those classes as the basis for credit by examination or as part of your experiential learning credit portfolio. For details about both options, read those sections of this chapter.

Degree Requirements

Generally speaking, most American colleges have a core set of classes in the liberal arts, mathematics, and sciences that all students must take. Different schools call these required courses by different names, but the idea is basically the same. These courses include knowledge that all college students should know.

The general requirements often include at least one English class on writing, one or two history classes, science classes, a mathematics course, a course in art and/or music, a social sciences class, perhaps a philosophy or literature class, and possibly one or two classes in foreign languages.

<u>Degrees</u>

College degree programs are generally divided into two- and four-year categories. Two-year degree programs (60 credits) lead to Associate degrees, whereas four-year programs (120 credits) lead to Bachelor's degrees. Both the Associate and Bachelor's degree programs can be either in arts or sciences. The Associate of Arts (A.A.) and Bachelor of Arts (B.A.) degrees usually have a foreign language requirement. The Associate of Science (A.S.) and the Bachelor of Science (B.S.) degree programs generally do not require a foreign language but may have additional mathematics or science course requirements.

For most people the distinction between these degree programs comes down to whether you have a two- or a four-year degree. There is, however, a difference between going to college for two years and earning an Associate degree: the Associate degree indicates completion of a planned program of approved course work. Similarly, four years of college and a Bachelor's degree are not the same: the Bachelor's degree indicates completion of a structured degree program. Additional degrees such as a Bachelor of Independent Studies are also available. However, the basic distinction for you to focus on is the two- or four-year degree program difference.

Because most students who begin college do not complete their bachelor's degree in four years, with many students leaving school only to return years later, it would be a good idea to earn an Associate degree on the way to your Bachelor's degree. If you should need to leave school before you complete your four-year degree, the completed Associate degree may give you a slight edge in the employment market.

Major

The major you select determines the area in which most of your courses will be taken. The faculty members of the department in which you major have probably listed a number of courses in their area along with some supporting courses from other departments that all students in that major must take. In addition, your major area requirement will often give you a number of different class choices, that is, choose either class A or class B. Finally, your major will usually have some elective classes that you may select from all of the remaining classes in your department. In essence, your major is an area of concentration for your college study. It will focus your study on a limited academic area.

Just because you decide to major in a specific area does not mean that you cannot have interests in other areas. Your major also does not mean that you are committed to working in that area. All your major means is that you have decided to focus a portion of your college classes on studying that topic. For example, many people choose to study in an academic area like art, history, sociology, or literature, but they work in the business world to earn a living.

Changing Your Major

Although your major is important because it controls a large number of classes that you will be required to take, it is not as crucial to your career as many people think it is. Less than 50 percent of the people who graduate from college actually work in the field in which they majored. At the University of Maryland at College Park where I work, almost 80 percent of the students change their major at least once before they graduate. If those two figures are combined (the percentage of students who work in their major field and the percentage who change majors), it turns out that the odds of your working in the field in which you first major are one to nine. Put another way, after graduation only 1 or 2 students out of every 10 work in the area in which they first majored when they started college!

What I am saying is that college majors don't make or break you. What is important is the quality of your education and that you learn the skills and knowledge that you need for whatever it is that you want to do.

Let's look at some examples to show you what I mean. In the "good old days," if you applied to a Masters in Business Administration (MBA) program, you were usually expected to have had a degree in business. Now, the admissions requirement tends to be 30 credits in business and a good grade point average. I recently met a student who had an undergraduate major in nursing. She was admitted to the MBA program and graduated with a 4.0 (straight A's) in a 60-credit program, which made her the top in her program. Note, she competed against students who had majored in business

even though her undergraduate major had been nursing.

Can you get a job as an administrator in a bank with a degree in English? Engineering? Art? Psychology? Business? The answer to all those questions is yes, as long as you have the skills that the bank wants you to have or if you can show them that you can rapidly learn the skills that you will need on the job.

Now, should you change your major? Yes, if changing your major will help you get more of what you want from college. Before you change majors, however, find out what the change will mean in terms of how long it will take you to complete your degree and how the change will affect your grade point average. Sometimes when you change majors, you end up in a position that will significantly lengthen the time it will take you to complete your degree program---courses you may have taken may not apply to your new major or there may be additional course requirements that you will have to take for a new major. Even if a change may initially look like it will keep you in college longer, it really may not. Read "Credit by Examination on Campus" in this chapter for an example of a student who changed his major at the beginning of his senior year and still graduated on time.

Because most students change majors while they are in college, changing your major really is no big deal. Just remember, before you change, be sure that you understand what the change will mean regarding the classes that you will have to take and the impact that the change will have on the length of time you will need to complete the new degree. Staying with the old major and taking elective courses in the area to which you'd like to change may allow you to finish sooner than changing your major.

Changing Major and Your Grade Point Average

A change in major could significantly affect your grade point average (GPA). Many schools have an academic clemency policy that allows you to drop the grades you received from courses that the new major does not require. For instance, if you were an engineering student who had D's and F's in several upper level math and engineering classes, if you change your major to business, for example, the grades from all classes in math and engineering might be dropped from the calculation of your grade point average or selected grades might be dropped, depending on campus policy. Note, however, the grades will still remain on your college transcript. Note also, if you had taken five classes in engineering and had one A and the rest were D's and F's, you could lose credit and the grade from all five of those classes, even the course in which you had earned an A. Your calculated grade point average would, at the same time, go up, because the D's and F's no longer pull down your GPA.

If you make a significant change in majors and have low grades in your old major, talk to your advisor about the possibility of getting academic clemency.

Minor

A minor is similar to a major; it just has fewer courses required. Minors usually do not have specific required classes, just a requirement that you have approximately 12 or more credits in one academic concentration. You can use a minor to support your major or as an area of interest like a hobby. Minors can also be used as "mini majors" that focus on the world of work. A literature major, for instance, could minor in business administration to have sufficient background in business to interest potential employers.

Electives

Electives can be just about any courses that you want to take. That is, any course that your college offers can fit into your degree program as an elective.

You can, of course, just take classes because they interest you, because they are easy, or because they are offered at a convenient time, etc. I would urge you, however, to think about a strategy for your electives before you take them. Three different strategies come to mind:

1. Select classes to produce competencies and knowledge in selected areas of interest.

Those areas could be:

<u>Hobbies</u> If you have an interest in an area such as literature, painting, music, computers, Africa, China, history, etc., you could select your classes in that area to formally learn more about that field.

<u>Broaden Your Education</u> Take classes in areas that are not required in your general education classes but would broaden your education. You could study a foreign language, other cultures, philosophy, history, government, astronomy, mathematics, etc. In essence, you could broaden your general knowledge in areas of study based on what you think your college education should be.

<u>Work Skills</u> Employers are interested in hiring people who have both the qualifications that are needed for the job and people who have skills that go beyond what I call "the expected." Take classes in subjects that would be of interest to employers in your field or that would give you skills that you know you will need on the job such as applied computer courses.

2.   Focus your electives on building course concentrations or "mini majors" that have special interest to you but that are not, for some reason,

an area that you want to major in. Take three or four courses in one area to develop more in-depth skills and knowledge. If, for instance, you love music, why not take several classes in the Music Department to study those areas that are of particular interest? If you enjoyed science classes in high school but chose not to major in one of those fields, why not take a collection of science classes that interest you? Many students are using collections of classes to study African-American studies, the role of women, great literature, history, foreign languages, and so forth.

In the work world, probably the most important skill that most employers want is the ability to write well, so take several courses to build your writing skills.

A.   Solid skills in the use of computers is an asset in almost any field.

B.   The ability to speak well in front of groups or the general public is valued in practically any job.

C.   Foreign languages are increasingly important in the business world.

D.   Knowledge of human diversity and different cultures is increasingly important in the modern world.

E.   Mathematical, statistical, and logical analyses are valued in almost every field.

In essence, think about the skills that a prospective employer would be interested in or areas of knowledge that you would like to know more about and create a collection of courses that produces the knowledge and skills that you want to learn at the level that you want to know them.

3.   Use your electives to create a second major. Most schools will allow you to have a double major or to work on two different degrees at the same time. For instance, you could work on a major in mathematics and physics at the same time. The electives in your math major could be required courses in your physics major and the electives in your physics major could be requirements in your mathematics major. You could tie just about any two major programs together to create a set of skills that would make you unique in the job market.

Two majors can usually be completed in about the same time that a single degree can be finished. Usually a double degree will take more time and credits to complete than a single degree. For example, a double degree such as a Bachelor of Arts in Music and a Bachelor of Science in Engineering will usually require about 150 credits.

The advantage of both of these strategies is that you show that you know enough to be able to create the program and that you have the personal characteristics or strength to complete both programs. You also have expertise in two different academic areas.

In most degree programs, the college and the academic department have created a structure that allows the institution to control some of the classes that you take for your degree. At the same time, you have some freedom to tailor that degree to your special needs. So, think about what you want from college. Then plan a degree program that gets you the education that you want.

Ways of Earning Credits

The most obvious way to earn college credits is to take college courses. For years that was just about the only way that you could get credit. However, as alternate forms of education became popular (noncredit classes at work or in the military, on-the-job training, and independent or personal self-study, etc.), colleges began acknowledging that you could learn college-level material without being inside an actual classroom. Whether you are 18, 50, or older, younger, or somewhere in between, you probably ought to take a look at the variety of ways that you can improve your education while gaining academic credit that will apply to your college degree.

Not all of the alternatives listed will be available to you at your college, and I have not, by any means, covered all of the alternative ways of earning college credit. What I hope you will gain from this

220

section is the realization that there are a wide variety of ways of gaining both an education and college credit.

In creating your degree program, you are limited more by what you do not know about options for earning credit than you are by your college or degree program. Pick and choose among the options that are available to you at your school to get the kind and quality of education that you want.

When I was in college, I heard about the concept "the junior year abroad." I knew it meant that students could go to Europe and study and apply the experience toward their college degree. I thought that the option was available to only "rich kids" and that it wasn't an option for me. It was! All or most of these options <u>are</u> available to you. Think about which ones are important to you and your education. Then try to develop a strategy that will get you the options that you want.

Let's return to my example. Although I knew about the availability of studying in a foreign country, I figured that I couldn't afford to go. Little did I know that there were some financial aid packages available that I might have made use of "if I had only known" they existed. First learn the options that are available to you; then strategize on how you can make your selection a reality.

Transfer Credit

You do know that there are other colleges that offer college credit besides the school that you are attending, don't you? Of course you do. Sometimes it can be a good idea to take classes at another school and transfer those credits to your school. For instance, if you are concerned with the cost of your education, you could begin by taking classes at a community college and transferring those classes to your four-year college. Before you take classes at the community college, check with your four-year college to see if they will accept the credits that you plan to take.

Sometimes there are restrictions on the classes that you can "bring with you" to the new school. For instance, four-year colleges will often restrict you to no more than 60 credits from a junior or community college. If you take more than 60 credits, they simply will not transfer. You'll have the education but not the degree credit.

If you are a student attending a college that is a long way from home, taking summer classes at your school could be inconvenient if you had planned to be home for the summer. Adults who are working could receive a temporary work assignment a long way from their home. Students heading to vacation jobs at the beach or other tourist locations often cannot take classes at their schools during the summer. In each case, it could be possible for you to arrange to take classes at a college near where you will be and transfer those credits back to your school.

Again, be sure the credits will transfer before you take the classes. Dean's Offices like to be in on the planning of any unusual or deviant plan to gain credit. Often, and perhaps usually, you can arrange for the credit to transfer even if you did not go through the Dean's Office first; it just may be a little more difficult.

Another reason for looking at transfer credit could be the programs and faculty at other local institutions that may be offering courses that are not available to you at your school. You can get permission to take selected classes at other schools and have them transfer to your program even if the specific classes do not exist at your school. Go through your Dean's Office to learn how to go about the process of having the courses accepted at your college.

Some areas that have several colleges have formed a consortium or association that allows students to take classes at another member school as long as the class is not offered by the home college. In the Washington, DC area, the organization is called The Consortium of Universities of the Washington Metropolitan Area. In general, students pay their tuition at their own college but can take classes at other area schools. There are, of course, specific rules for

these arrangements, so read the fine print before you register. If a similar program is available to you, why not check it out? You may find that there is a much larger variety of classes available to you than you thought.

National Exchange Program

The National Exchange Program allows students at member colleges the opportunity to study at over 100 different public colleges and universities in the United States, including Alaska and Hawaii, as well as in colleges in territories of the United States. International options at universities around the world are also available through the Exchange.

To participate in the program, students pay the tuition and fees charged by their college for the semester or year of the exchange or the in-state (resident) fee charged by the host college, depending on the arrangement established by your school. Room and board are charged at the host school rate.

The exact conditions for an exchange are established by each member school and are summarized in a booklet published by the National Exchange. The information booklet describes campuses that are members of the exchange, including material about the majors that are available, the size of the campus, the location of the college, costs, the ethnic diversity of each campus, and the limitations, if any, for the exchange program on that campus. (A few years ago I worked with a student who did an exchange with the University of Hawaii. While we were shoveling snow, she was in Hawaii!)

For information about the National Exchange Program, check first with your registration office or write

National Student Exchange
State University College at Buffalo
1300 Elmwood Avenue
Cleveland Hall, Room 417
Buffalo, New York 14222

Telephone: (716) 878-4328.
Fax: (716) 878-3054.

Semester at Sea

The University of Pittsburgh offers what sounds like an exciting program: a semester sailing around the world for academic credit! When I first heard of the program, I thought that someone was pulling my leg. The program does exist.

The S.S. Universe is the campus of the Semester at Sea, a campus of approximately 500 students. All students must enroll in the core course, International Studies 100, an overview of the countries and cultures that will be visited during the semester. The remaining courses are selected from among 40 or 50 classes that are offered each semester. Although the itinerary for each semester varies, the Fall 1992 voyage will give you an idea of what to expect. Ports of call for that semester include Vancouver, British Columbia; Kobe, Japan; Keelung, Taiwan;

Hong Kong, China; Panang, Malaysia; Madras, India; Odessa, Russia; Istanbul, Turkey; Cadiz, Spain; La Guaira, Venezuela; and New Orleans, Louisiana.

For a catalog and additional information about the Semester at Sea program, write

Semester at Sea
University of Pittsburgh
811 William Pitt Union
Pittsburgh, Pennsylvania 15260

Telephone: (800) 854-0195.

In Pennsylvania: (412) 648-7490.

Independent Study

Most of the courses that students take in college are designed and delivered by faculty members. Independent study is the option that allows you, the student, to implement a course that you design. Basically, independent study is an experience that you create. You take an area or subject that interests you and study it. All you have to do is find a faculty member to supervise your work.

Often, you will find that your department has independent study as a course offering in the catalog with course numbers like 389, 399, 489, or 499. When you have determined your topic, you will need to identify a faculty member to supervise your work. Each faculty member has her own standards as to what she will require for the credits you receive for your project. Usually you will have to write a paper, like a term paper, that summarizes the information that you learned from the experience that you create.

When I supervise independent study contracts with students, I require three hours of work each week for each credit taken. Students registering for three credits are therefore expected to work at least nine hours each week on their independent project.

If you are planful in your independent study, you can create a paper or document for the project that you can show prospective employers. Your work can show that you are willing to go beyond the expected, to work on your own to learn and do things that you wanted to know more about.

Internships

An internship is a hands-on experience outside of the normal college classroom. Interns earn academic credit and gain experience applying their collegiate knowledge on the job. Internships give students an opportunity to integrate the theoretical learning that they have had in the classroom with the practical experiences they gain working at a job in their chosen field. An internship gives you an opportunity to learn practical information and skills through day-to-day experience at work.

The best time to get an internship is during your junior year. At this point in your academic career you have enough knowledge to be of some

value to an employer. You are also at a point that practical knowledge can help you select your final college courses. That is, your work experiences might cause you to rethink the courses that you were planning to take to complete your degree.

For an internship, you need both an internship placement and a faculty member to supervise your work. Some agency on your campus coordinates internship programs and placements. It could be an experiential learning office, a career development office, a student services agency, or an academic dean's office. Your advisor should be able to refer you to the appropriate agency.

On the other hand, you can also find or create your own internship placement. Think about the kind of work that you want to get, the kinds of experience that you want to have, and then think about the type of business that would give you what you want. Talk to a manager in the company that you select about your interest and see if she or any other member of the company would be interested in supervising you.

The faculty member you select to be your academic supervisor can be either an instructor you have had in one of your classes or someone who is interested in the type of experience that you are planning to have. Remember that different faculty members will have different expectations for the academic side of your internship. Some faculty members will expect an in-depth paper about your experiences, others will only expect a short paper and log, whereas others may only want you to give them a verbal report about your experiences and your learnings.

Remember, you can receive both academic credit for an internship and a salary. That's right. You may be able to get paid for the same work for which you receive academic credit. Plan carefully.

One of my favorite stories about internships occurred about 15 years ago. The student was a 38-year old woman who was an accounting student with a 3.4 grade point average. The student, I'll call her June, wanted to get a job with one of the big eight accounting firms. (In the field of accounting, there were eight large firms that dominated the national accounting field. Today there are only six.) When June talked to her advisor about her goals, she was told that it was very unlikely that she would ever be hired by a big eight firm because (1) she only had a 3.4 grade point average and the firms she was interested in seemed to want recruits with extremely high grade point averages, perhaps in the 3.8 range; (2) the firms that June was interested in were seen as mostly interested in males who were in the 22- to 25-year old age range; and (3) the big eight accounting firms appeared to be most interested in having male employees, and June was clearly not a male.

When I heard the story, I suggested that June investigate an internship, preferably with the Internal Revenue Service (IRS). After all, accountants are working against paying unnecessary taxes to the IRS. June liked the idea and tried to get the internship cleared through her advisor. "That's not the way we work" she was told, "we don't recommend internships for our students." Because the only possible option to reach her goal was the internship, June went to the IRS to find out about their internship program.

IRS didn't have an internship program, but they referred her to the Government Accounting Office (GAO). The GAO had an internship program and offered June an internship that started in their auditing department. June had an excellent internship experience; she learned a great deal, and she received excellent recommendations from her supervisors.

Six months after June completed her internship, she entered the job market. She applied to several big eight accounting firms as well as to other accounting companies. In mid February, I received a phone call from June saying that she had been offered a position with one of the big eight accounting firms. Two days later, June called again to say that she had turned down the job offer! I couldn't believe my ears! It turned out that the firm across the hall from the first company, also a big eight accounting company, had offered June $2,000 more starting pay and a middle management training program, which she gladly accepted.

The opening for June had been her superb performance on her internship coupled with an excellent academic record. Use an internship or a cooperative education experience to create credentials that will help you get the job offers that you want.

Co-ops

Cooperative education, or co-ops, are very similar to internships, only they are usually longer and more intensive. Often co-op students work full-time for an entire semester for their co-op experience. Some programs will alternate semesters of attending college classes with semesters of full-time work. Other cooperative education arrangements may entail part-time work and academic credit over a number of semesters.

As with internships you will have to find an employer who will allow you to create a co-op experience. In contrast to the internship experience, most cooperative education experiences are for pay. Thus, your co-op program can be both a part of your educational program as well as part of your financial planning program. The same office that handles internships at your campus probably handles the campus Cooperative Education Program, so if you are interested in co-ops, start there.

A couple of points of possible concern in many cooperative education programs are the requirements that your campus may have for you to qualify for a co-op experience. Most programs will require you to have some kind of advanced standing such as junior class standing. They may also require you to have a grade point average of 2.0 or higher before you can qualify for a co-op placement. Both requirements, advanced standing and the grade point requirement, are there to ensure that you have an academic background that will assist you in benefiting from the experiential learning experience.

Remember, too, that when you have either an internship or a cooperative education experience, at least two people will get to know the quality of your work from the supervisory standpoint--your employer and your faculty advisor. Both of those supervisors should be excellent references for you to use when it comes time to look for employment.

Experiential Learning Credit

Basically, the idea behind experiential learning credit is, if you can earn credit from internships and co-op placements, why can't you go back in time and get college credit for learning that has taken place without faculty supervision?

In experiential learning programs, credit can be earned for college-level equivalent learning that has taken place outside of the classroom. Older students returning to college may find that they can earn between 30 and 45 credits for just showing what they have learned while they have been out of school. The learning could have been "on the job" or learning that has come from participation in volunteer work, hobbies, outside reading, etc.

Experiential learning students create a portfolio or report that summarizes the experiences they have had and what they have learned from those experiences. The credit is given for the learning that has occurred, not for the experience itself. For example, one of the students I taught in an experiential learning class had been very active in politics and had held a local elected office for several terms. She had 8 or 10 years of experience in local and state government. Do you suppose that what she learned was equivalent, or perhaps superior, to the information that students would have learned in a course on local and state government? The student wrote about how local government works, how legislation really gets passed, the difference between "politics" and administration in local government, etc. The faculty evaluator who reviewed her work gave her credit for her knowledge that was similar to what students would have learned in regular government and politics classes.

Other students I have worked with have gained college credit for their college-level learning that was gained working with computers; managing their own business; working in the business world;

studying art, music, dance, and woodwork; writing reports, proposals, and technical papers; conducting training programs; making oral presentations; conducting volunteer programs; etc.

The Council for the Advancement of Experiential Learning (CAEL) has written a publication Opportunities for College Credit which reviews credit for experiential learning programs across the country. You can contact CAEL at

Council for the Advancement of Experiential Learning
10840 Little Patuxent Parkway
Suite 203
Columbia, Maryland 21044

Credit by Examination

Regular college classes include reading assignments, lectures, discussions, writing papers or lab reports, and course examinations. As older and more experienced students began to return to college, they often asked why they couldn't just take a test to show that they had mastered course content without ever having taken the actual class. Today there are at least four different methods of earning college credit by simply taking an examination on which you show your knowledge. With some of the options, you only receive credit for the course; with the on-campus option, you may be able to receive both credit and a grade for passing the examination.

On-Campus Credit by Examination

Many, if not most, colleges have a system in which students can earn credit for courses that are taught in that school by taking a departmental course examination. The examination is aimed at finding out whether you really know the course content, that is, the basic information that is usually covered by that class. The examination does not assume that you have been in the actual classroom with the instructor who is teaching the class. That is, if Professor Smith is teaching the general introductory psychology course, you do not have to know the specific information that she teaches in her class. You do, however, have to demonstrate that you have mastered the information and concepts that are usually taught in a general psychology course.

Several years ago, a student I knew decided to study calculus on her own. She bought the textbook that was used in the course and studied it "at pool side." Her boyfriend tutored her when she needed help. She passed the two calculus courses with A's. The two four-credit A's are on her transcript and are calculated into her grade point average.

A second student decided that she really disliked her major at the end of her junior year. She wanted to change her major but was advised not to because she had never taken a class in the department that she wanted. There were eight required courses in the new major and several had to be taken in a sequence that could not be completed in one year. Over the summer the student studied the texts for the first two classes in her new department. When she arrived on campus in the fall, she passed the two classes by taking an examination. The department head allowed her to concurrently enroll in two classes that were usually taken in sequence. In addition, she took a third unrelated required class, bringing her total in the department to five.

Over the Christmas break, the student studied another class on her own, taking the course examination when she returned for the spring semester. During the spring semester, she took the final four classes that she needed to graduate in the major. She graduated on time with the degree and major that she wanted because she used the credit by examination option.

CLEP

The College Level Examination Program (CLEP) is a standardized national credit by examination program that is produced by College Board Publications. The program has five general examinations that cover English composition, humanities, mathematics, natural sciences, and social sciences and history, as well as approximately 30 specific area examinations such as general psychology, introductory sociology, American literature, college algebra, general biology and general chemistry.

CLEP tests are given at testing centers across the country.

After taking the CLEP test you receive a numerical grade, such as 52, in a specific subject area test. The score has no meaning until you check with your campus to see what the passing score is on that campus for that subject area examination. One campus could set passing at 50, whereas another could set it at 55. If you should transfer campuses, the "cutting or passing score" at your new college is the one that counts. That, of course, means that you could have credit at one school for your CLEP score but lose it when you transfer to another school that requires a higher score.

For additional information about the College Level Examination Program and the location of local testing centers, write

CLEP
P.O. Box 6601
Princeton, N. J. 08541-6601

Telephone: (215) 750-8420.

Because each college sets its own standards for receiving CLEP credit, be sure to check with your advisor about your campus's passing scores and policy before you take any of the tests.

Dantes

The Dantes Program began shortly after World War II to provide military personnel with a method of obtaining college credit for knowledge that they had gained through nontraditional experiences. The Dantes Program (Defense Activity for Nontraditional Education Support Program) was expanded to include nonmilitary students in 1983. The current program offers credit by examination for 50 different academic courses such as geography, criminal justice, astronomy, principles of real estate, introduction to business, personnel/human resource management and principles of public speaking. Study guides are available for each Dantes examination.

For additional information about the Dantes examination program, write

The Dantes Program
Educational Testing Service
Princeton, New Jersey 08541

Telephone: (609) 951-6264.

Before you sign up to take any of the Dantes examinations, be sure that your campus accepts Dantes credit.

ACT-PEP

The American College Testing--Proficiency Examination Program (ACT-PEP) has 42 college-level proficiency examinations in areas of business, education, nursing, arts, and sciences. A numerical score is earned on the examination, which colleges then use to determine whether credit will be awarded or not. Each school sets its own passing score. The credit is awarded by the college, not by ACT-PEP.

A study guide is available for each ACT-PEP examination, which contains a detailed outline of the content that will be covered by the exam, a bibliography of textbooks that could be used in preparation for the exam and a section on sample questions and answers that show typical items that can be found on the actual examination.

For additional information about the ACT-PEP, write

ACT-PEP
American College Testing
2201 North Dodge Street
P.O. Box 168
Iowa City, Iowa 52243

Telephone: (319) 337-1387.

As with the other credit by examination programs, be sure to check with your college to see if they will award credit through ACT-PEP examinations before you register for any exam.

Military/Business Course Credit

Students who have taken noncredit classes in the military, through their employer or from local colleges, may be able to convert some of those courses into college credit. The American Council on Education (ACE) has a noncredit course accreditation program that reviews company, college, and noncredit college courses and makes recommendations as to whether they are at the college level.

Suppose, for example, you work for IBM and take several of their staff development courses. If the classes have been submitted to ACE for evaluation and ACE has recommended those classes for college equivalent credit, your college can give you credit for the IBM classes.

Credit recommendations for military training are listed in The Guide of Evaluation of Educational Experiences in the Armed Forces, and business and industry credit recommendations are in The National Guide to Credit Recommendations for Non-Collegiate Courses. Copies of both guides are probably located in your Admissions or Registrations Office.

Of course, not all colleges will give you credit for this kind of learning. Many of the classes that you have taken will not have been reviewed because your company or college has not submitted them for review. To find out whether noncredit classes that you may have taken can be converted to college credit at your school, contact your academic advisor. If she does not know about getting credit for your training classes, contact your Registrar's Office, the head of your advising office, or your Dean's Office.

If the noncredit classes you have taken do not convert to college credit, they may still be useful to you in receiving credit either through a credit by examination program such as CLEP or through an experiential learning program.

Correspondence Courses

Many college-level courses may be taken without ever sitting in a classroom. Correspondence classes can be taken from a number of different colleges. If you are planning to transfer credits from a correspondence course to your current college, be sure to find out if your school will accept those credits.

Before you begin taking correspondence courses, think about your work habits. A large portion of students who take correspondence courses never finish them. Are you able to work independently, without supervision or the structure of a class? If you are able to read and study on your own, you can save both money and time through these classes.

The Peterson's Independent Study Catalog provides information on over 10,000 credit and noncredit correspondence courses. For additional information, write

Peterson's
P.O. Box 2123
Princeton, N. J. 08543-2123

Telephone: (800) 338-3282.

Remember to check with your school to see if they will accept credit from the correspondence program that you select.

Louisiana State University

Louisiana State University (LSU) is one of the many college programs that can be completed by what is called distance learning. In distance learning, the student, the instructor, and the school are not in the same geographic

place at the same time. Students may view TV lectures or read assignments that have been mailed to them. At LSU, there is an Independent Study program in which students complete their college work in their own homes. Faculty supervise and evaluate the academic work.

"Louisiana State University and Agricultural and Mechanical College is accredited by the Commission on Colleges of the Southern Association of Colleges and Schools to award bachelor's, master's, doctoral, and professional degrees" (p. 44, 1996-97 College Bulletin).

For additional information write

Office of Independent Study
LSU
Baton Rouge, LA 70803-1508

The email address is

study@lsuvm.sncc.lsu.edu

Their fax number is

504 388-3524

National Universities Degree Consortium (NUDC)

In 1990 nine universities created the telecommunications oriented National Universities Degree Consortium to make college-level courses available to students throughout the country. Courses are broadcast via satellite or cable through the Mind Extension University (ME/U channel) distribution system. All courses are offered by accredited colleges and universities. A bachelor's degree in management is available through the University of Maryland University College.

For additional information, call

(800) 777-MIND

If you are planning to transfer your credits to your present school, check to see that the courses you plan to take will be acceptable in your degree program.

Study Abroad

Many students build studying in a foreign country into their college degree programs. Study abroad can be an essential ingredient for degree programs such as majors in foreign languages, international business, and international law. If a student is majoring in Spanish, wouldn't it be a good idea for her to live in a Spanish-speaking country for a semester or a year in order for her to more fully understand both the language and the culture?

Several years ago I talked to a student who was majoring in Chinese. I asked her if she intended to go to China as part of her college education. She had thought about the idea but hadn't gotten specific plans set. She ended up going to Taiwan for a year. While there, she began teaching a few English language classes to help her with her living expenses. After a few months she had her own television show teaching English. By the time the year was over, she had earned all of her expenses for her entire stay.

Often the cost of studying abroad seems to be excessive for your college budget. Before you give up on the idea, think about whether you really want to go and if you are willing to do all the work that may be needed to earn the money for your program. Many times scholarship or other financial aid packages are available to you to help with the additional expenses.

If studying abroad is really important to you, would you be willing to take out a bank loan to cover the additional expenses? If you are reading this a year or two before the time that you would like to go abroad, can you set aside some time to research the costs of a semester or a year overseas and to strategize alternate ways of funding the program? Remember, it will often take a lot of both time and effort to get what you want in life. Study abroad can be an educational experience from both the planning and implementation standpoint as well as from the actual experiences you can have by living in another culture.

Check with your international student services office or your Dean's Office for information about the study abroad program that is available on your campus.

Senior Citizens' Programs

Many colleges have special admission and fee programs for senior citizens. Eligibility for these programs tends to

232

require U.S. citizenship, being over 60 years old, and being retired. If you are interested in finding out about the program available at your school, call your campus Admission Office.

Summary

College degree requirements are typically broken down into at least three categories:

1. General college course requirements such as English, mathematics, science, fine arts, and social sciences;

2. A major or area of concentration; and,

3. Elective courses.

Associate or two-year degrees usually require approximately 60 credits, whereas four-year or bachelor degrees necessitate between 120 and 128 credits.

Although traditional classroom instruction is one way to earn college credits, other options include independent study, credit by examination, internships and cooperative learning experiences, correspondence course credit, study abroad programs and experiential learning credit.

In most cases, students are limited in their degree options more through lack of information than by the credit options that are available. Look for the best options that are open to you to get the education that you want.

13 SPECIAL NOTES

While putting this book together, I found that there were a number of topics that I wanted to comment on that didn't comfortably fit into any previous chapter. I have put this potpourri together to adapt the basic techniques of this text to a variety of issues that are specific to student subpopulations and to learning in what students call "the hard subjects"---mathematics, engineering, and the sciences.

Student Subgroups

Not all students are treated equally in higher education, nor do they have the same problems. Some of the difficulties that students encounter are predictable and can be overcome with a little bit of foresight and effort.

Commuter Students

Commuter students get less involved in campus than students who live in residence halls. Commuters are less likely to use campus support agencies, are less likely to get involved in student organizations, will work more hours off campus and will tend to focus their attention on off-campus activities. The off-campus focus of commuter students reduces the impact of college and lowers the probability that the commuter student will graduate.

If you are a commuter student living at home, it is difficult for your family to understand that your life is any different from what it was last year when you were in high school. Your need to study more will not be apparent to anyone.

Commuter students need to focus their attention on college even if they work and live off campus. Try thinking about college as though it is your full-time job. (It is, you know. Your job in college is to learn all that you can to prepare yourself to enter the work force.) Try using the 9-to-5 approach: Monday through Friday from 9 a.m. to 5 p.m., you go to work on campus---you go to class, study, write your papers, and meet with members of your support team. When you finish your work (studying) you leave campus to go home or to go to your paid employment.

Residence Hall Students

My primary concern with students living in the residence hall is to help them make their room their home away from home. Security and privacy can easily become issues---security because most students don't remember that everyone isn't honest, and privacy because you will usually have at least one roommate in a residence hall. Security can be taken care of easily if you do simple things such as engrave your valuables and lock your room. Privacy issues are more complicated and will require talking and negotiating with your roommate(s). Because most residence hall issues will involve your roommate in some way, can you arrange regular times to talk with your roommate so that concerns can be addressed before they become issues? If you need a neutral mediator for some of your discussions, why not try using your resident assistant?

For many residence hall students, it is a good idea not to study in your room. Your room is your home, a place to sleep, play, and relax. Make the library or study room your office, that is, the place you go when you want to work. Home, your room, is for fun; the office, the library, is where you get all your work done.

Women in Higher Education

Women in higher education are not treated the same as men are. During the 1980s, articles about women in higher education talked about the "chilly climate" on campus for women. Women students are called on less than their male counterparts, they are interrupted about 10 times more than men are, and they receive less mentoring than men do. At first the solution to these problems was for women to try to find women instructors. Unfortunately, women faculty members were almost as guilty as their male counterparts in most areas of support.

On every campus there are male and female faculty and staff who will assist both male and female students. The best way to find these facilitators is through women's support clubs and agencies on campus. Their referral network can help women students with most gender-

related campus problems.

Minorities in Higher Education

Although this country is supposed to be a melting pot of different cultures and races, there is abundant evidence that everyone is not treated equally. For most minority students, there are significantly fewer role models on campus than there are for White males. The graduation rates for Black students, and especially for Black males, are below those for White students.

On-campus mentors and networking are two aids that may assist minority students in their quest for a college degree. The race and gender of the mentor is not as important as the mentoring that can be provided. During the 1970s and the early 1980s many minority students sought mentoring from faculty of their own race. Although many students did receive support, many of the faculty that were supporting them did not receive tenure (permanent faculty status), in part because of the time they spent assisting students--- promotion in higher education is often tied to research productivity. The more time a faculty member puts into research, the greater the probability that he will be promoted or granted tenure.

Minority organizations on campus can be good sources of information about faculty and staff who are likely to be good mentors. Other students can also be good referral agents. A good mentor can be an important part of your success on campus---find a faculty or staff member to help you through the college maze!

Returning Students

Students who are returning to college after they have been out of school for a number of years often feel as though they are at a disadvantage when they compare themselves with the traditional-aged students. In reality, returning students have at least two distinct advantages that they can use to aid their success on campus: maturity and work experience.

Maturity is an advantage because having experienced more of life allows returning students to keep college and their reason for being in college in perspective---learning becomes more valued.

Work experience translates into skills and knowledge that have been learned on the job that are directly applicable to the college setting. For instance, papers that are written by returning students are usually neatly typed (or printed on a laser printer), are well organized, and tend to have fewer grammatical and spelling errors in them (returning students use business standards for most of their assignments). Returning students also tend to be willing to ask questions in class and to see their instructors during office hours.

The one major disadvantage that returning students may have is that their lives are often more complicated that those of traditional-aged students.

Returning students tend to be married, to have children, and to work, often full time, while they are attending college. Goal setting and time management are especially important to balance home life with work and college classes.

Talking with other older students, perhaps in a returning student support group or student organization, and sharing your college experiences with them can also be a fruitful endeavor. It is comforting to know that other students are also experiencing similar problems and concerns and to see the variety of ways that adult students can resolve what appear to be very complicated predicaments.

Fraternities and Sororities

Social fraternities and sororities can facilitate success in college or be extremely detrimental to it. A lot depends on the organization; a lot depends on you.

In working with one fraternity on the College Park campus of the University of Maryland, I got the feeling that most of their students were graduating. When we checked the graduation rate for men who entered that fraternity during three different years, we found that about 94% of members completed their college degrees!

On the other hand, during the pledge period on most campuses both the members of the sororities and fraternities and their pledges fall behind in their academic work and receive low grades on their examinations.

It all seems to come down to priorities; if your academic work is important to you and you keep up with it, you will do well in your classes. The members of your fraternity or sorority can be a tremendous help to you in finding good faculty, selecting your classes, and tutoring you in some of your classes.

Membership in one of these organizations means that you will have a built-in support network that can help you get through college.

On the other hand, the activities of sororities and fraternities can become so interesting and demanding that it becomes easy to forget the primary purpose for being in college. (That does not mean having a good time!) Can you find a junior or senior in the organization who would be a good mentor or model for you to follow?

Remember, if you join one of these groups, it will be up to you to keep your focus on your college education. Socializing is great but not if it comes at the cost of your education.

Transfer Students

Transfer students are at a disadvantage because they do not know the school and its support agencies as well as students who started at that college. When community college students transfer to major universities, they often experience what is called the "transfer student syndrome"--- their grades drop about half a grade point for the first semester as they get adjusted to their new school. There are two main reasons for the grade point decrease:

1. Most transfer students move up academically when they transfer, that is, they tend to go from a community college to a four-year college or university; and

2. Transfer students lack information about classes, instructors, requirements, and support services on their new campus.

The solution to the first problem, transferring up--- moving to a more rigorous academic program---can usually be solved by studying more or by taking advantage of support services such as the learning center on campus or tutoring services.

Getting involved in activities and meeting other students at the new college is often the solution to the second problem, lacking information about your new campus. Joining the student organization in your academic department can be crucial to making a smooth transition to your new program. Third- and fourth-year students in your department can help you learn information about courses, instructors, requirements, and support services. If you are a transfer student, keep in mind that students who started at your school have had time to learn both the formal and the informal structure of your college; they know their way around your campus. Learn from those who are "in the know."

First-Generation College Students

Students who are the first in their families to go to college do not have family collegiate experiences to learn from. Many times their family cannot understand the academic demands of college, the costs that are involved---tuition, fees, materials, textbooks, etc.---or the social activities that tend to go with being a college student.

Mentors and networking become important compensations for first-generation college students. If family members have not experienced the maze of college, faculty and staff on campus have. Mentors will share their experiences and offer you advice on how to succeed on campus.

Creating your own academic support network is also very important for first-generation college students. Look back at the sections of this text on networking and assertiveness. Your family may be very supportive of your efforts in college. However, support from campus personnel---students, faculty, and staff---will increase the probability of being successful on campus.

Learning Specific Subjects

Some academic areas present predictable problems for students. Often these classes are in mathematics and the sciences. Here are a few

suggestions about getting through classes that may be difficult for you.

Hard Classes In General

A class that is hard for you can be in any academic discipline---some engineering students find English classes difficult, many liberal arts students find mathematics difficult, a history student may have problems with his foreign language class, etc. Often, the biggest single problem that students have with a difficult class is the block to learning that they create just to prove how demanding the class is.

My graduate degree comes from a counseling department in a College of Education. One of the most difficult courses that students in my major had to take was statistics. Statistics courses were extremely difficult for most students in the department, even though there was a clear logic to most techniques that we were being taught. On the other hand, the material from the personality class was relatively easy for most students despite the fact that we had to know between 30 and 50 different theories that used the same words to explain different concepts. The complexity of human behavior was easy; statistics was impossible! Why? A significant part of the answer was because students thought that they couldn't learn statistics; they blocked their own learning.

You, too, may have had

experience with making learning difficult. Did you study a foreign language in high school? Did you learn it? A tremendous number of students study a foreign language, all the time saying to themselves "I can't learn this." Sure enough, they spend hours memorizing vocabulary lists only to forget what the words mean by test time.

If you have a difficult class, try to remember that most people can learn most subjects. You may have to work harder and more often on difficult material, but you can learn it.

For your difficult classes, it will be important for you to stay slightly ahead in your assigned readings. By reading ahead, you will familiarize yourself with the vocabulary that will be used during class sessions as well as introduce yourself to the main ideas that will be presented. The extra work gets you prepared and creates cognitive anchors on which you can attach new information.

Going To Class Is Essential

If you miss a class that you enjoy, it will be easy for you to get caught up. You will probably talk to other students about what you missed or perhaps even speak with your instructor. For difficult classes, however, most students that I talk with never seem to bother trying to get the material that they missed. They tend not to know other students in the class, and they rarely get together with their classmates to discuss the

subject matter. Missing classes creates gaps in your learning that will ultimately make the course more difficult for you.

Try never to miss any classes for those subjects that are hard for you. When you go to class, be prepared. Stay up on your reading so that you are familiar with the concepts and vocabulary that will be presented in lecture. Review your notes from the previous class session so that you are warmed up on the subject matter and ready to learn new material.

Remember, attendance in class is highly correlated with success in that class. The more difficult a course is for you, the more important it is for you to attend every class session.

The Vicious Circle

For me, learning German in high school was difficult. Why was it so hard? I didn't like my low test scores. Why were my scores low? Because I didn't study. Why didn't I study? Because German was hard. Why did I think it was hard? Because I received low test scores.

That's crazy! Not really. I created what I considered to be a logical explanation for German being difficult for me that allowed me to rationalize getting poor grades because I didn't study enough.

I had created a vicious circle. In part, because I received low grades, I thought that I didn't like German. Since I didn't like tha class, I didn't study. Because I didn't study, I received low grades.

To break this vicious circle, try either mentally changing your impression of the course or studying more. Let's return to my German. What would have happened to my test scores if I had studied German as little as 30 minutes each day? Yes, I would have scored higher on my German tests. That in turn would have made me feel better about my German class and my assignments. If I had liked it more, I probably would have studied even more. Had I studied more, my grades would have been even higher. The down spiral would have been broken and replaced with an upward spiral that would have helped me learn more.

Try breaking the negative thought pattern you have about your difficult classes; try to think positively about why you are studying the material and what you will get out of it. Most important, increase your study time to the level that you need to learn all the information that you need for that class.

Learning Time

Often when you are studying material that is difficult for you, it is necessary for you to study longer and more systematically than you may usually study. In a literature class, for instance, if you get behind, you can take a day or two and read several books to get caught up. In mathematics, the sciences, and engineering

it is very difficult to get caught up just by studying intensely for a day or two. You need time to digest new information and to assimilate it into your total learning.

Study difficult material every day if at all possible. Even better, study it two or three different times a day. If you study a couple of times a day, several things will happen:

1. Your dislike of the subject will begin to go down---for instance, it will take too much energy to keep fighting statistics; eventually you will wear down some of your resistance and you will learn more;

2. Because you are studying regularly you will forget less, which should help build your confidence a bit; and

3. As you remember more and fight learning less, you will learn new material more easily and retain it better.

No, it won't be magical; it will take a lot of time, but the results should be worth it.

How much should you study? That really depends on a lot of different factors. In general, for a very difficult course, figure on studying three hours or more for every credit hour. A difficult four-credit chemistry course would then require 12 or more hours of study each week!

Mathematics And Statistics

Math classes are difficult for many students for two primary reasons:

1.   The vicious circle that I mentioned above, and

2.   The fact that mathematics requires sequential learning and the utilization of information that has been learned previously.

If you find yourself locked in a vicious downward spiral, try talking to a learning skills specialist, studying mathematics two or three times a day in short learning sessions, or thinking about the various ways that mathematics could help you in the future.

As you begin learning new concepts in your math class, review, perhaps even write down, the old concepts that you need to know to be able to understand the new material. For instance, if you are about to learn to multiply fractional exponents, you must be able to multiply fractions first. Once you are sure that you understand multiplying fractions, you can concentrate on what it means when you multiply fractional exponents.

If you want additional help in improving your ability to learn mathematics, read <u>Building Self-Confidence in Math</u> by Drs. Sally Wilding and Elizabeth Shearn (1991, Kendall/Hunt Publishing Co.).

<u>Engineering And The Sciences</u>

You should follow the same advice for studying engineering and science as for studying mathematics. But I have three additional pieces of advice for engineering and science courses. First, lab reports can often improve your grade in these classes, so take them seriously. You will earn higher grades with neat, well-written reports. If possible, type your report on a word processor to give it a professional look. (I recently talked with a student who turned in typed lab reports. Only one other student in his section had typed his report!)

Second, in many engineering classes, examination questions will demand that you work on problems that are more difficult than those you have had in class. That is, test questions will often require you to go beyond the level of knowledge that you have been taught in class. I have seen cases where scores of 20 or 25 out of 100 were the top grade in the class.

The rationale that I have been given for the demanding examinations is that engineers always go beyond their current knowledge. For example, a civil engineer doesn't build a bridge that has been built before. Even if he is building the second span beside an existing bridge, the forces on the new bridge will be different from those on the first span; the new span will usually require some changes in construction. In these cases use the knowledge and skills that you have to at least get started on solving the problem.

<u>Word Problems</u>

Often I have heard students in both science and engineering

classes say things such as "I can't handle the word problems. I know the material, but it's the word problems that kill me." Word problems are science; word problems are engineering. What I mean is, the word problems that you encounter in these classes have two different parts: setting up the problem and solving the problem.

Solving the problem or equation requires you to use your math skills. Some people refer to the solving of equations as "plug and chug"---once you plug the numbers into the appropriate equation all you have to do is chug through to the answer. That means that the mathematical manipulations that you need to use in solving the problem should be automatic for you; if they aren't, you need to work on the necessary math skills.

The essence of word problems then becomes knowing what to do with all the information that you have been given. The scientist and the engineer learn the thought flow of solving problems. They sort out the information that has been given, determine what needs to be done, select the appropriate equations for the task, and then plug in the numbers to get the solution.

If you are having difficulty with word problems, try breaking your studying or your problem-solving skills into two separate tasks:

1. Learn the theoretical information, the equations, and the how and why to use them;

and

2. Learn the necessary mathematical skills you need to master in order to the solve the equations you have learned.

Foreign Languages

Studying a foreign language once a week for three or four hours will not help you learn the language. As with mathematics and science courses, you should spread your study time out. Study five or more days a week. Study several different times during the day rather than studying for several hours at a time.

Use is important in learning a foreign language; the more you use the language the better you will learn it. Why not get together with a couple of students who are learning the same language and have some conversations in the language? Locate restaurants in your area where the language is spoken, and go there for an occasional lunch or dinner. Are there film groups around that show films from the countries that you are studying? Seeing films can help you learn about that country's culture and give you some background for your language study.

Suppose you really wanted to learn a foreign language at a faster, more natural rate. What would be the best way to do this? Spending a year or a summer in a country where the language is spoken is the best experience. In a very short period of time you will have learned how to be understood. In fact, some studies indicate that being immersed in a language for an entire summer is better than one year of classroom study in the United States.

Most students, however, are not able to live abroad for a year or even a summer. Another approach to learning the language faster and more naturally would be to ask yourself, "What kinds of activities can I get myself involved in to duplicate living in the country while I am still in college here?" Some schools have foreign language houses where students try to use their new language skills in daily interaction. Also, you might try tutoring a foreign student in English in return for being tutored in the student's language. Still another option is to room with someone who speaks the language you are studying.

Literature, History, And Other Heavy-Reading Courses

Literature classes can often have 6, 8 or even 10 books on their required reading list. Other disciplines such as history can also have long reading lists. Getting through all of that reading can take a great deal of time. Two different techniques can be useful in completing your reading efficiently: survey the book before you read and study critical analyses of the assigned books.

In the first case, read through the book rapidly, reading the introduction to each chapter, the first sentence of every paragraph, and the summary of each chapter. In an hour, you can have a good understanding of the book and then go back to read the complete text. As you read the second time you will know how all the pieces go together; you will understand the structure of the book, and the main ideas that are presented, and you will know some of the supporting material that the author has used. The key to this approach is learning to survey, that is, to get the author's main idea before you begin to read every word of the text.

Reading critiques of a book can give you a condensed summary of the main ideas that the author is presenting and a few criticisms of the work before you read. In literature, books like Master Plots, published at Yale, can give you a good overview of a book, information about the main characters, and a general idea of some of the significant factors about the work. Then, when you read the assigned book, you will be able to read with greater understanding and in a much shorter period of time.

For reading literary works it is a good idea to learn about how to read and understand different kinds of literature. Your college English instructor may expect you to know how to study literature and therefore he may not spend much time discussing how to analyze characters, to interpret figurative language, or to understand the relationship between an historical period and literature of a period. If you do not understand these approaches, it is your responsibility to build an adequate background. You can start by asking either your instructor or a campus librarian to assist you.

For many history and government and politics classes it is often a good idea to get a general overview of the time period and subject area before you begin to study your textbooks. Suppose you are going to study the American Revolution. What was going on in Europe during the 50-year period before the war? Where were all the European colonies in the new world, what European governments did each belong to, and what was the general history of each colony? An hour or two spent in getting a good overview of the time period will help you to understand why many of the Revolutionary War events happened as they did.

The idea of reading literary reviews or general overviews may sound like cheating to you. It isn't. You are actually going beyond your instructor's expectations by laying a solid foundation for your learning. Professors read critiques that are written by other scholars. That was part of their professional training. Why shouldn't you take advantage of other scholarly thinkers as you prepare to learn?

Summary

I strongly urge all students to create an on-campus support network to help them through the collegiate maze. Mentors are also important, especially for anyone who sees himself as a member of a minority group on campus. Why make mistakes that others have already made and can help you avoid?

Difficult classes are usually demanding for two reasons:

1. The subject matter requires sequential learning and the retention of a great deal of information and

2. A student makes the course more difficult by not systematically studying and not being adequately prepared for both classes and examinations.

Difficult subjects need to be studied practically every day. If new material requires mastery of previous knowledge, you must go back and review the old information if you are going to assimilate the new.

Difficult subjects must be reviewed regularly because you are bound to forget material that you do not use. Frequent reviews and regular study help you to break the negative spiral that is associated with classes that you do not like.

INDEX

246